IMAGES
of America

JEWISH COMMUNITY OF NORTH MINNEAPOLIS

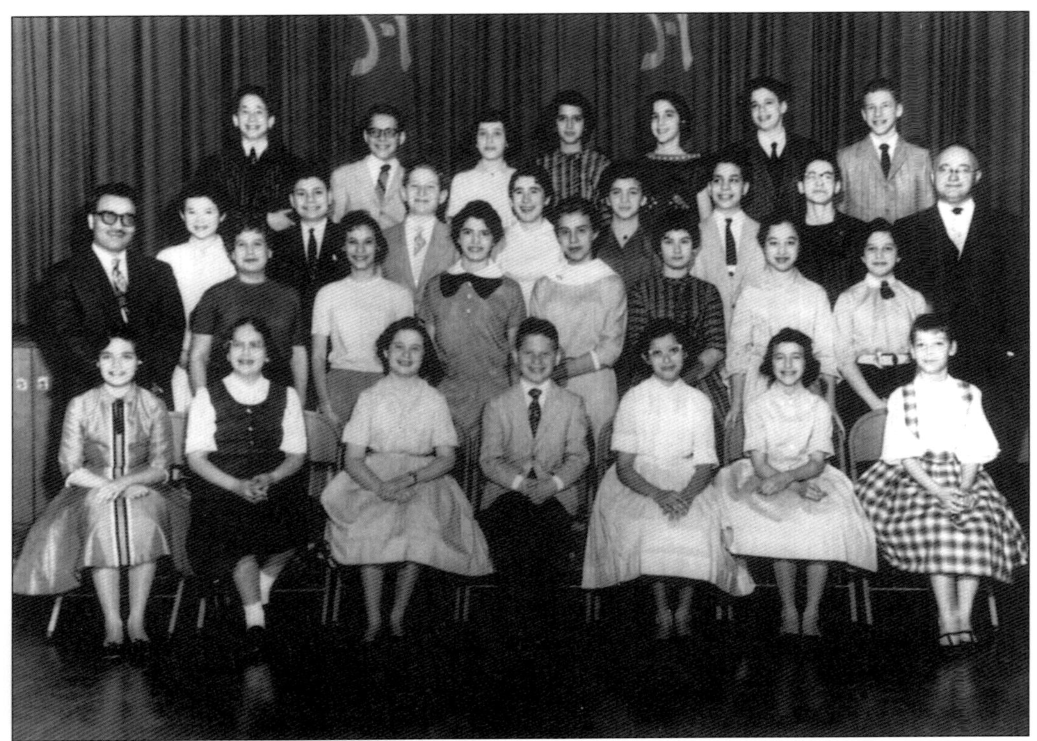

IT'S GRADUATION TIME! Almost every Jewish child who grew up on the North Side attended Talmud Torah Hebrew School, with two-hour classes after school Monday through Thursday, and on Sunday morning. Smiling for their elementary school graduation photo in 1958 were, from left to right: (front row) Laurie Rosen, Marcia Cohen, Betty Sue Gordon, Chuck Turchick, Naomi Joshua, Melanie Steinman, and Caroline Katz; (second row) Assistant Principal Dr. Samuel Nachshon, and students Arden Fingerhut, Stephanie Lehrman, Cathy Friedman, Harriet Malin, Miriam Herman, Eileen Singer, and Sarah Appleman; (third row) Elaine Lapidus, Jules Beck, Elliot Bailess, Jamie Evidon, unidentified student, Joey Kopstein, Larry Kivens, and Rabbi Unger; (back row) Ron Salzburger, Jay Rovner, unidentified student, Eileen London, Roberta Stein, Jay Milstein, and David Bermans. (Courtesy of Jewish Historical Society of the Upper Midwest.)

About the cover: Quien Sabe was a friendship group organized by young women on the North Side. Many of its members went to elementary school together, started partying in junior high school, and are still close friends more than 60 years later. Members and their dates—some of whom they later married—gathered for a formal dance at the Glenwood Park Chalet in November 1947. Left to right, standing, are: Bernie Laiderman, Frances Schirmer, Bernadine Garfinkle, Mike Jaffe, Irv Lebow, Shirley Weinberg, Rhoda Neimark, Paul Jaffee, Myrle Lebowske, Royal Aren, Sally Dann, and Marcia Schnitzer; (seated) Helen Broude, Bob Perwien, Ruth Meltz, Blanche Sherman, Pat Blumenthal, Joyce Finkelstein, Steve Perlman, Charlotte Kenis, Irv Nudell, Joan Korengold, and Israel Mirviss. Not pictured are Roberta Cohen, Manny White, Joyce Rothman, Stan Leibo, Don Finkelstein, Mervin Tomsky, and the chaperones, Mr. and Mrs. Broude. (Courtesy of Marcia Schnitzer Hinitz.)

IMAGES
of America

JEWISH COMMUNITY OF NORTH MINNEAPOLIS

Rhoda Lewin

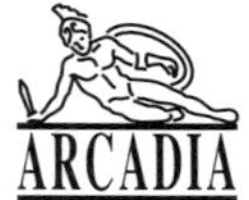

ISBN 0-7385-0817-9

Published by Arcadia Publishing,
an imprint of Tempus Publishing, Inc.
3047 N. Lincoln Ave., Suite 410
Chicago, IL 60657

Printed in Great Britain.

Library of Congress Catalog Card Number: 2001094983

For all general information contact Arcadia Publishing at:
Telephone 843-853-2070
Fax 843-853-0044
E-Mail sales@arcadiapublishing.com

For customer service and orders:
Toll-Free 1-888-313-2665

Visit us on the internet at http://www.arcadiapublishing.com

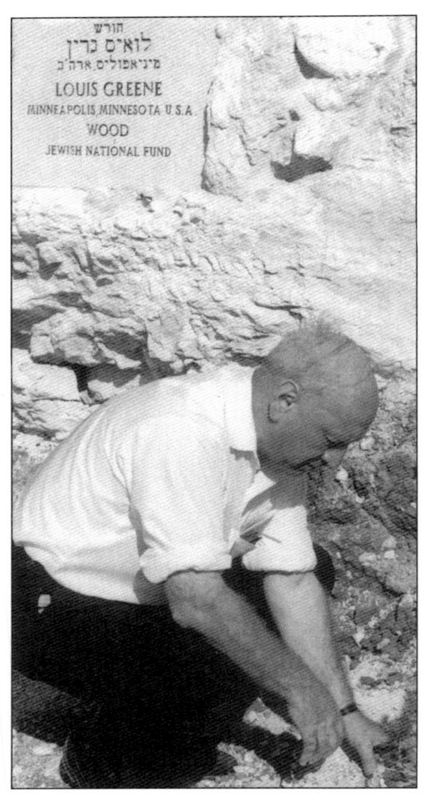

This book is dedicated to my family—those who came before and those who will follow—and to the state of Israel, where a forest was planted in September 1964, in honor of my father's dedication to community service. To my grandparents, Chaim and Sophie Greene and Nehemiah and Minna Glick, and my parents, Louis and Florence Greene, of blessed memory. And to my husband, Tom Lewin, and our four children—Ellen Lewin and her daughters, Salome and Amalya, and granddaughter Iris, Susan and James Roth, Kate and Scott Shamblott, and Jeffrey and Jennifer Lewin and their children, Max, Simon, and Devra.

Contents

ACKNOWLEDGMENTS

In the 1970s, I began tape-recording interviews with East European Jewish immigrants who had come to Minneapolis in the early part of the 20th century as part of my research for my doctoral dissertation in American Studies at the University of Minnesota. It was a new approach; history books would no longer be a dull collection of documents and "just the facts, ma'am," but would be history as if "real people" mattered. Since that time, I have lectured on oral history, taught "how-to" classes, and have done many more oral histories—including interviews with Holocaust survivors, American liberators, and Righteous Gentiles for my book, *Witnesses to the Holocaust: An Oral History*, which is used as a textbook by many high schools, colleges, and church groups.

My parents always had wonderful stories to tell. My mother, Florence Glick, was born on January 1, 1900, in Muscatine, Iowa, shortly after her parents had come to America from Lithuania. When she was a child, pearl buttons cut out of Mississippi River clam shells were Muscatine's major "industry," and she helped support her family by sewing pearl buttons on cards for a penny a gross! My father, Louis Greene, was born in Romania and came to America as an "illegal immigrant" when he was just a few weeks old. His father was already in Minneapolis, and while his mother was waiting for him to send her tickets to America she had another baby—my father. So she brought with her to America a pillow with a slit in one side, and when she had to go through a ticket stall or customs inspection, she'd put her newborn little boy into the pillow and hope he wouldn't start to cry! He grew up in Minneapolis, where newspapers were always a part of his life; he sold papers as a child to help support his family and became a sports reporter and then the copy editor for the *Minneapolis Tribune*. So now I've returned to my "roots" after many years of teaching journalism, editing corporate and community publications, writing newspaper editorials, book reviews, and histories of community organizations, and so on, to write this book about those East Europeans who came to Minneapolis beginning in the 1890s, and settled on the North Side of Minneapolis, which was where I grew up.

Words cannot express my gratitude to my husband, Tom Lewin, who spent so many hours taking photos, researching city records, and scanning for reproduction every photo and document in this book. Other people who deserve a thank you include: Linda Schloff, Jewish Historical Society of the Upper Midwest; Mordecai Specktor, *American Jewish World*; Janice Goldstein, Jewish Family and Children's Service; Bob Janssen and LaVette Rainer, *Minneapolis Star Tribune*; and staff at the Minnesota Historical Society, Hennepin History Museum, and Minneapolis Federation for Jewish Service. People who generously shared their photographs and memories include: Aaron Isaacs of the Minnesota Transportation Museum, Pacey Beers, Dr. Reuben Berman, Ruth Davis, Merrill Fischbein, Morris Fruen, Arnold Glick, Norman Goldberg, Bobbi Goldfarb, Bonnie Heller, Marcia Schnitzer Hinitz, Tillie Jaffy, Robert Kleinbaum, Joe Kopstein, Bob Latz, Harry Lerner, Marshall Levin and Deborah Levin Stillman, Dr. Fred Lyon, Earl W. Miller, Jill Orbuch of the Minneapolis JCC, Sheldon Pinck, Beryl Richman, Beverly Roberts, Mort Ryweck, Joe Tschida, Helen Broude Tomsky, Chuck Turchick, Fern Wolf, and Helen Wolk. A special thank you to my University of Minnesota professors and oral history mentors, David Cooperman and George Hage, and to Stephen R. Silberfarb, executive director of the Jewish Community Relations Council of Minnesota and the Dakotas, who so eloquently says, "The rich and vibrant Jewish neighborhoods like the one on the North Side of Minneapolis reflected the changing face of America. We look forward with great anticipation to the publication and distribution of this important work."

INTRODUCTION

For those who ask why Jewish immigrants were so successful in America, one answer could be that the Jews' identification with the underdog, which had been a Jewish dog for centuries, was what led the newcomers to be so innovative and to promote new industries. Others say that the Jew could innovate and invent because his religion told him he was free to question and discard the old ways, and that Jews are "stamped with the values" that make for success—a love for study and learning, the willingness to save and sacrifice for a future goal, and the courage to take a chance on new ventures.

In the 1850s, the world was just beginning to industrialize, but almost two-thirds of Europe's Jews were already working in factories or had mechanical jobs. One-third of them owned little shops or were wholesale merchants, and only three percent were still farmers. In Russia, members of the nobility hired Jews to manage their estates, and Jewish merchants bought and sold the peasants' crops and cattle. The fledgling Russian clothing industry was almost entirely owned by Jews, practically every tailor and shoemaker was a Jew, and Jews were highly visible in the building trades and in the metal, wood, and tobacco industries.

But then in 1881, Czar Alexander II was assassinated. His successor claimed that the Jews were the villains and announced that he would force one-third of them to leave the Russian Pale of Settlement, one-third to convert to Christianity, and the rest to die of starvation.

Although they had to say goodbye, probably forever, to relatives, friends, and the world they'd grown up in, one-fourth of the world's Jews—more than 3,000,000, most of them from Eastern Europe—were living in the United States by the time Congress passed the Johnson Act in 1924, which virtually closed off immigration and would later make it impossible for thousands of European Jews to escape the Holocaust.

The journey to America was not easy. Most of them traveled to port cities in overcrowded third-class railroad cars or by horse and buggy. Although the price of steerage passage to America was only $12, many could not afford to buy tickets for the entire family, so a husband would have to leave his wife and children behind, hoping they could get along without him and promising to send money for tickets as soon as possible. When they boarded their ship, they might receive a mattress and, if they were lucky, a towel, a bar of soap, and a life preserver. The price of a ticket also included food, but the food was usually inadequate, often spoiled, and Orthodox Jews couldn't eat most of it because it wasn't kosher. As many as eight of them would be crowded into a small cabin or would end up eating and sleeping on the floor in the crowded, smelly, airless quarters in steerage.

It took at least a week to cross the ocean, and when they finally arrived at Ellis Island, or Galveston, or some other port of entry, some were sent back to Europe because they couldn't pass a physical exam, or didn't have enough money to live on until they found jobs, or because the young man who was supposed to pick up his immigrant bride-to-be for a marriage arranged by a *shadchan* didn't show up.

Many of those who were permitted to stay were "welcomed" at Ellis Island by German Jews, who had begun coming to the New World in the 1840s. Many of them were already very successful businessmen, and they engaged in "philanthropic farming" by offering the tired, dirty, hungry newcomers free railroad tickets to the Midwest, where they said they were sure to find work. Others came to the Midwest because they already had friends or family there, or because they'd seen advertising booklets circulated throughout Europe by the Canadian Pacific Railroad advertising prairie land for sale as "the richest soil in the world," or the Northern Pacific Railroad, promising jobs and temporary housing for newly-arrived immigrants. By 1924, when the Johnson Act effectively closed off immigration to the United States, there were 40,000 Jews living in Minnesota, most of them from Eastern Europe.

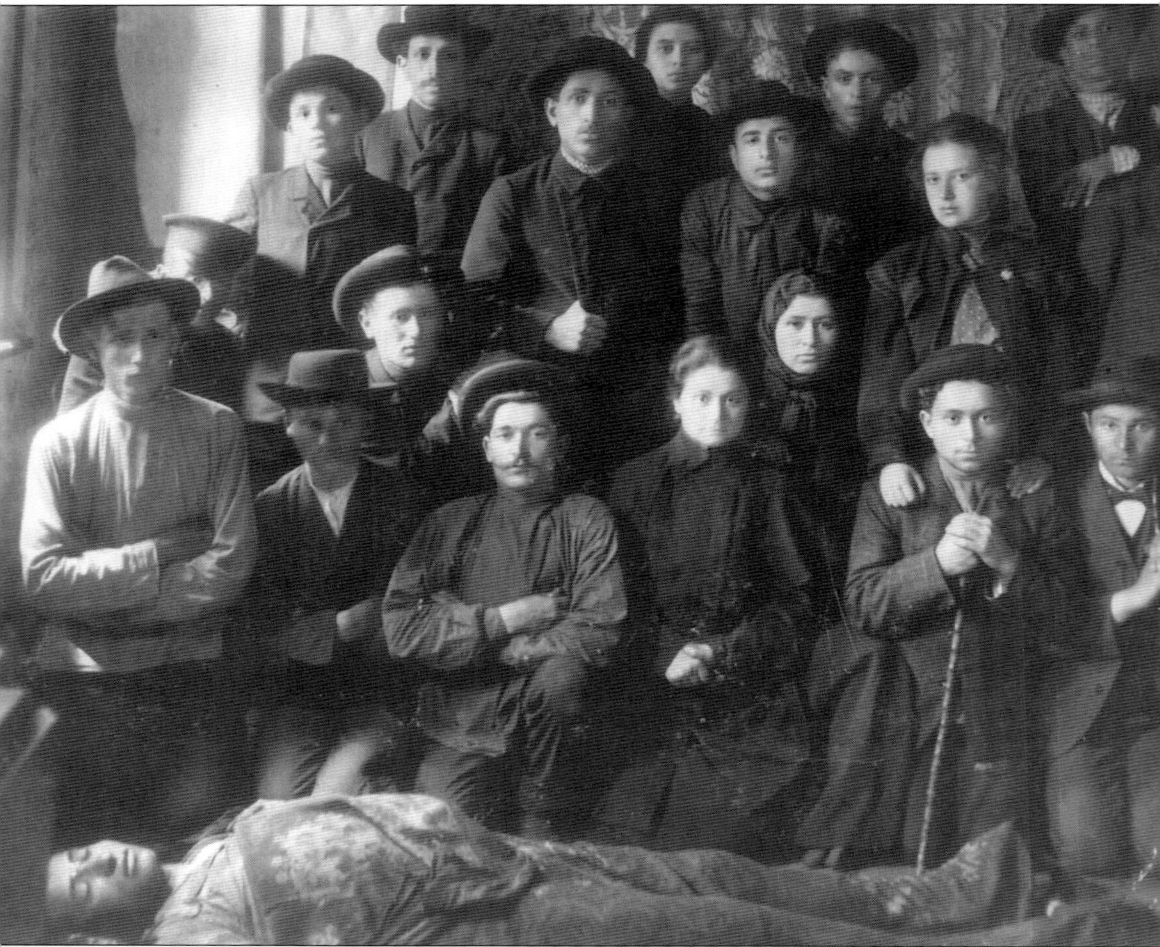

Family members and friends gathered to mourn another victim of a pogrom, the anti-Jewish riots and killings that sometimes destroyed whole villages in Eastern Europe. Harry Lerner's father, on the far right, left for America, the Promised Land, a few years later where his children, and now his grandchildren, would indeed fulfill the American dream. (Courtesy of Harry Lerner.)

One

Journey to the New World

Destination Minneapolis

East European Jewish immigrants came to Minneapolis because relatives were already there, because it was the spot on the railroad where their money ran out, because Minneapolis was rumored to be a rich lumber town where there was money to be made, or perhaps because a sack of flour they'd seen in Vitebsk, Russia, said "Pillsbury Company, Minneapolis, Minnesota"—and there had to be jobs in a town where mills produced flour that traveled all the way to a Russian *shtetl*! Others had seen booklets like *Minnesota: The Empire State of the New Northwest*, published in 1878, which invited them to exchange "the tyrannies and thankless toil of the Old World for the freedom and independence of the new," and promised that in Minnesota they would find "unparalleled opportunities . . . good schools and churches, healthy climate, pure water, and happy, intelligent, and prosperous people." The state's Immigration Board also sent agents to tap the incoming flow of immigrants in Quebec, Milwaukee, Chicago, and New York, and port cities in Sweden and Germany, urging them to come to Minnesota because it was such a healthy place to live that their death rate was only half the rate for the entire United States, and they would be sure to find jobs, as well as "lofty hills, graceful slopes, verdant nooks, crystal streams, limpid lakes, innumerable pleasure resorts, boating, fishing, and outdoor sports," which would make them "physically and mentally stronger, purer and nobler!"

As many as 40 percent of the newcomers arrived penniless, having spent all their money just to cover the cost of passage. And, of course, their job prospects were poor, because they could not speak English and knew nothing about America except what they'd read or heard. When the first 200 Russian Jews arrived at the St. Paul Railroad depot on July 14, 1882, the community was shocked at how "hungry, dirty, and impoverished" they were, but Minnesota Governor Lucius Hubbard, St. Paul Mayor Edmund Rice, the City Council, and the Chamber of Commerce quickly offered "emergency aid" and housed them in a temporary tent city on St. Paul's West Side. Many of the German Jews and second- and third-generation American Jews who had begun coming to the "Minnesota Territory" in the 1840s were already successful businessmen and civic leaders, and they helped the "removalites" find jobs and places to live.

In Minneapolis, members of B'nai B'rith, a men's club organized by German Jews and volunteers like insurance agent Joseph Schanfeld, an immigrant from Romania, and medical student Max Seham, who would later become chief of staff at Minneapolis's Mt. Sinai Hospital, were getting up as early as 5:00 a.m. to meet the trainloads of immigrants that began arriving on a daily basis. One of their assignments was to make the rounds of local factories where, if a worker hadn't shown up, they could place a new arrival in the job. They placed about 25 per month this way, and B'nai B'rith and other community groups also provided many of the newcomers with food and other necessities, and a place to live until they were ready to be on their own.

The newcomers also saved money to buy steamship and railroad tickets for family members they'd left behind. They wrote letters to friends and relatives, telling them that in America they'd find jobs, good food, equality of opportunity, very few beggars, and most of all, freedom. By 1924, there were 40,000 Jews in Minnesota, most of them from Eastern Europe, and in 1937, the state's Jewish population peaked at an estimated 43,700.

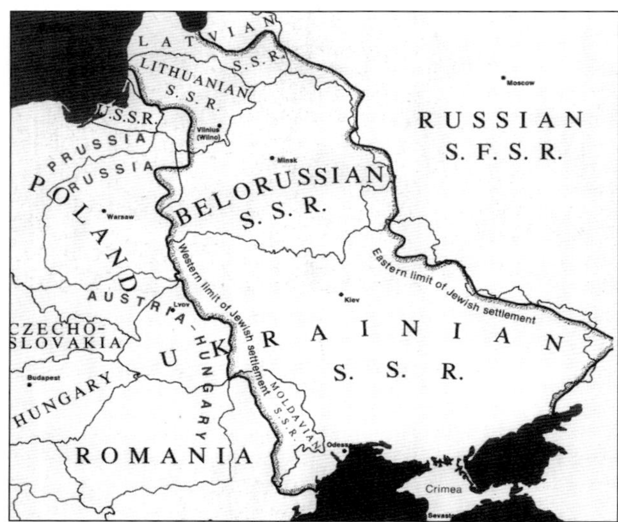

Most of the Jewish immigrants in Minnesota came from Russia, Lithuania, and Romania. (From *They Chose Minnesota: A Survey of The State's Ethnic Groups*, edited by June Drenning Holmquist. Courtesy of *Minnesota Historical Society Press*.)

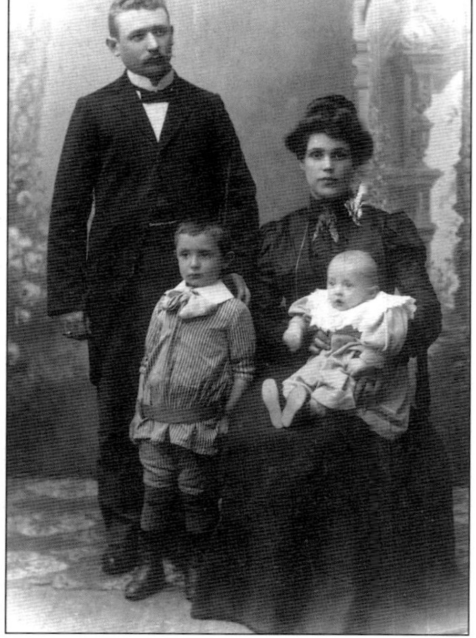

Not all the families fleeing East European pogroms came to the United States. Nehemiah Glick never saw his brother's family again after they emigrated to Stockholm, because he and his wife, Minna, settled in Muscatine, Iowa, and then moved to Minneapolis in 1918 because their son, George, who was a professor at the University of Minnesota Law School, had lost his wife in that year's influenza epidemic and he needed them to care for his two young children. (Courtesy of Florence Greene.)

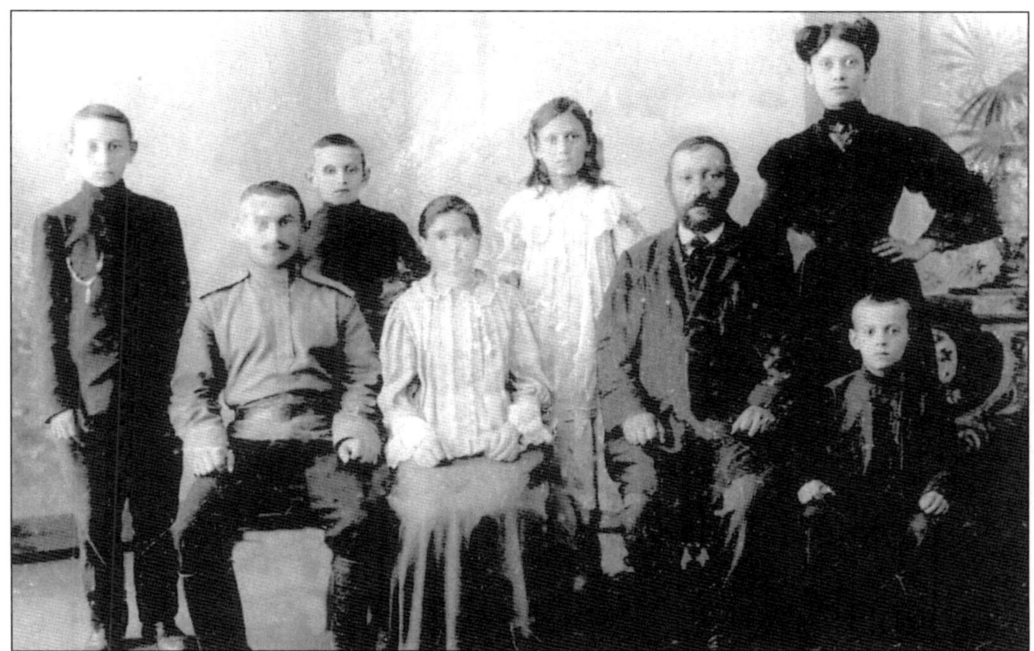

When pogroms began in Minsk in 1900, the Rossook family fled to America, where some of them changed their names to Rose and others to Rosen. Left to right are: Ben Rose, Kabulakov (Cabel) Rose, Bill Rosen, Grandma Chaya Rochel, Ida Rosen (Frailich), Moishe Rossook, Bessie Rosen (Overbach), and Louis Rosen. (Courtesy of Harold Rosen.)

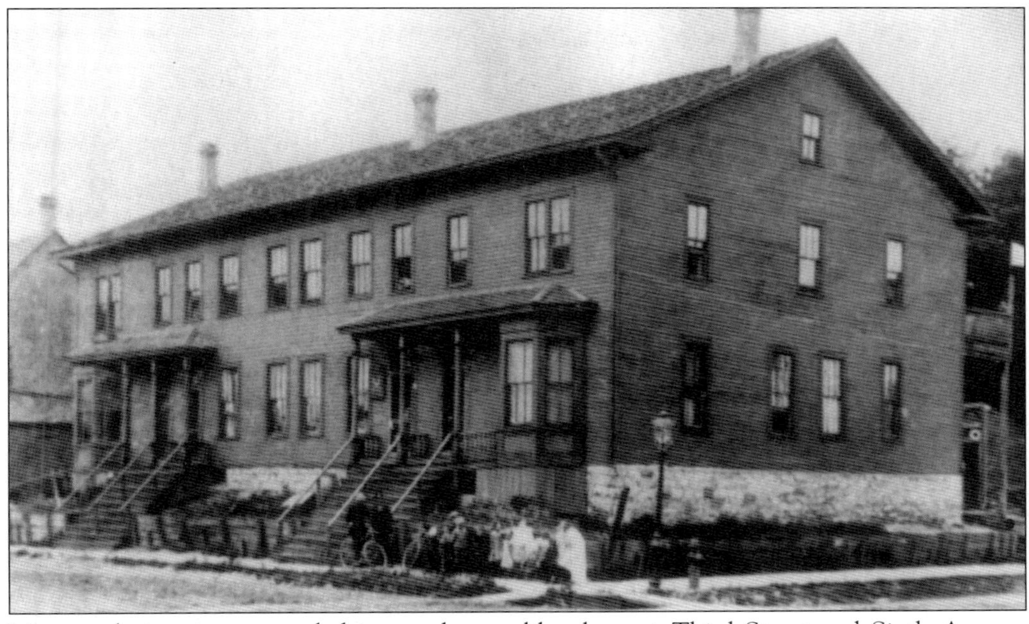

Many early immigrants settled in row houses like these at Third Street and Sixth Avenue North. They were demolished in later years to make way for new housing, business buildings, and the construction of Olson Highway and the city's first freeways. (Courtesy of Jewish Historical Society of the Upper Midwest.)

STATE OF MINNESOTA | DISTRICT COURT
COUNTY OF HENNEPIN | FOURTH JUDICIAL DISTRICT.

In the Matter of the Change of name of William Gittleman to William Guttman, } ORDER

This matter came before the Court on the petition of William Gittleman for leave to change his said name to William Guttman, and the said matter came duly on to be heard pursuant to proper petition on file herein, and was heard before the undersigned, one of the Judges of said Court, ~~at a Special Term thereof~~ in Chambers, held November ~~15~~ 19, 1919, Messrs. A. H. Karatz and Carl C. Meixner appearing as attorneys for petitioner.

Now upon hearing the evidence adduced by the petitioner in support of his application to so change his said name, by his own evidence and the evidence of witnesses testifying hin his behalf, and the Court being fully advised in the premises, finds the following

FACTS

That the petitioner is twenty-five (25) years of age. That he has used and has been known as William Gittleman during practically his whole life. That his birthplace was Russia; that for the past seven years he has baen and now is a resident of the United States of America and has been duly naturalized as a citizen of the United States as of August 1st, 1918. That he now resides in the said Hennepin County, City of Minneapolis, where he is steadily engaged in work. That he is a single man of good character. That he has no interest whatsoever in real estate except as appears under the name of William Guttman and the Court finds that he is not under guardianship or other impediment as to his legal rights. The Court also finds on evidence that in the use of said name of Gittleman, by which name he is known, petitioner has been considerably annoyed from time to time, due to the fact that said name is not the name used and adopted by his brothers and relatives now residing in this country, and in this city. That the name of Guttman, which ~~your~~ the petitioner prays that he may adopt, is the name now used by his said brothers and relatives living in said City of Minneapolis and that the name of Guttman will be of much more convenience and less liable to confusion in this country, where he intends permanently to dwell, and that the application is made in good faith and for a proper purpose. The Court grants the petition and finds that the petitioner should be and is entitled to use the name of Guttman by which he may hereafter be known with like force and effect as the name of Gittleman, by which he has hitherto been known, and the Court finds

HIS CONCLUSIONS OF LAW.

That the petitioner is entitled to judgment herein to have his name changed from William Gittleman to William Guttman.

Let judgment be entered accordingly.

By the Court.

Charles S. Jelley

Judge of District Court.

Dated November 19, 1919.

attest
P. S. Neilson Clerk
By Geo. H. Hamperley
Deputy

Many immigrants changed their names when they came to America. William Gittleman, a Russian who became an American citizen in August 1918, petitioned a year later to change his name to William Guttman. Another newcomer changed his name to "Johnson" after he discovered how difficult it was for his Scandinavian neighbors to pronounce a name like Gazhonsky, and Mr. Marayatzin changed his name to "Morrison." (Document courtesy of Jewish Historical Society of the Upper Midwest.)

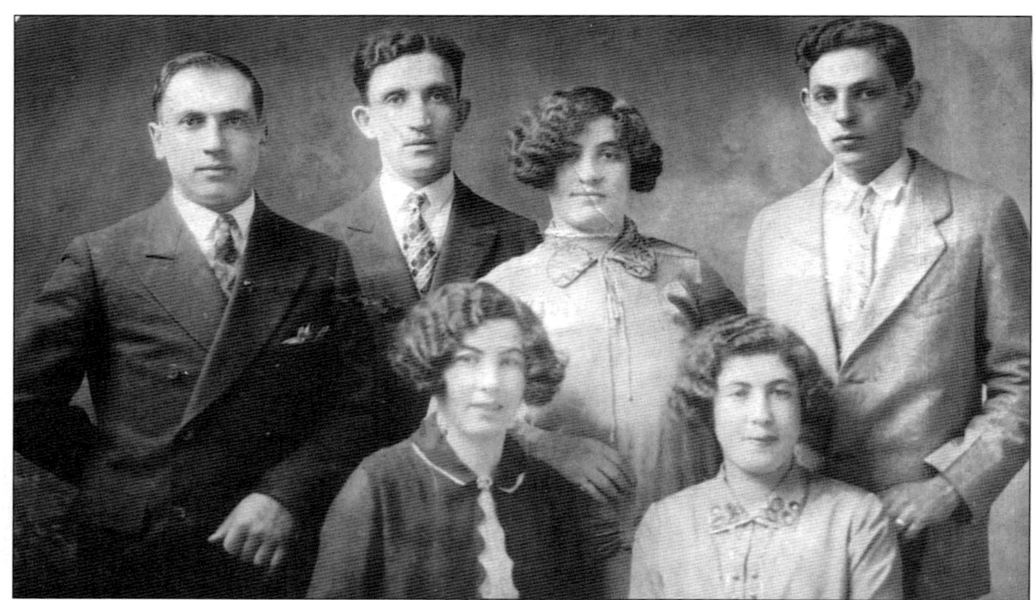

When William Schnitzer came from Poland in 1917, he married newcomer Goldie Rapaport from Belarus. He painted streetcars for a living until he saved enough money to buy a horse and wagon and start peddling fruit. Later, William and his brother, Harry, built a very successful business as dealers in scrap metal. In this family photo—the three women are the Rapaport sisters—are, left to right: (front row) Goldie Schnitzer and Judith Fox; (back row) William Schnitzer, Ray and Edith Banwell, and Harold Fox. (Courtesy of Marcia Schnitzer Hinitz.)

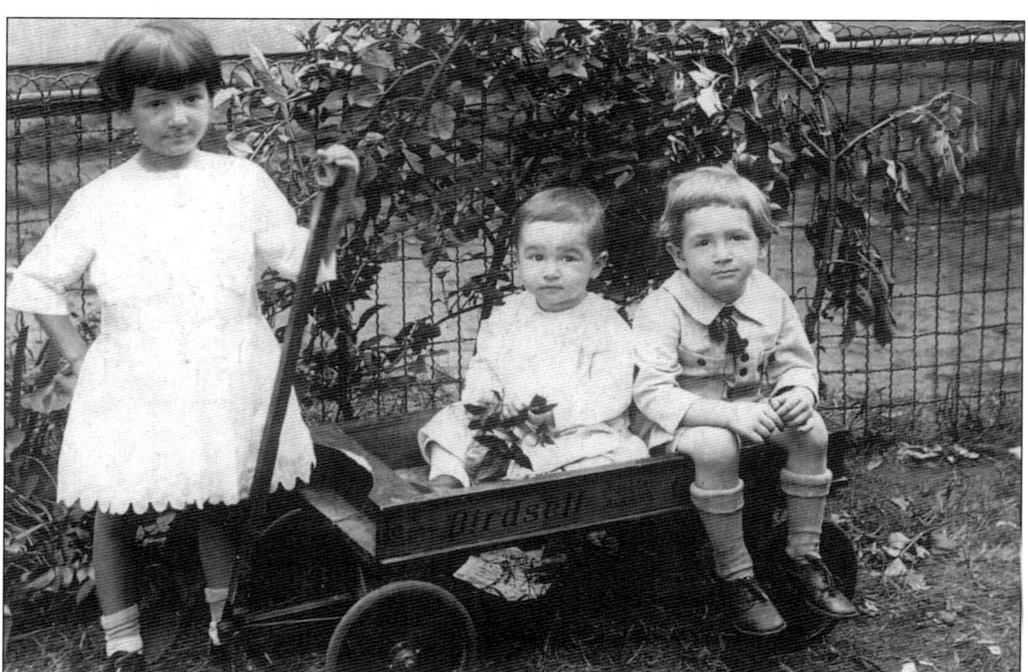

Miriam, Aaron, and David Lerner posed for a photographer in August 1923, to create a picture postcard their parents wanted to send to family and friends. (Courtesy of Harry Lerner.)

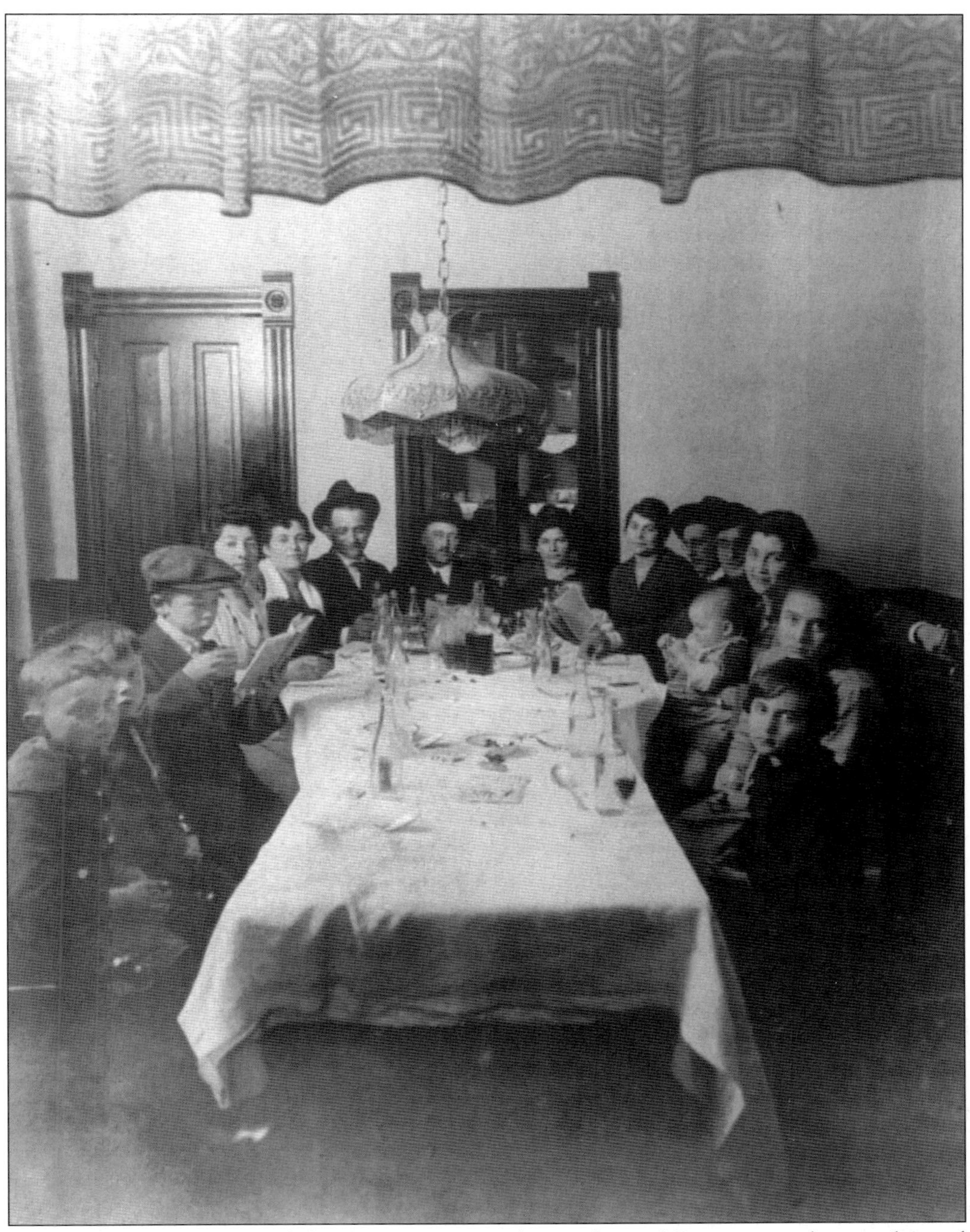

The Plitman family dressed for the occasion as they welcomed Passover at their traditional family Seder in 1917. (Courtesy of Jewish Historical Society of the Upper Midwest.)

THE AMERICAN JEWISH WORLD

VOL. II
NO. 1

JULY 30
1915

SPECIAL ARTICLES
IN THIS ISSUE

TRUE AMERICANISM - - - -	Louis D Brandeis
WHY THE JEWISH CHILD SHOULD BE TAUGHT HEBREW - -	Dr. S. N. Deinard
THE ZIONIST CONVENTION - - -	Dr. M. Silber
THE MINNEAPOLIS COUNCIL OF JEWISH WOMEN - -	Mrs. Leopold Metzger
THE WAR AND THE JEWISH QUESTION - - - -	Dr. Stephen S. Wise
THE LADIES' AUXILIARY OF THE TALMUD TORAH - - -	Mrs A. Berman
THE PRESSING PROBLEM OF THE JEWISH CHARITIES - -	Julia I. Felsenthal
ELLIS N. HARRIS An Appreciation -	Louis L. Schwartz

Reform Judaism viewed its members as Americans of the Hebrew faith, rather than as Orthodox Jews who happened to be living in America, and Rabbi Samuel Deinard of Congregation Shaarai Tov (now Temple Israel) worked to bridge the gap between the East European newcomers and his German-Jewish congregants, most of whom had arrived in the 1850s. In 1914, Rabbi Deinard began publishing a weekly newspaper, the *American Jewish World*, now in its 87th year and still independently owned in an era when such newspapers are mostly published by Jewish community organizations. (Courtesy of *American Jewish World*.)

Two

Where We Lived and Shopped

Our Neighborhoods

About a dozen families settled in an area they called the *veld* to raise dairy cattle, poultry, and fruits and vegetables. The land was cheap, and the two-story house that Elliot Royce's parents built at 33rd and Dupont Avenues North in 1895 cost only $1,000, with $50 down and monthly payments of $10 plus interest, but Elliot says, "The horse-drawn streetcars were 11 blocks away, and there were no sidewalks, sewers, or gas or electric power . . . and it took us all—parents and seven children—14 years to pay for that house."

Their real estate salesman had convinced the Royces that many Jewish families would soon be living there, and a few did arrive soon after, including the Greensteins, Cooperman the grocer, and the Landys, Blooms, Weinsteins, and Rosenfields. The Greensteins bought several lots on 36th and Knox, and rented an additional 40 acres where they raised crops, bought some cows, and started the Flour City Dairy. Allen Greenstein recalls that the cows had to be milked by hand every 12 hours, usually at 4:00 a.m. and 4:00 p.m., and the milk had to be chilled immediately, so they put it in big cans and set the cans in troughs filled with cold water from a well they had dug—and they'd also built the windmill they needed to pump the water out. They sold their milk door-to-door in a horse-drawn wagon. The housewife would bring out a dishpan or a jar, and they'd measure out as many quarts as she wanted, at 5¢ a quart—but if she bought $1 worth of "tickets," Allen says, she'd get an extra 4 quarts free, 24 quarts of milk for only $1, delivered to her door! Meanwhile, Allen's mother kept house, baked bread every day, had 13 children—nine girls and four boys—to take care of, and if her husband got sick she had to milk the cows and drive the horse and wagon to deliver the milk.

She also took care of the "synagogue room" that her husband built behind their house, where neighborhood families came to worship on Saturdays. Later the families in the *veld* built a little synagogue on 34th and Colfax and hired a *melamed* to teach their children Hebrew. But then, one by one, they moved away, and their *shul* had to close when they no longer had the 10 men they needed for a *minyan*.

Most of the newcomers from Eastern Europe settled near downtown, however, where they found jobs with garment manufacturers and other companies eager to hire new immigrants. Then they began moving toward Lyndale and Glenwood Avenues, and then Sixth Avenue North, a beautiful wooded area with two lakes that no longer exist—Hoag Lake, where the railroad tracks are under the Seventh Street bridge, and Oak Lake, where International Market Square and the Farmers Market are now.

The immigrant's dream was to go into business for himself, and some of them saved enough money to buy pushcarts or a horse and wagon. Some lined up by the railroad stations downtown to pick up and deliver freight, and others sold fruits and vegetables or other items in nearby neighborhoods. Sometimes two or three men would pool their savings or borrow money from loan societies like Gemelus Chesed to start up a business. They could borrow $25 interest-free to open a store, and when they'd paid it back, for as little as 50¢ a week, they could take out another loan, this time for $50.

In 1906, Solomon Brochin opened his grocery store on Glenwood Avenue. In addition to selling groceries, corned beef, schmaltz herring, tobacco, cheeses, and smoked and canned delicacies from all over Europe, he also had a foreign exchange office which was one of the first American Express agencies in the city, so immigrants could telegraph money to their families in Europe, and he was an agent for the Cunard Steamship Line, selling tickets to men who had saved enough money to bring their wives and children, or relatives, to America. He sold 800–1,000 Yiddish newspapers every week, as well as religious supplies, Yiddish-English dictionaries, citizenship booklets, Jewish sheet music, and books by Jewish authors, and he became the ticket box office for Jewish plays, concerts, movies, and lectures. People could also pay their utilities bills at Brochin's, and it was the unofficial post office box for newcomers who were still living in rooming houses. In 1916, attorney Alex Kanter brought Supreme Court Justice Brandeis, who was on a nationwide tour to see how immigrants were adapting to life in America, to Brochin's, "so he could see how Americanized Jews and new immigrants rubbed elbows in the Midwest between barrels of pickles, herring, sauerkraut, and other Jewish foods." In 1919, Chaim Weizman, who was touring the United States and would later become president of Israel, visited Brochin's on a day when community leaders happened to be meeting in the "caucus room" at the back of the store to plan a protest against Ukrainian pogroms.

By 1907, there were so many Jewish families along Glenwood Avenue that the area was almost like a European *shtetl*, although their neighbors included Scandinavians, Finns, and a few Italians. By the late 1920s, though, many of the immigrants were also living in the neighborhoods known as Homewood and Willard-Hay. In 1936, a canvass by the Minneapolis Federation for Jewish Service found that more than 11,000 of the 16,260 Jews in Minneapolis were living on the North Side, and at Willard Elementary School there might be only three or four children left in each classroom on the Jewish holidays. And even at North High School, which also served the mostly Scandinavian community living north of Golden Valley Road, almost half the students were Jewish. Others remember that "we walked everywhere, as far as 2 miles to school and to the Talmud Torah, and when it was winter we could stop at all our friends' houses along the way to warm up! Only in the worst weather did parents give us a dime to ride the streetcar to school."

The Depression was a difficult time. Brochin's sometimes delivered food baskets to people who couldn't afford to buy groceries, and Sander and Susie Abramovitch had very few cash transactions at their dry goods store. They would send their sons Jay and Lee out to try to collect what people owed them, because Sander's motto was "they'll pay if they can." And if a man came in asking for charity, he would give him some money, or if there was no cash in the register, he'd at least give him a pair of socks.

Then in 1936, their neighborhood began to change. The City Planning Commission decided that housing along Sixth Avenue North was deteriorating and that "the neighborhood largely serves as a ghetto for low-income African-American and Jewish families," and received permission from the federal government to build the Sumner Field Housing Project. The Public Works Administration financed 45 percent of the total cost and issued a loan to cover the balance, which would be amortized over 60 years by rental receipts from the project. Residences and businesses in the area bordered by Emerson and Aldrich and Sixth and Eleventh Avenues were torn down, and in December 1938, the Sumner Field Homes officially opened for occupancy. The project included 464 dwelling units ranging in size from two-room flats to two-story, three-bedroom townhouses, all in 48 flat-roofed red brick apartment buildings centered around Sumner Field Park, and designed by local architects Magney and Tusler.

Meanwhile, Plymouth Avenue was replacing Sixth Avenue North as the community's shopping and entertainment area. There were so many food markets that Max Fallek regularly visited them to collect "leftovers" for the Oak Park Children's Home. Malcoff's was now a favorite restaurant and deli, and it was the first area distributor for a frozen cheesecake from Chicago that became known as Sara Lee. Rose Margolis owned a children's clothing store, Margolis Dry Goods, from 1935 until the 1960s. Her shop was next door to Malcoff's until she moved across the street, where her husband had an auto repair shop. Stillman's, a forerunner of today's supermarkets, was competing with Brochin's, which was now its next-door neighbor at Plymouth and Newton. Soon there were four drugstores—Strimlings, Desnick's, Rosoffs, and Homewood Drug—and four delicatessens—Malcoff's, Abe's, Polar Grill, and H&S (which later became Flitman's). There were four Jewish bakeries within five blocks of each other—People's, Lehmann's, Lincoln, and the North Side Bakery—and People's and North Side Bakery family members delivered fresh-baked breads and bagels to customers' homes. There were two fish markets—Fidelman's and Pessis—and Greenstein and Post, which sold kosher meat, and four barbershops—Lester Swaiman, Jack Blicker, Kaplan Brothers, and Abe and Dave Garfinkle's.

Now the North Side was beginning to change. The Bell family had been in the wholesale fruit business, but when a garage fire destroyed most of their trucks in 1942, they couldn't buy new trucks because of wartime vehicle shortages, and their business was going downhill. Then they heard that the Malcoff family had decided to retire and move to Phoenix, and on June 6, 1944, they bought Malcoff's delicatessen and restaurant at the corner of Plymouth and Newton. It continued to be a family business and Marty Bell remembers working in his father's deli at age 11, when he had to stand on a soda pop box behind the counter so he could reach the slicing machines and then weigh the corned beef and salami, which sold for 50¢ a pound, or make corned beef sandwiches, which they sold for 15¢ or 20¢ each.

A number of other North Side families who began on a shoestring built multi-million-dollar businesses after World War II. In 1926, for example, five years after they'd left Russia, the Friedell family began raising chickens. They sold the chickens to kosher butchers and peddled their eggs to neighborhood grocery stores—and their business eventually became Crystal Foods, listed on the New York Stock Exchange and producing eggs, cheese, butter, margarine, and other products in plants in 22 states. Jack Fiterman started Liberty Box Co. in 1919, and his son Ben had to leave North High School in 1937 to work in the family business. During World War II, they sold boxes at 5¢ a pound, because the government set the price, but in 1966, they started manufacturing boxes and became a worldwide business. Max Levin started his produce business in 1932, in the depths of the Depression, and got up at 4:00 a.m. every day to go to work. His sons, Phil and Sheldon (Corky), worked in the family business and became pioneers in the frozen food business in the 1960s. Max and Fred Rappaport started selling auto parts in 1918, published their first catalog in 1921, were a nationwide business by 1930, and by 1948, had a worldwide business that included parts for military vehicles gleaned from government war surplus after World War II. Harvey Ratner and Marv Wolfenson, who'd been award-winning athletes in high school, invested some of their business profits in professional sports as owners of the Minnesota Timberwolves, until they sold them to New Orleans in 1994. And the list could go on and on. The most popular explanation for why their community and their businesses grew and prospered was that "you never give up!"—also known as tenacity—which was something kids learned if they grew up on the North Side.

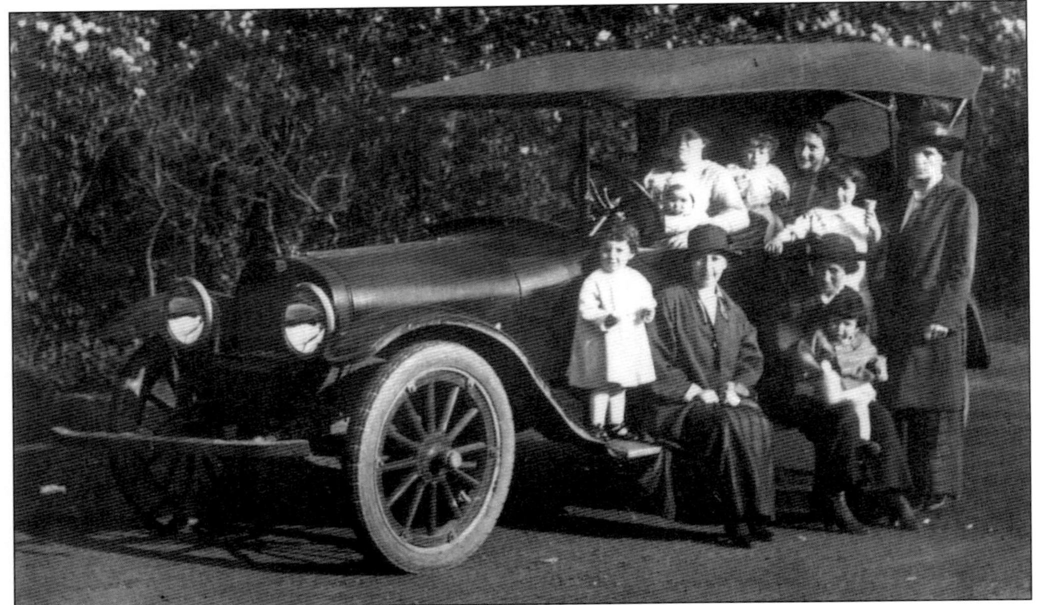

The Bloom family took up farming in the area known as the *veld*. They lived on 26th and Lyndale Avenues North, but as they prospered and their family grew—they had five sons and three daughters—they built a larger home on Aldrich Avenue North. Here they are on a Sunday outing with their neighbors. (Courtesy of Fern Wolf.)

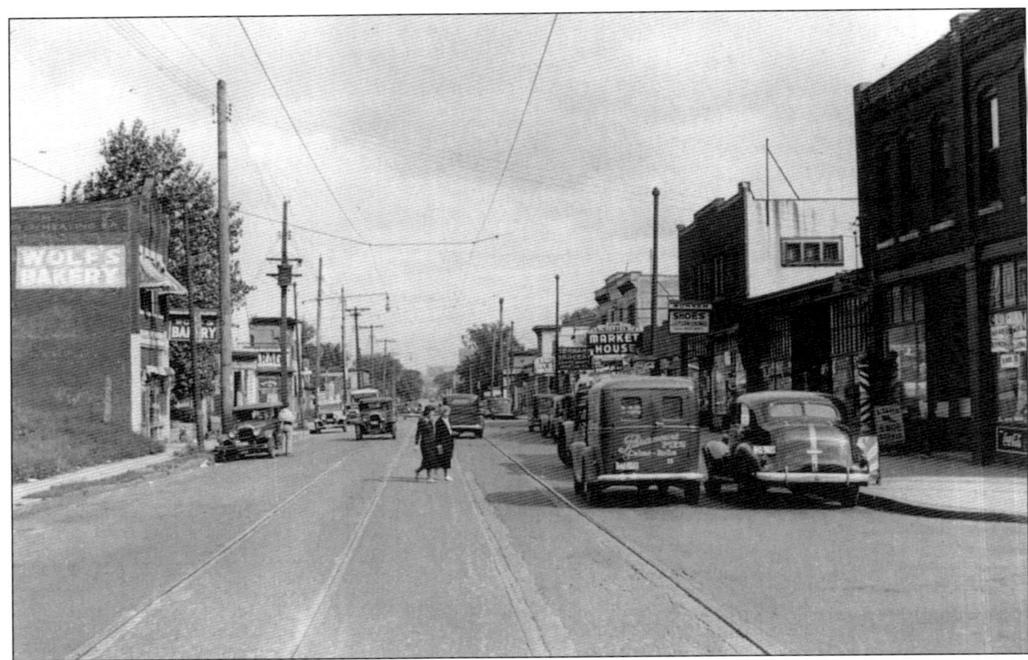

In the early years of the 20th century, however, few people could afford automobiles. People were used to walking, and it cost only 5¢ to take the streetcar downtown, or to go shopping, or go to work, so streetcars were the preferred method of transportation for almost everyone. (Courtesy of Aaron Isaacs, Minnesota Transportation Museum.)

Teresa (Tessa) Bloom Lexier is pictured with her two children and her aunt, Ossie Bloom Weinstein, *c.* 1910. Later the Weinsteins moved to 1207 Washburn Avenue North, a home designed by architects Liebenberg and Kaplan, who also designed Temple Israel, Beth El, and many Art Deco theaters. (Courtesy of Fern Wolf.)

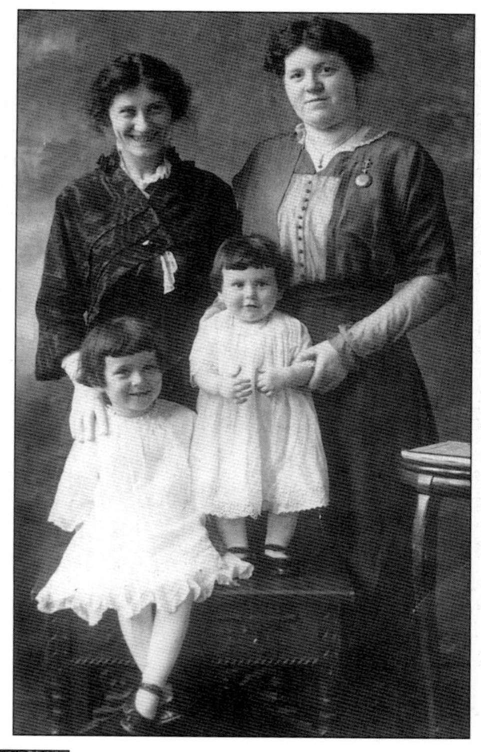

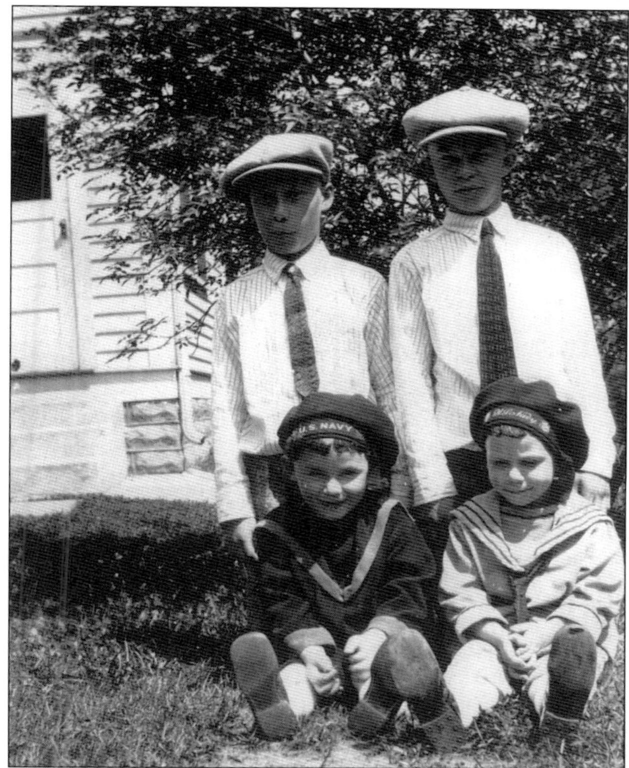

Sabbath was dress-up day for the Beers family. Posing in their back yard at 922 Girard Avenue North were Carl and Emil, who'd already learned to tie their own neckties, and their little brothers, Pacey and Joe, *c.* 1924. (Courtesy of Pacey Beers.)

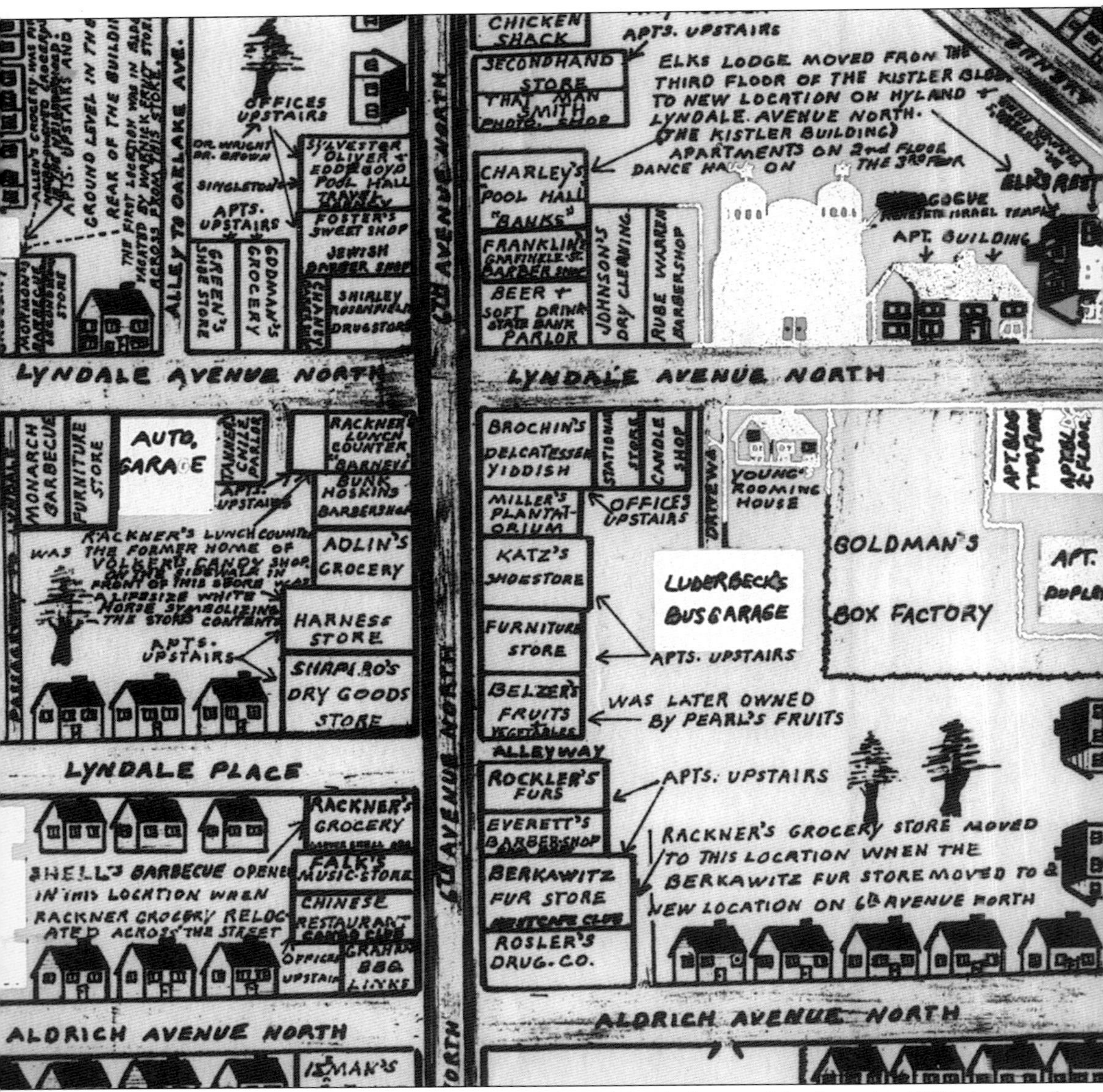

This detailed map of the intersection of Lyndale and Sixth Avenue North in the 1920s is part of a "neighborhood history" map created by Clarence Miller and published by the Phyllis Wheatley Center. Grade-school boys worked the area selling what they called "extras" for 2¢ each—local newspapers specially printed to report on events like boxing matches, natural disasters, and train crashes. Small businesses, most of them owned by members of the Jewish community, lined the streets, and the four-story Kistler Building on the southeast corner of Sixth and Lyndale included an ornate ballroom that could be rented for weddings and social functions. A group of Jewish men who called themselves the Atlas Club—which later became the Gymal Doled Club and then the Standard Club—met there regularly to socialize, play cards, and eat dinner, which was usually corned beef sandwiches they ordered from Brochin's, their "corner grocery store," at a cost of 5¢ or 10¢ each! Doctors and businesses had offices on the second floor, and the first floor included a pool hall and a bar, which later became known as "the infamous Keystone Club." (Courtesy of Earl W. and Clarence Miller and Phyllis Wheatley Community Center.)

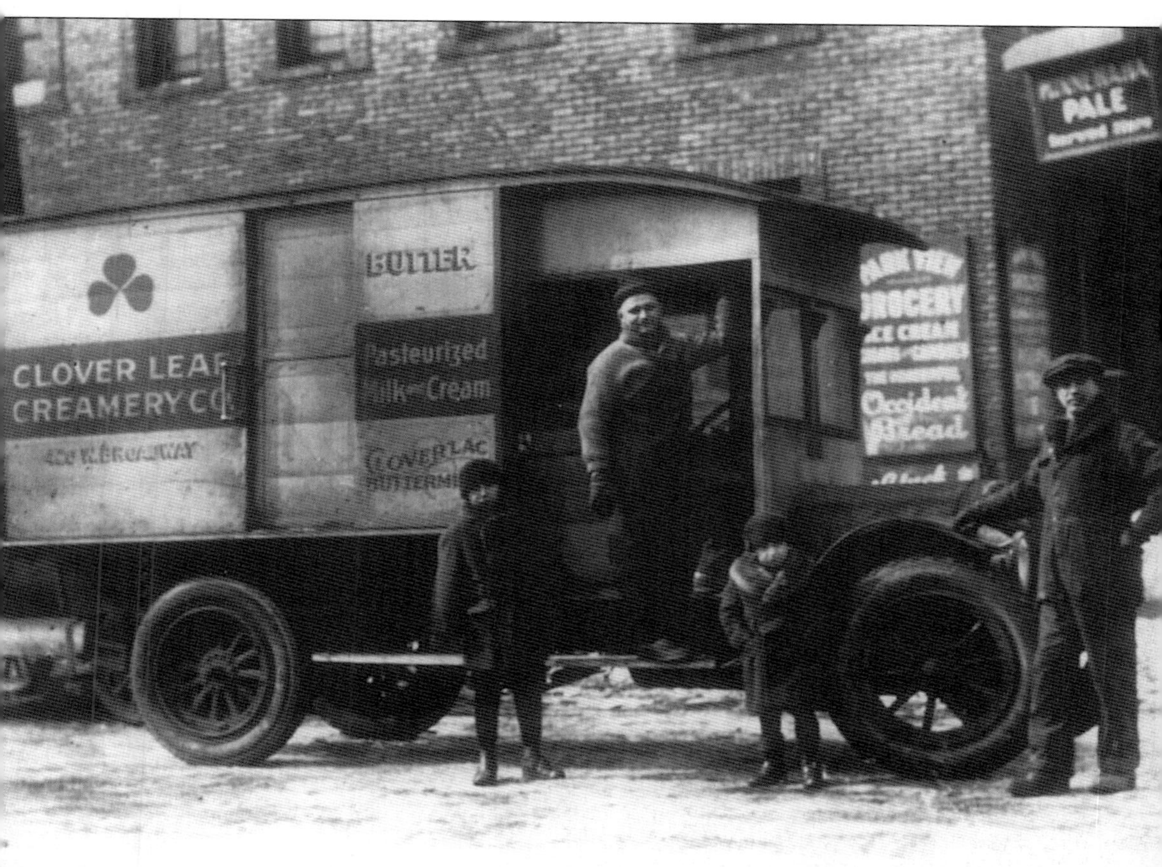

Not all newcomers could afford to go into wholesaling, but Max Ratner, shown here in 1922 with his two young employees, David and Meyer Fingerman, sold so much milk that he could afford to lend money to start-up businesses if they would become his commercial accounts. (Courtesy of Harriette Fingerman and Jewish Historical Society of the Upper Midwest.)

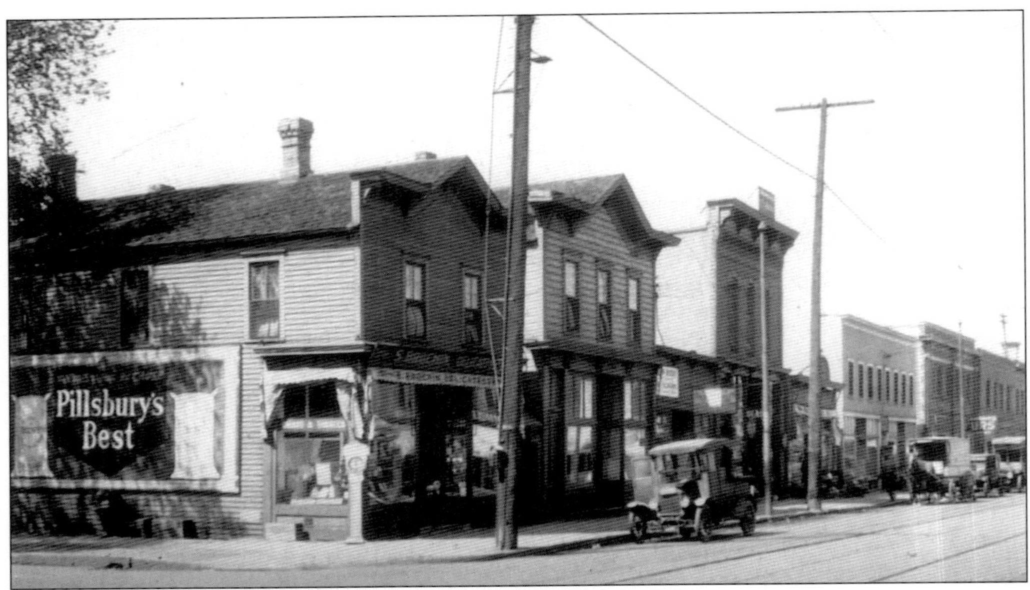

A conglomeration of little Jewish-owned grocery stores, butcher shops, fish markets, clothing stores, barbershops, restaurants, and other small businesses sprang up along Glenwood Avenue and then on the 14 blocks from Oak Lake to Penn on Sixth Avenue North. (Courtesy of Jewish Historical Society of the Upper Midwest.)

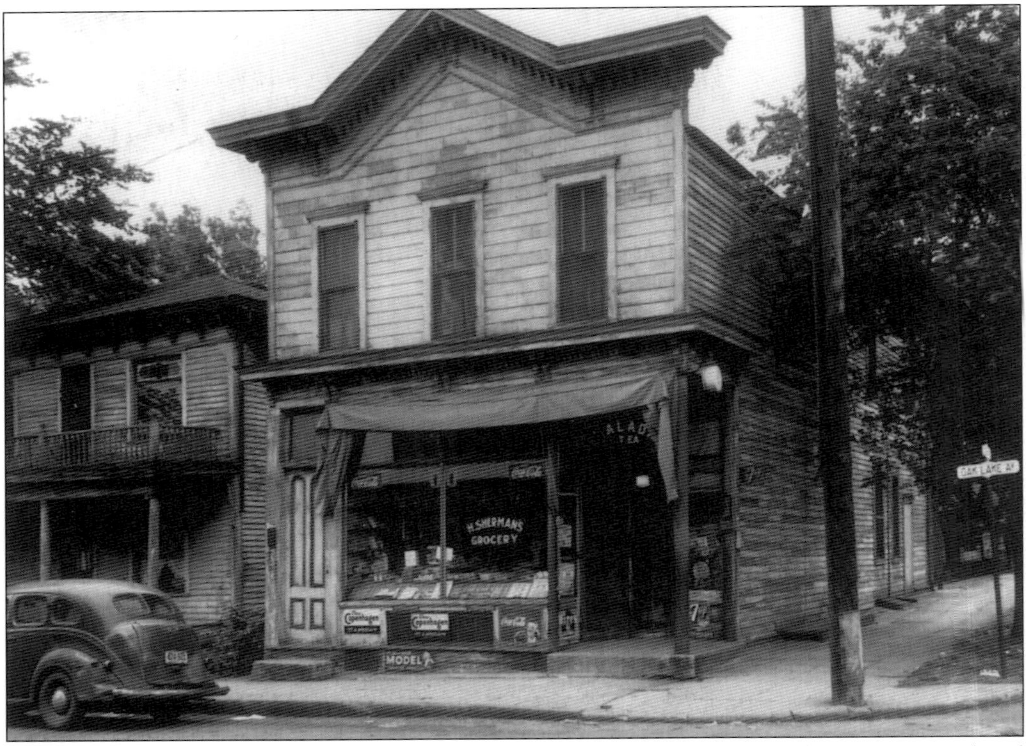

Like so many families, the Shermans sold groceries in their store on Oak Lake Avenue and lived upstairs. (Courtesy of Jewish Historical Society of the Upper Midwest.)

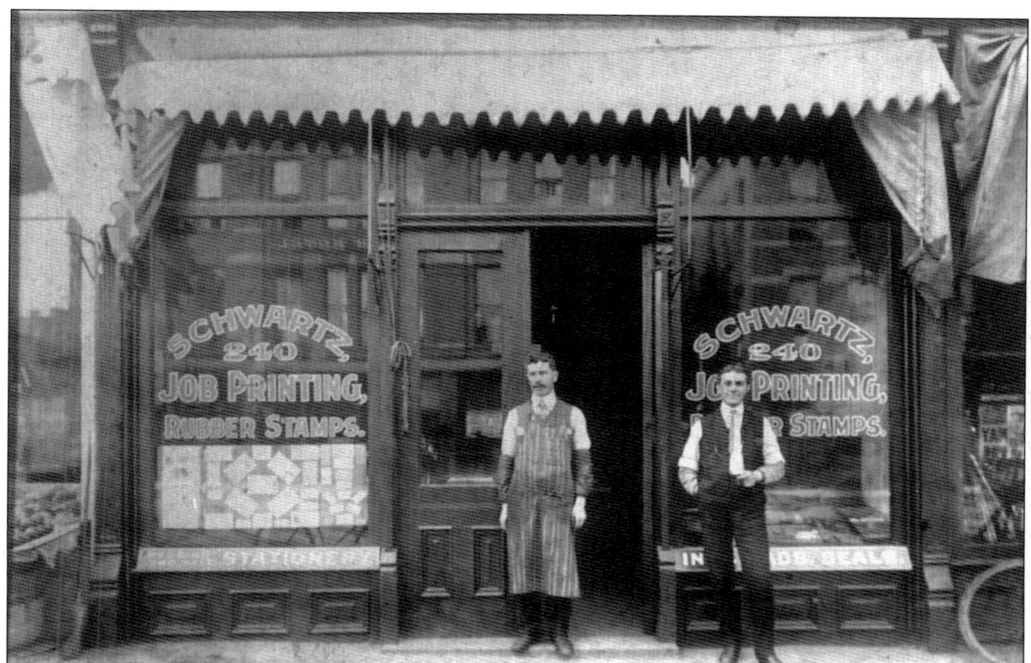

The predecessor to Eddie Schwartz's lifetime Ad Art Advertising and Printing Co. was this family business on Glenwood Avenue. (Courtesy of Jewish Historical Society of the Upper Midwest.)

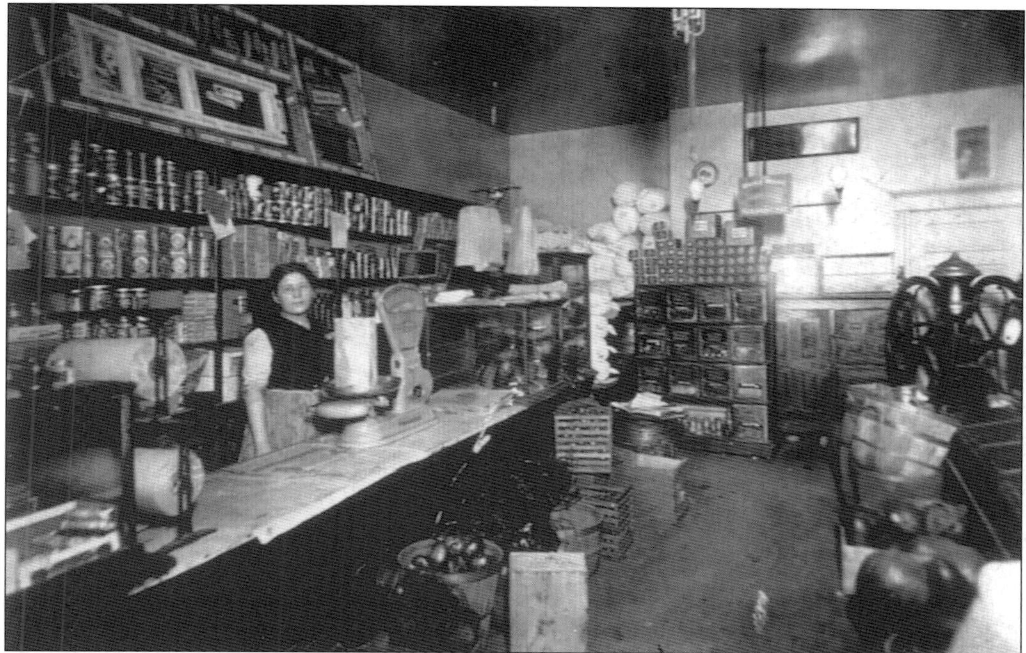

Rose Zipperman put in long and very tiring working days in her family's grocery store on Lyndale and Eighth Avenue North. This photo was taken in 1915. (Courtesy of Jewish Historical Society of the Upper Midwest.)

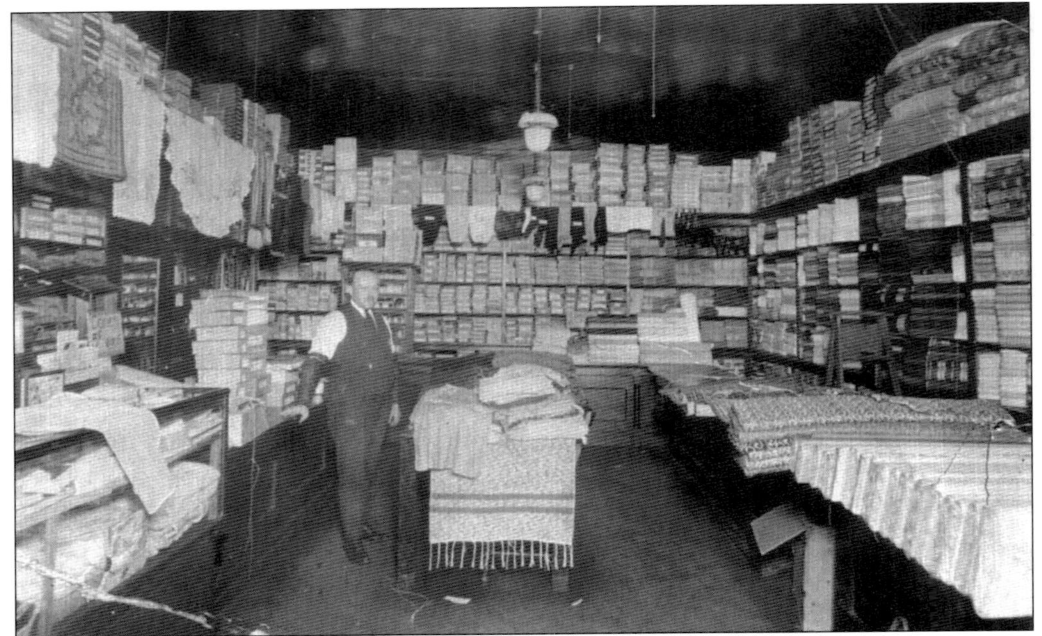

Isadore Swatez came to America in 1914, and opened his dry goods store in 1917, in a small building on the corner of Girard and Sixth Avenue North. The Swatez family lived upstairs of their store. Their son, Manny, was born at home in 1923; Manny's first job was trying to collect the bills his parents' customers ran up during the Depression, when they let people charge clothes and shoes with no interest and no carrying charges. (Courtesy of Celia Swatez Heilicher.)

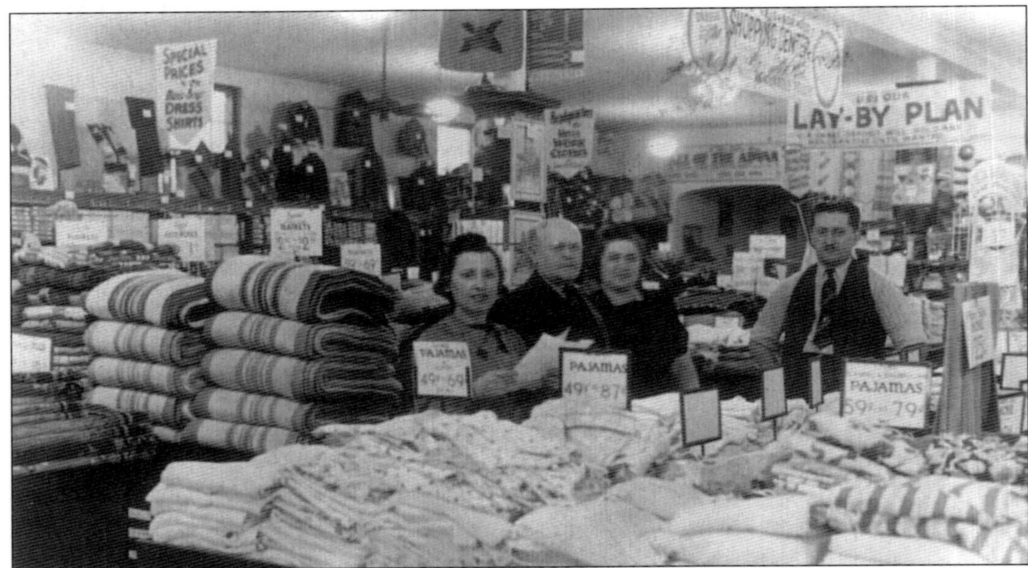

When he moved across Sixth Avenue North to a much larger store and began calling his business Swatez Department Store, his nephew, Bert Swatez, and Rose Sherman and Molly Schloff worked with him until urban renewal projects took over the area in 1956, and he had to close. (Courtesy of Celia Swatez Heilicher and Jewish Historical Society of the Upper Midwest.)

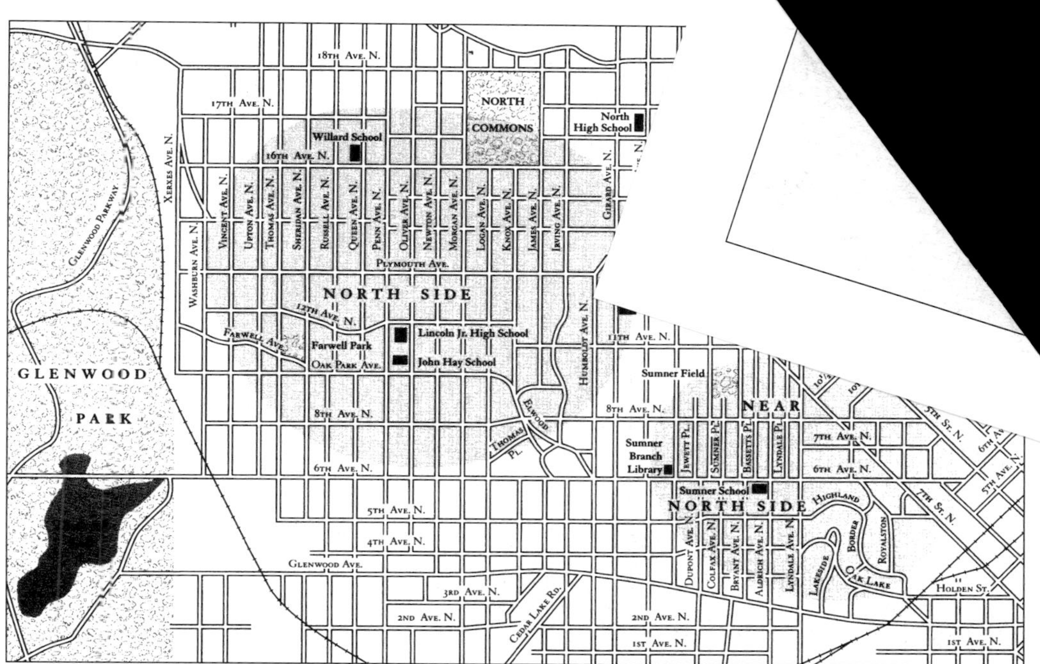

This is a map of North Minneapolis in the 1930s, before Sixth Avenue North became Olson Highway, and Glenwood Park was renamed in honor of Minneapolis Park Systems designer Theodore Wirth. (Courtesy of Jewish Historical Society of the Upper Midwest.)

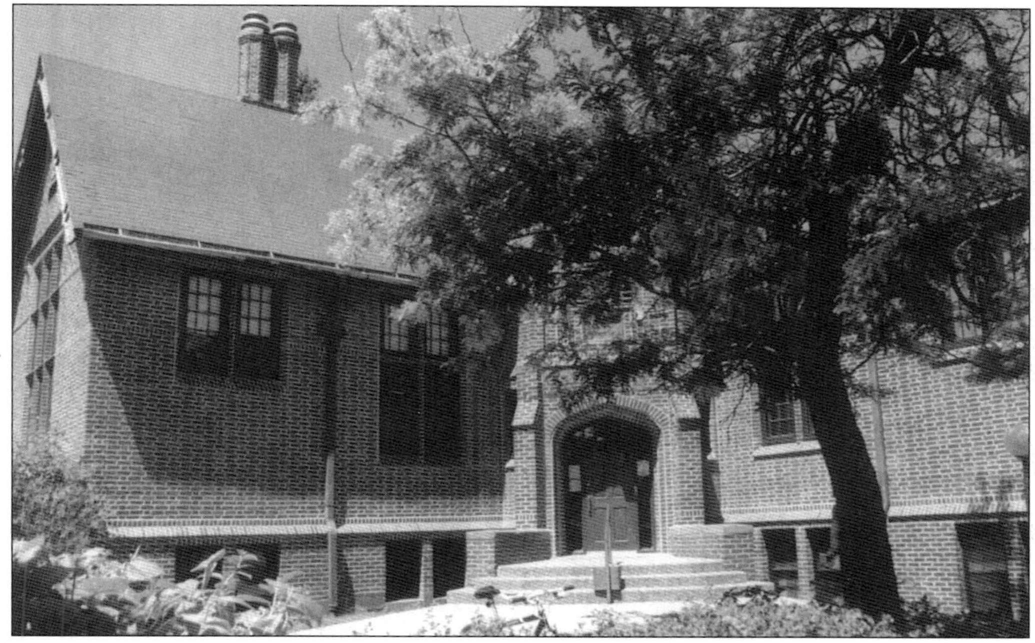

Sumner Branch Library at Sixth and Emerson was a "second home" for many young people. It was a meeting place for Boy Scout troops, and students did their homework there, signed up for the summer vacation Honors Reading Program, and got counseling and inspiration from the librarians. (Photograph by Tom Lewin.)

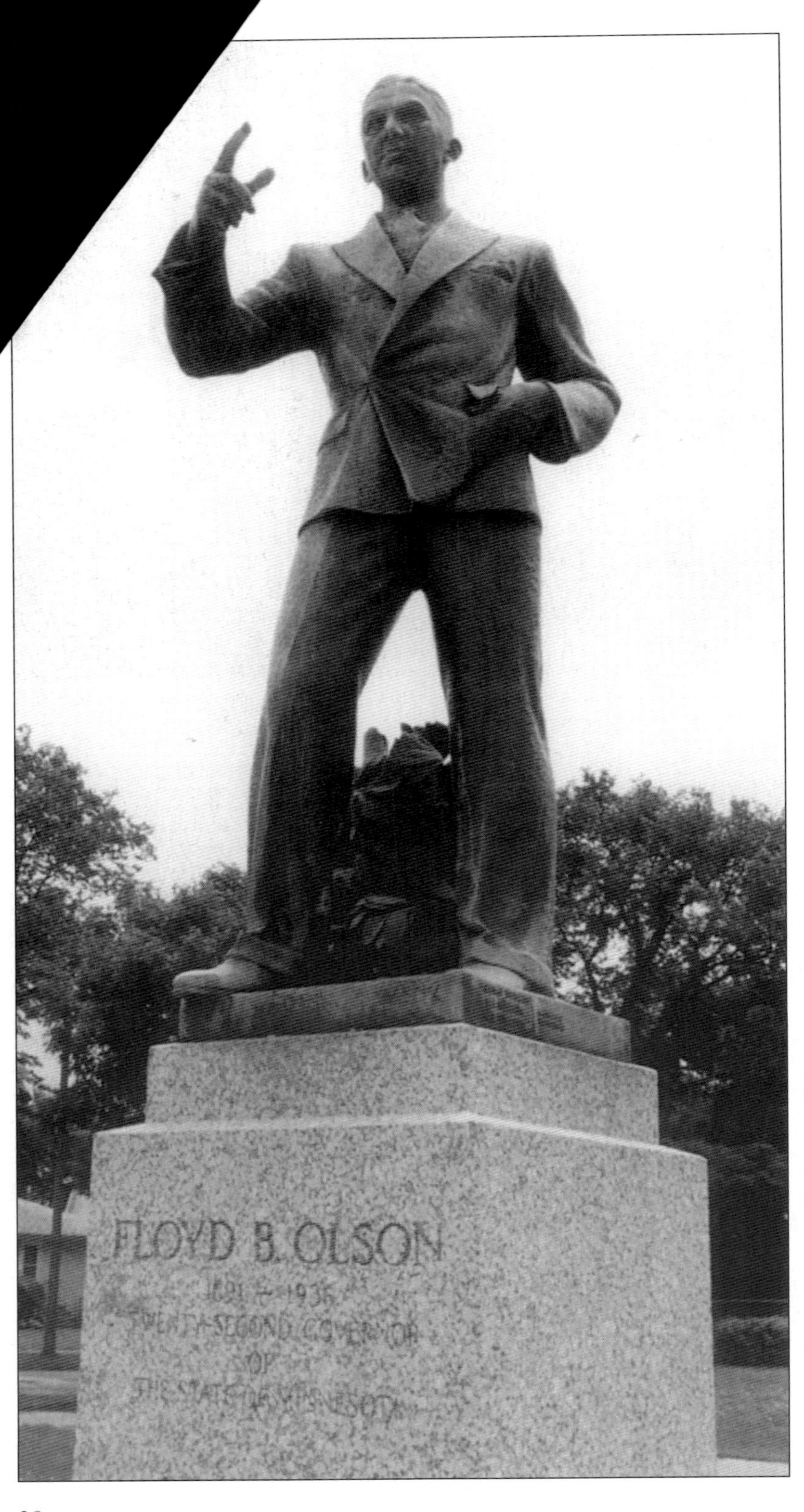

Floyd B. Olson learned Yiddish from his playmates and became a *shabbos goy* for his Jewish neighbors and business owners on Sixth Avenue North, lighting their stoves and gas lights and tending their furnaces on Sabbath and the Jewish holidays. When he was elected governor in 1932, he appointed many of his Jewish friends to state office, including Harry Fiterman as Tax Commissioner and Roger Rutchick as Assistant Attorney General. He died of cancer during his campaign for re-election in 1936, and in December 1939, Sixth Avenue North was renamed Olson Highway, and this statue was erected in his memory. (Photograph by Tom Lewin.)

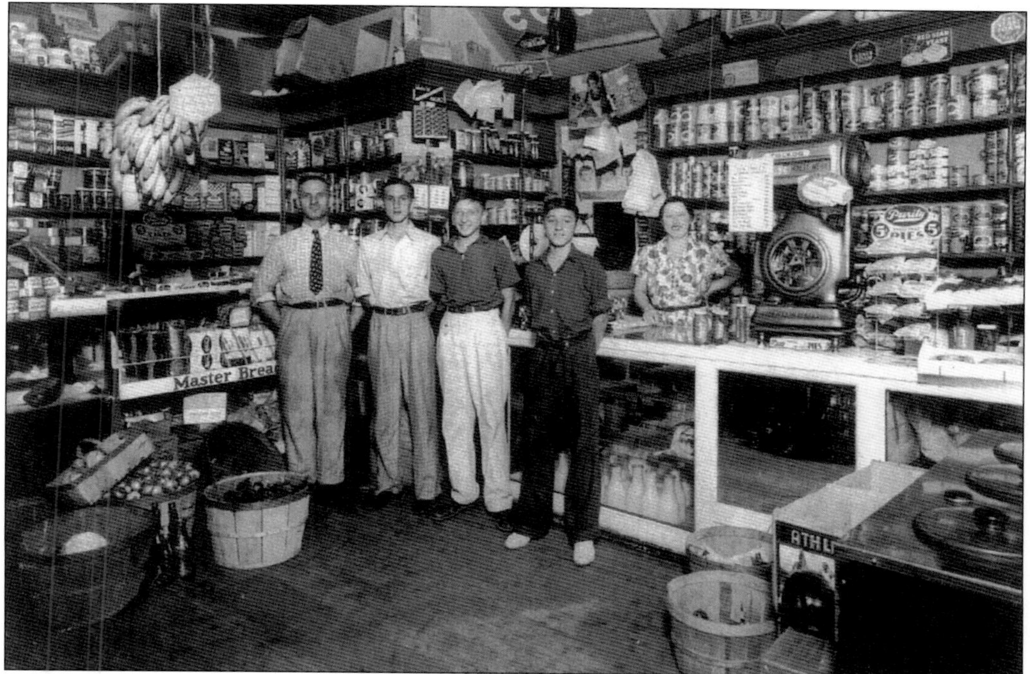

In their family grocery store at Twelfth and Fremont Avenue North, Jake and Eva Bearman's sons, Norman, Sidney, and Morton, came to work every day after school and on Sundays too. (Courtesy of Jewish Historical Society of the Upper Midwest.)

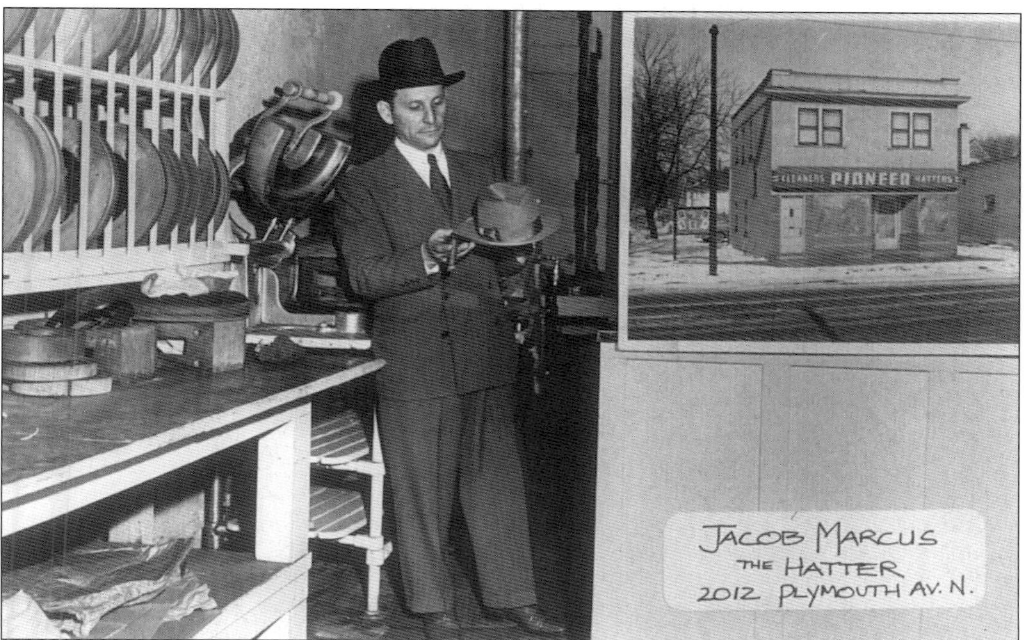

Jacob Marcus made, sold, and cleaned the hats men wore in those days. His first store was on Sixth Avenue North, but he relocated to Plymouth Avenue in the 1930s. (Courtesy of Jewish Historical Society of the Upper Midwest.)

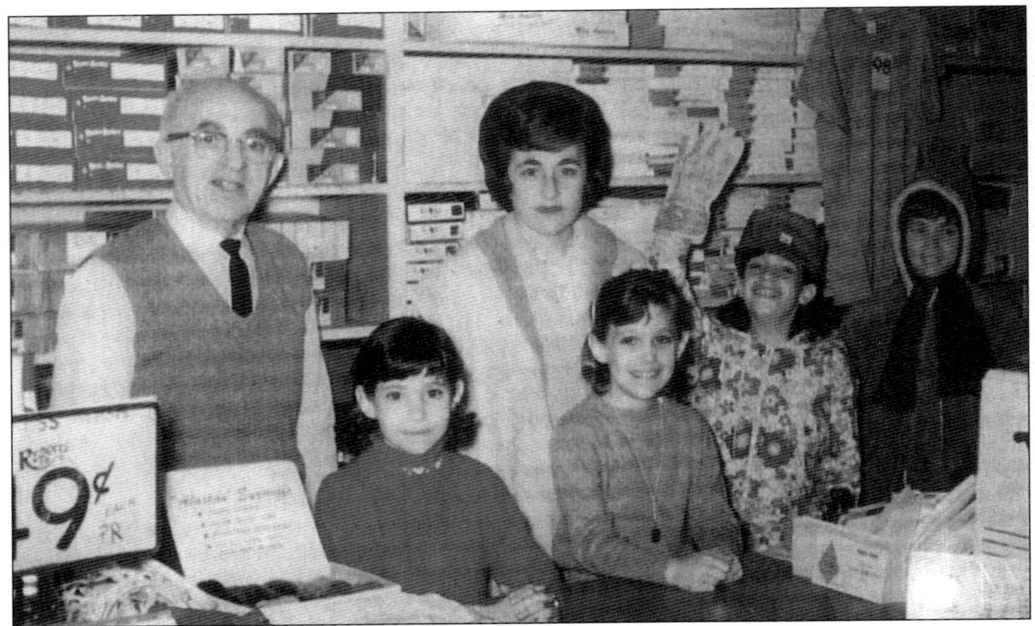

George Berman's daughter, Nessalee Berman Laiderman, and his granddaughters, Amy, Mary Jane, Beth, and Reida, liked to go shopping at Grandpa's Minneapolis Shoe Store on Plymouth and Oliver Avenues North. (Courtesy of Jewish Historical Society of the Upper Midwest.)

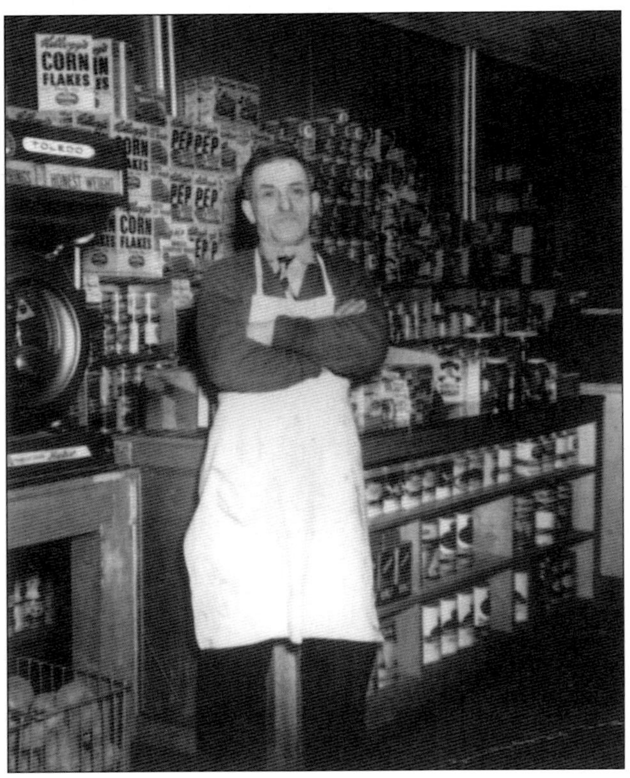

Harry Goulin and his wife, Bertha, owned and operated Goulin's Grocery Store at Girard and Plymouth Avenues North from 1934 until 1960, when they moved to St. Louis Park. "We were just four blocks from North High," Goulin recalls, "and the kids all stopped for snacks on their way to the Talmud Torah." (Courtesy of Jewish Historical Society of the Upper Midwest.)

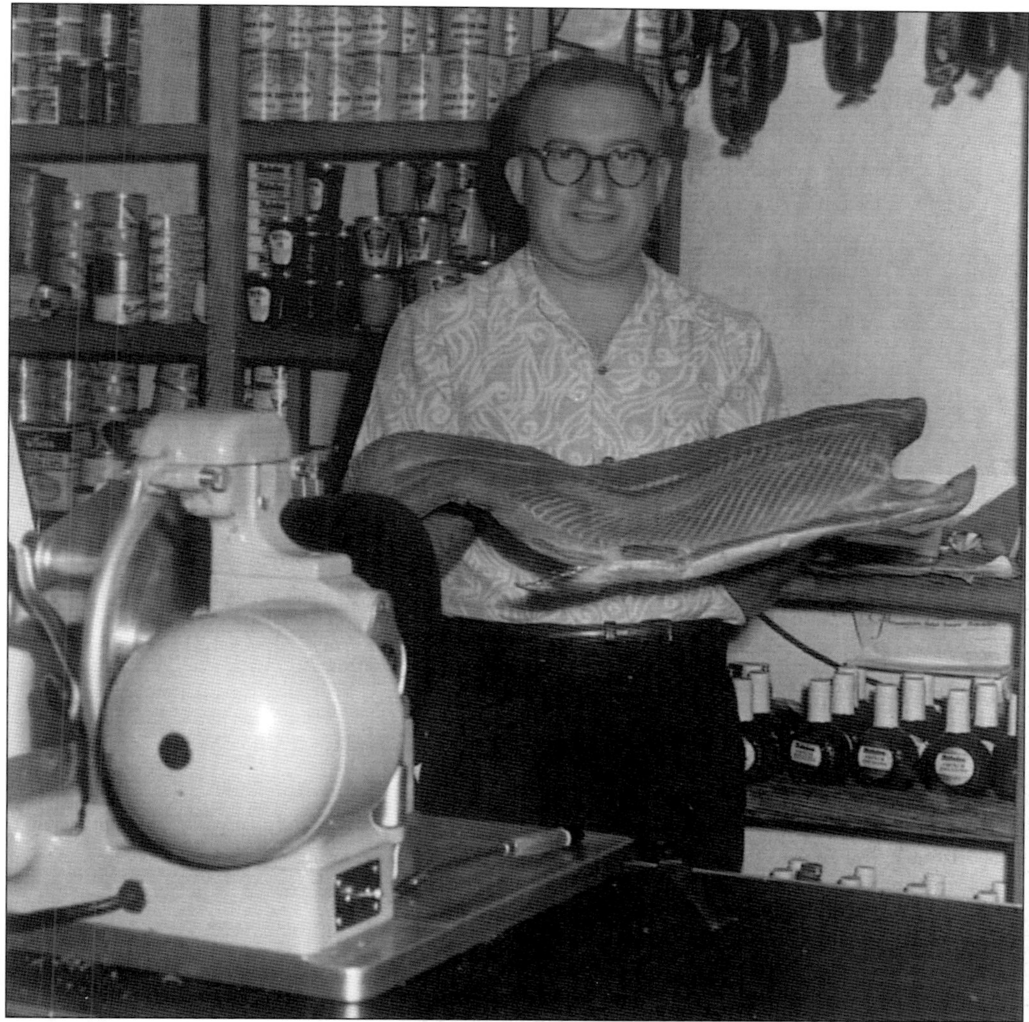

For Ben Brochin, shown here holding a freshly smoked salmon which his father had taught him how to "cure," the delicatessen and grocery store his father, Solomon Brochin, had started on Sixth Avenue North at the turn of the century became a lifetime career. As a child, Ben worked for his father six days a week. He and his friends would pick up bundles of New York Jewish newspapers at the railroad station early in the morning, and after school he would sit on top of the counter in his father's store, selling cigars and the newspapers for prices ranging from a penny to 10¢ each. When he grew up and took over his father's business, Ben packed and shipped Passover orders to customers in the Dakotas, Montana, Wisconsin, and Iowa, shipped delicacies as far as Seattle, sent herring to Alaska, and packed salami for Minneapolis students away at college. Schmaltz herring came to the store in barrels filled with brine, and Ben would use a pointed stick he'd made out of a wooden slat from an orange crate to reach down into the barrel and stab a herring through the eye. Then he'd hold it up to drain, slap it into the newspaper he was holding in his left hand, and take it to the scale to be weighed! By the 1940s, Brochin's had moved to Plymouth and Newton Avenue North, and every member of the family worked there, including his brother Joe and four sisters, Ida Lazarus, Adele Goldblum, Dorothy Wittcoff, and Gloria Leavitt, who managed the store while her brothers served in the army during World War II. (Courtesy of Jewish Historical Society of the Upper Midwest.)

Some 1939 City Directory listings

Plymouth Avenue:

#	Name
829	Ravitz, Nathan – groceries & meats
	Bryant Avenue
900	Farnham & Hawkins Fuel & Oil
901	Weiss, Frank – groceries
918	Mill City Launderers & Cleaners
	Dupont Avenue
1000	Mandel, William – hardware
1006	Jaffa Transportation
1028	Carpenter Drug Store
	J. L. Krishef – dentist
	Samuel Leonard – physician
	Emerson Avenue
1101	Beyer, Ralph – groceries
1103	Beyer, Alex – meats
1107	Della's Beauty Shop
	Skully Millinery & Dresses
1111	Versteger, Margaret – restaurant
	Fremont Avenue
1203	Bolduc, Louis – pile driving
1230	DuPew, Kenneth – filling station
	Girard Avenue
1304	Stavnaw – ice
	Humboldt Avenue
1400	Scharf Brothers Pharmacy
1401	Zeesman, Georg – undertaker
1402	Wolf, Joseph – baker
1408	Fitzsimons, John F & Co.– wholesale grocers
1413	Safeway Steel Scaffolding Co.
1423	Conway Filling Station
	Irving Avenue
1521-23	Javinsky, Jos. – groceries
	James Avenue
1600	Rosenker, Chas – groceries
1601	Rosoff, Samuel – drug store
1603	Schuster, Max – meats
1605	Quaker - Dr. Pepper – bottling company
1619	I. L. Friedman – dentist
1620	Rod, Howard – meats
1621	Volkenant, Raymond – electric applianc
1623	Feldhandler, Morris – shoe repairs
1627	Phillips & Feldman – meats
	Knox Avenue
1709	Abramovitch, Alex – dry goods
1711	Blinder, Ben – groceries
1719	Saldoff, Louis – barber
1721	Simons, Norman – beauty shop

#	Name
	Logan Avenue
1800	Bordman, Harry – cigars
1801-05	Peoples -Lehman Baking Co.
1802	Blicker, Jack – barber
1811	Kirshbaum, Irving – dry cleaners
1815	North Side Bakery
1817	Pesis, Morris – meats
1819	North Side Plumbing & Heating
	Twin City Upholstering
1821	Strimling, William – drug store
1822	Ratner, Louis – filling station
	Morgan Avenue
1901	Dubinsky, Abraham – confectnr
1903	Tenenbaum, C.A. – dry goods
1904	Peoples Printing
1905	Grossman, Harry – groceries
1906	Fidelman, Louis – fish
1907	Greenstein & Post – meats
1907½	Radke, Louise – beauty shop
1909	Schwartz & Evidon – meats
1911	Herskovitz, Jack – beverages
1912	Grossman, Harry – garage
1913	Margolis & Sons – garage
1916	Plymouth Hardware Co
1918	Schaefer, A.N. – ax mfr
1919	Homewood Theater
1922	Margolis, Jack – dry goods
1924	Malcoff, Jake – confectioners
1925	Katznelson, Sol – jeweler
	Newton Avenue
2001	Brochin, Ben – groceries
2003	Sporen, Hermand – restaurant
2005	Bank, Charles – beverages
2007	Central Bakery
2012	Marcus, Jack – hat cleaner
2016	Kaplan, Sid – barber
2018	Sklar, Harold – billboards
2020	Sachs & Karkoff – plumbers
2021	Goldman, David – shoe repair
2021	Soferman, Louis – tailor
2023	Wolstein, Meyer – meats
2024	Swaiman, Mrs. Shirley – barber
	Gordon, Philip – physician
	Shaperman, Eva – physician
	Swatez, Ben – dentist
2025	Schermer, Harry – groceries

[Pl]ymouth Avenue (continued):

	Name
	Oliver Avenue
1	Gordon, Harold – filling station
8	Hechter's Realty Company
6	Kaplan, Betty – beauty shop
	I. M. Goldstein – dentist
	Penn Avenue
1	Berman, Charles – filling station
6	Aaron, Meyer – monuments
8	Rosenfield, H. L. – furrier
6	Freier, E. F. – printer
8	Fingerhut & Pliam – window shades
6	Rudick & Rovner – groceries
	Shamus, Paul – meats
	Queen Avenue
9	Homewood Presbyterian Church
	Russell Avenue
0	Murman, Abe – groceries
	Murman, Irving – plumber
2	Russell Beauty Salon
6	Belzer, Samuel – groceries
8	Homewood Northside Pharmacy
	Goldberg, Maurice – dentist
	Sheridan Avenue
0	Peters, Mary – groceries

Penn Avenue North...

#	Name
929	Lazarus, Max – groceries
1000	John Hay School
1001	Calvary Methodist Church
1124	Lincoln Junior High School
	Lincoln Evening School
1254	Homewood Hospital
1301	Desnick Brothers – pharmacy
	L. E. Erdman – dentist
	R. H. Lundquist – dentist
	Sheinkopf, Jacob – physician
1302	Hubbard, A. M. – plumber
1304	Gifis, M. B. – bicycle repairs
1349	Beth El Synagogue

Plymouth Avenue businesses were almost 100 percent Jewish-owned in the 1940s. (Research by Tom Lewin, Minneapolis City Directory, 1939.)

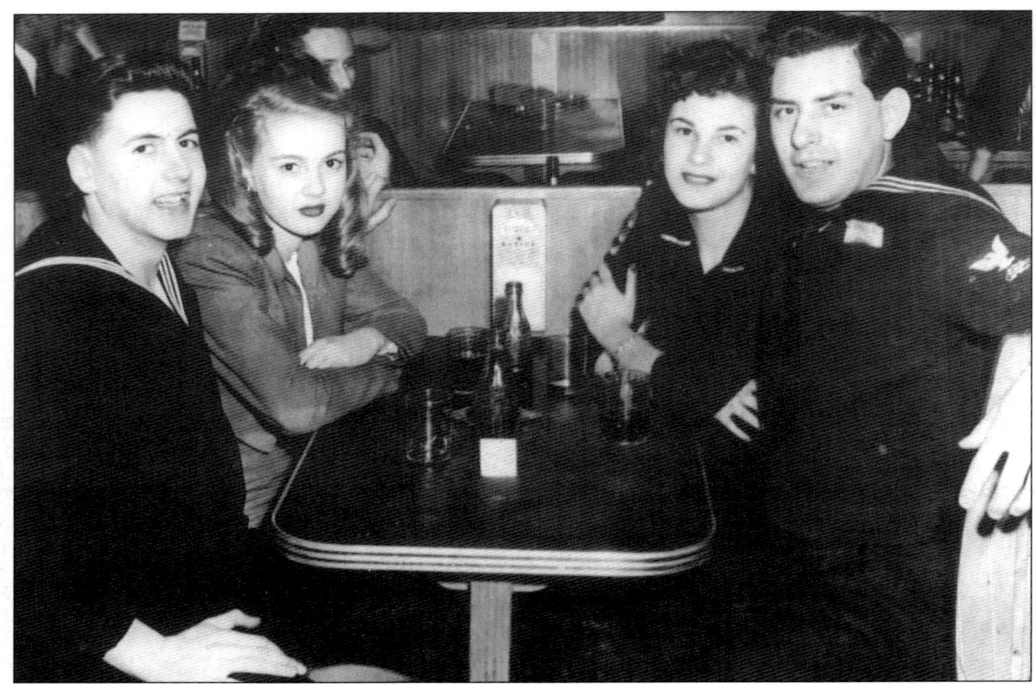

The restaurant at Malcoff's Delicatessen, across the street from the Homewood Theater, was a popular hangout for young people. Marcia Schnitzer, Mel Maisel (right), and Don Horwitz and his date ate dinner there in the 1940s. (Courtesy of Marcia Schnitzer Hinitz.)

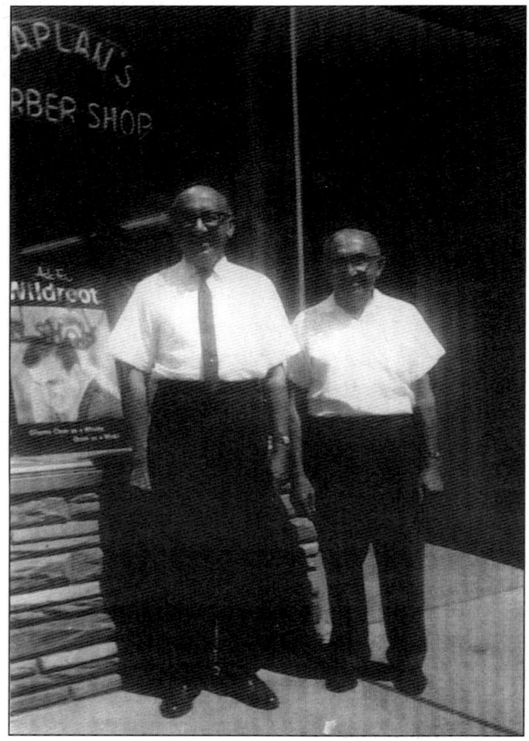

George and Sidney Kaplan opened their Barber Shop at 2020 Plymouth Avenue North in 1929. Their slogans were "A Million Dollar Haircut for Two Bits" and "Stick With Kaplan and the Girls Will Stick With You." They could do a haircut in 10 minutes, but many customers stayed after their haircuts to *shmooz* and play pool. (Courtesy of Jewish Historical Society of the Upper Midwest.)

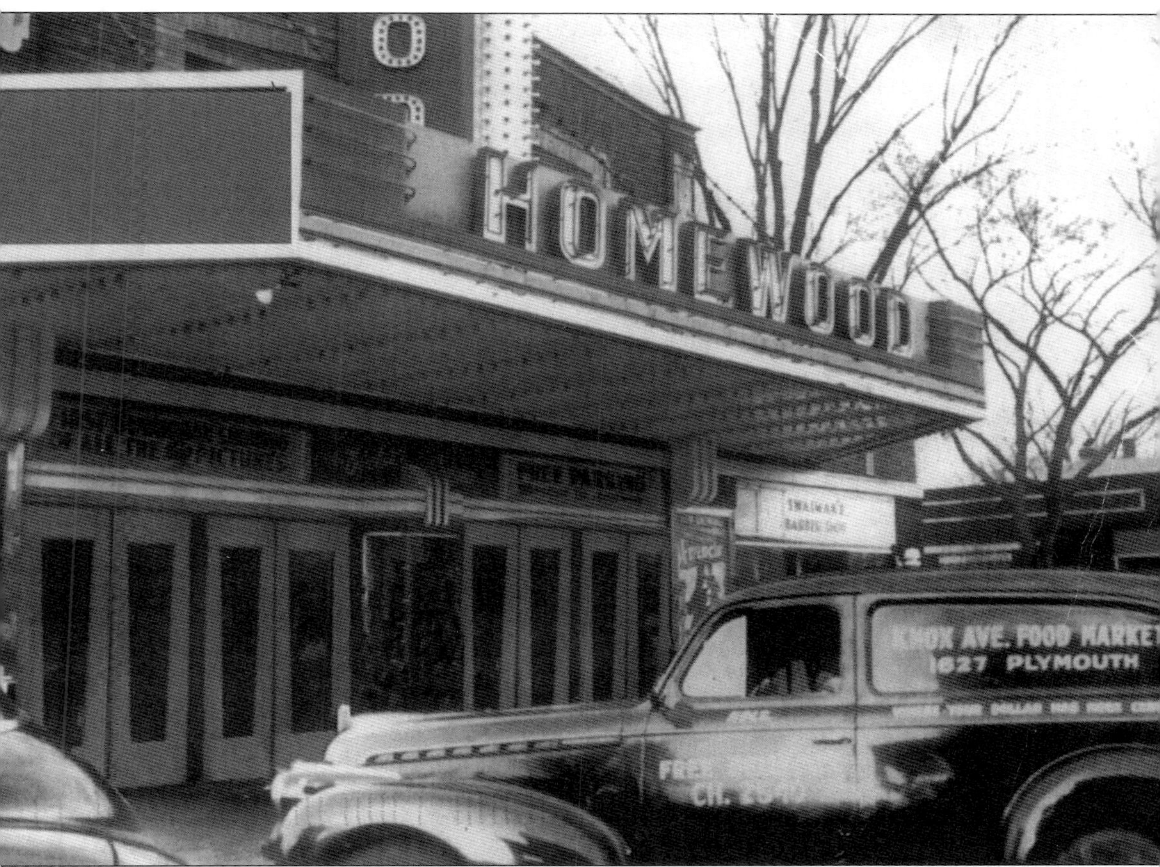

There was plenty of entertainment on Plymouth Avenue, including Charlie Bank's pool hall, the bowling alley next to Brochin's, and most of all, the Homewood Theater, owned by S.G. "Sol" Lebedoff. On Wednesday evenings—Bank Night—the theater was full of people hoping to win the evening's dollar jackpot, a set of dishes, or other prizes. In the 1930s and '40s, a box of popcorn cost a dime and tickets were 15¢ for adults, 10¢ for children, and 5¢ for Saturday matinees that included a double feature plus cartoons and news. Hollywood made about 600 movies a year, according to Lebedoff's son Martin, who owned the Brynwood Theater on Glenwood Avenue, so they showed three or four different films every week and had midnight shows and double features two or three times a week. Harry Lerner still laughs about earning $1 a week by climbing up a ladder to change the listings on the theater's marquee—but he also got to see the movies for free and bring a friend. The theater was cooled by an artesian well in the basement, and people stood outside on hot summer nights waiting for someone to open a door so they could feel the cool breeze wafting out. (Courtesy of Jewish Historical Society of the Upper Midwest.)

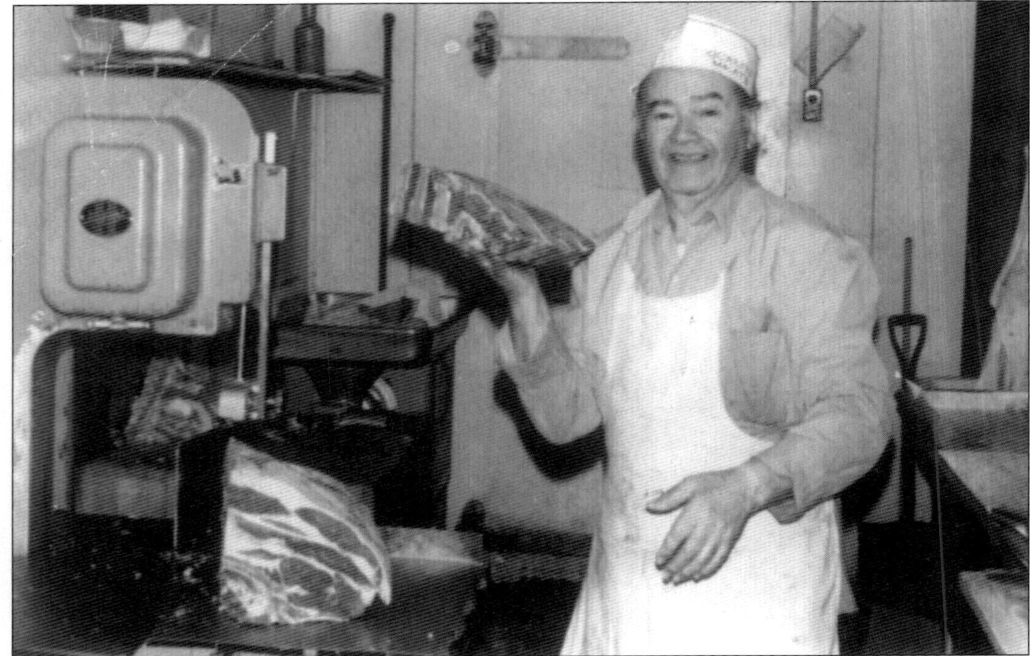

Louis Post and Moe Greenstein went into business together, selling fish and kosher meats. People said Louie Post always smiled and called all the housewives who came to shop by their maiden names, and here he is, still smiling, as he shows off kosher prime ribs at Greenstein and Post, which by then had moved to Plymouth and Newton Avenues North, next to Brochin's. (Courtesy of Jewish Historical Society of the Upper Midwest.)

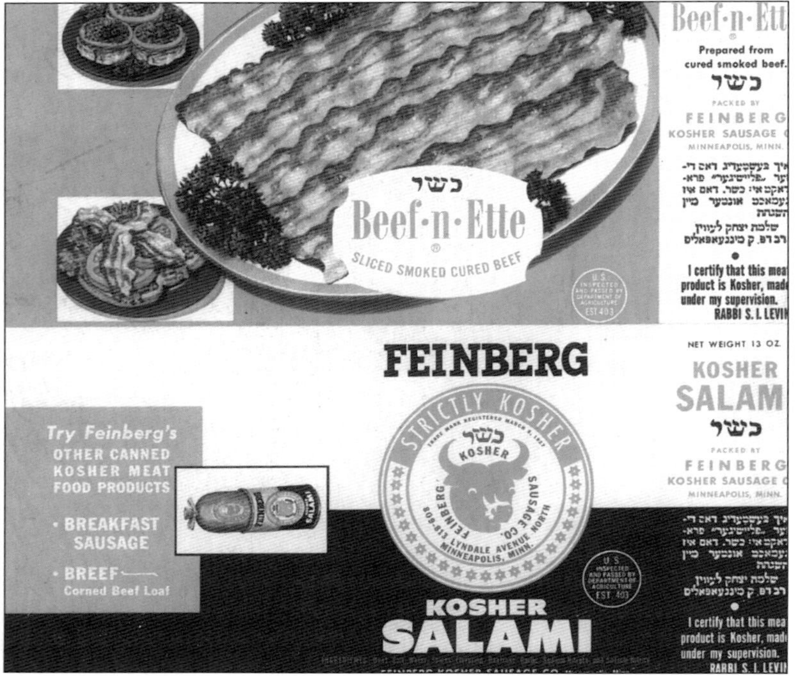

Feinberg Kosher Sausage Co. began their manufacturing business at 811 Lyndale Avenue North in the 1920s. They sold their salami, hot dogs, and other kosher meat products to Malcoff's, Abe's, and other neighborhood delicatessens and meat markets like Greenstein and Post. (Courtesy of Jewish Historical Society of the Upper Midwest.)

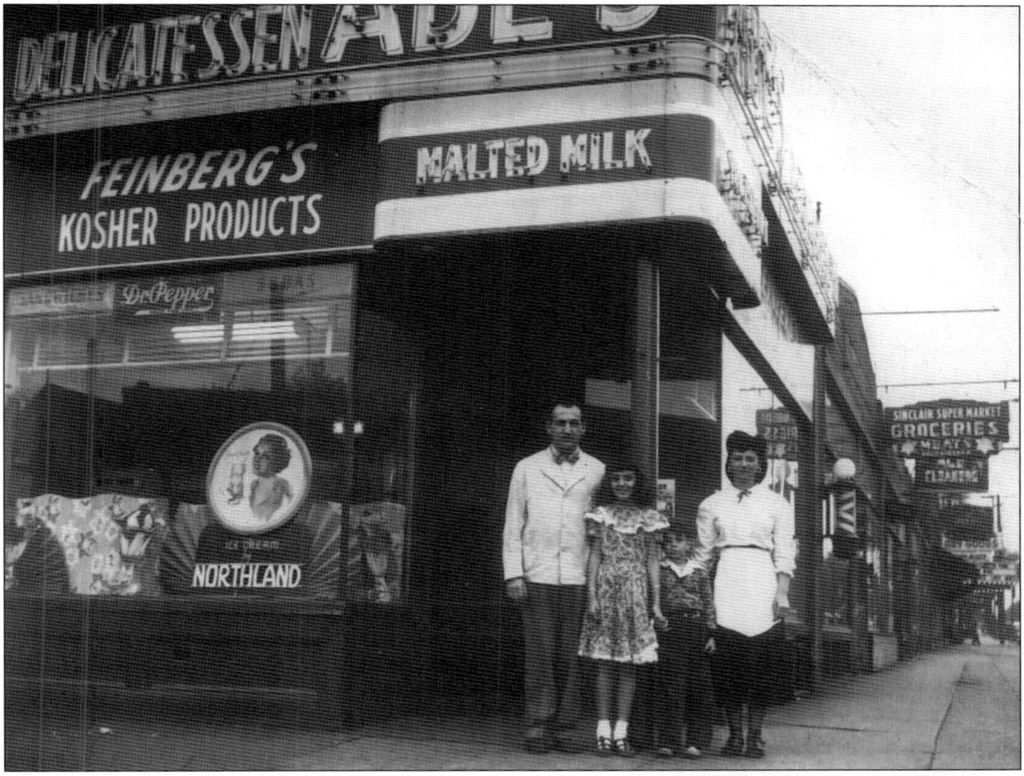

Abe's Delicatessen at Plymouth and Logan was a family-run business where corned beef sandwiches cost 25¢, chocolate malted milks were 15¢, and you could get a three-scoop ice cream cone for a nickel. (Courtesy of Minnesota Historical Society.)

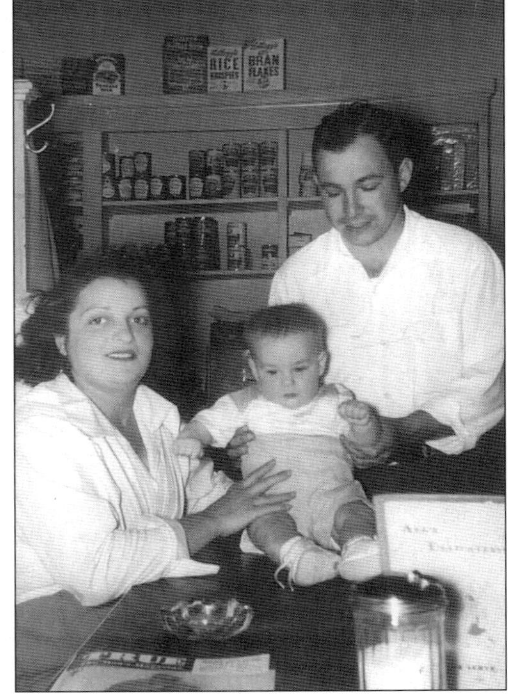

This is a June 1949 photo of Tilly Dubinsky Jaffy with her husband, Sam, and their six-month-old son Stanley, at the Dubinsky family's Plymouth Avenue deli. (Courtesy of Tillie Jaffy.)

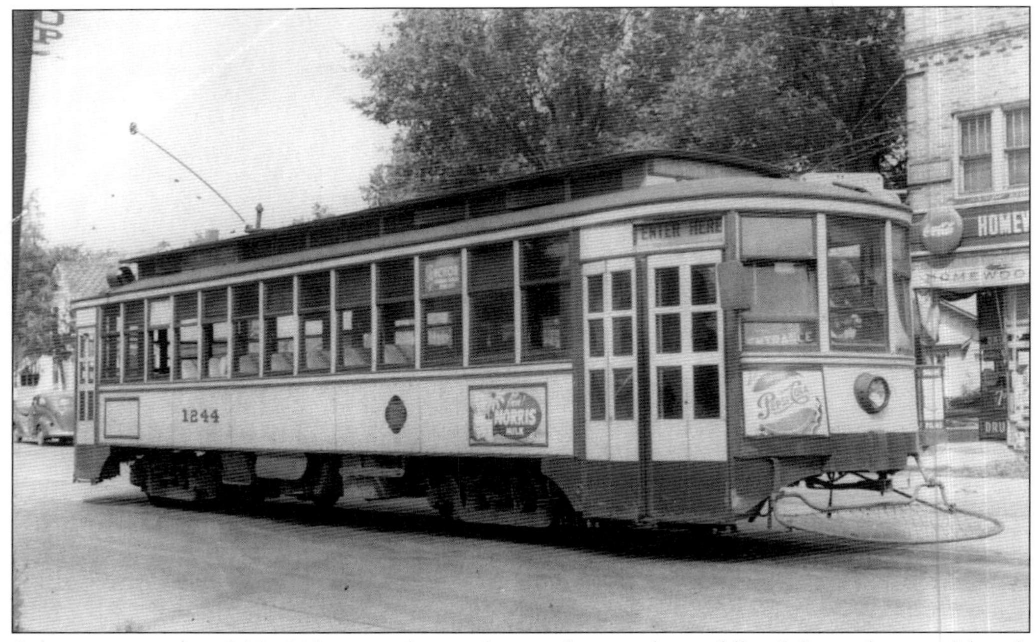

Streetcars were available 24 hours a day, and even if it was the middle of the night, you felt safe walking home alone once you got off. (Courtesy of Minnesota Transportation Museum.)

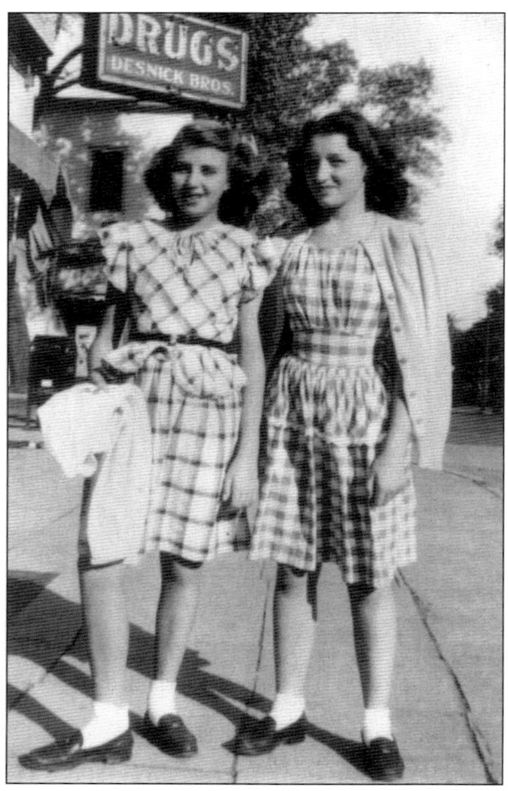

Ruth Lurie and Reva Margolis shopped at Desnick's, their neighborhood drugstore, on Penn and Plymouth Avenues North. This photo was taken in 1946, when the move to the suburbs was about to begin. (Courtesy of Jewish Historical Society of the Upper Midwest.)

Three

Were We Really the Antisemitism Capital of the United States?

Unfortunately, antisemitism was spreading to America. The "Old Yankees," for example, blamed the recently-arrived immigrant workers when the Industrial Revolution began sprouting strikes, riots, rising prices, political corruption, and what some considered the vulgarization of Americans' tastes and traditions. In the farming area known as the *veld*, one resident recalls that Norwegian children in the neighborhood would throw ashes in front of the Jewish kids' sleds when they went sliding in the wintertime, and on July 8, 1906, the *Minneapolis Journal* printed a story about the "North Side Jewish quarter," saying that some residents objected to having their children attend the same school with Jewish children, "and it became the mission of the principal and teachers to convince the prejudiced ones that the Jewish children had neither hoofs nor horns, and were as companionable as their own children."

Because working on the Sabbath is a sin, Jewish shopkeepers kept their stores open on Sundays instead. In 1900, however, the United States Supreme Court upheld an 1884 Minnesota Statute that prohibited "all labor on Sunday. . . excepting the works of necessity or charity . . . needed for good order, health, or comfort of the community," and ruled that "keeping open a barber shop on Sunday for the purpose of cutting hair and shaving beards" was therefore illegal. And six years later, on January 19, 1906, the Minnesota Supreme Court ruled in State vs. Weiss that the section of a 1903 state law "prohibiting the public traffic in certain merchandise on Sunday" was also constitutional: "That the defendant was of the Hebrew Race and of the Jewish Church, regularly attended such Church as his place of worship on Saturdays . . . and believed in the doctrines of that Church . . . that Saturday is the Sabbath or Lord's day, to be observed and kept by him as a day of worship, does not in any manner effect the constitutionality of Chapter 362, p. 652, Laws of 1903," and therefore the defendant would not be permitted to sell groceries on Sundays just because his religion required him to keep his store closed on Saturdays.

With antisemitism already ingrained and legalized, a book called *Protocols of the Elders of Zion* quickly gained a large audience. First published in Russia in 1902, the *Protocols* described a supposed "Jewish plot" to destroy Christian civilization and create a worldwide Jewish empire. According to the *Protocols*, movements like women's suffrage and giving every American equality before the law, freedom of religion, a free press, universal education, and the right to vote, would eventually destroy both America and the entire world by encouraging Socialism,

Anarchism, and Bolshevism! The *Protocols* also accused the Jews of inciting workmen to demand higher wages and to strike, and blamed the Jews for instilling a "passion for drink" in the laboring classes, and for wars, epidemics, and famines. In 1920, automobile magnate Henry Ford read the *Protocols*, and for the next seven years he carried on a relentless antisemitic campaign in his own newspaper, the *Dearborn Independent*.

Then came the Depression, and a group that called themselves the Silver Shirts organized in 1932. As goose-stepping, brown-shirted admirers of the Nazis, they quickly became the most visible antisemitic organization in the United States, with an estimated 800 members in Minneapolis alone. They blamed Jews for Depression unemployment, bank failures, Prohibition, racketeering, and widespread poverty, and their teen-age admirers wore brown shirts to school, put knives in their boots, and threatened Jewish students with billy clubs and brass knuckles.

Developers in suburbs like Edina distributed brochures saying they would not sell lots to Jews. Building lots in some areas of the city and its suburbs were sometimes advertised as "not available to buyers of Chinese, Japanese, Moorish, Turkish, Negro, Mongolian, Semitic, or African blood or descent," and deed restrictions in certain suburbs included Jews on the list of "non-Caucasians" who could only live in the suburb as servants!

Jews also were excluded from many resorts and social clubs, and you might not even be able to reserve a vacation cabin in northern Minnesota if your name "sounded Jewish." The elite Minneapolis Club voted in 1922 to keep its Jewish members, but to deny their sons membership. When a *Minneapolis Tribune* reporter was assigned to cover a national golf tournament at the Minikahda Club, he was told he couldn't come into the clubhouse because he was a Jew. Toastmasters and Lions and Rotary Clubs didn't accept Jews, and Jews couldn't even join AAA, because some board members didn't want them dining or attending special events in their luxurious clubhouse! Rev. William Bell Riley's Sunday morning sermons at First Baptist Church were almost always antisemitic diatribes, and in 1938, a whispering campaign about incumbent governor Elmer Benson's supposed "Jewish connections" helped elect Harold Stassen governor.

A survey of 15 Minneapolis employment agencies in 1931 showed that more than half of them had clients who wouldn't hire Jews, so Jews were told to forget about landing a good job in most local businesses, including banks, insurance companies, and department stores. Advisors at the University of Minnesota's Dental Hygienist School were reportedly telling Jewish students to withdraw because it would be impossible to place them in jobs after graduation. Even Jewish business owners sometimes hesitated to hire Jewish receptionists or sales clerks for fear of "offending" clients or customers. In 1930, the now world-famous Mayo Clinic and St. Mary's Hospital in Rochester had only two Jewish doctors on staff, and Jews, Greeks, Afro-Americans, and members of "other minorities" had to deposit $100 before being admitted as patients. A 1936 editorial in *Minnesota Medicine*, the journal of the State Medical Association, focused on the "problem" of the increasing number of Jewish physicians in the "already overcrowded" medical profession, and since Minneapolis hospitals wouldn't permit Jewish doctors to care for patients who had to be hospitalized, a Jewish doctor who had to hospitalize a patient had to turn his patient over to a non-Jewish colleague.

Many Jewish businessmen couldn't buy property insurance because of their supposed "well-known tendency" to burn down their own businesses to collect the insurance, and a Minneapolis insurance company wrote to an agent in Wadena that it was canceling a policy "owing to the fact that Mr. Fink is a Hebrew, and Jewish people are not insured by our companies." Some downtown office buildings refused to rent to Jewish professional men, and the Board of Realtors didn't accept Jewish members.

Meanwhile, though, the Jewish community was beginning to fight back. In 1931 they opened Oak Ridge, their own country club. In 1934, they organized a Minnesota chapter of the B'nai B'rith Anti-Defamation League, which later combined with the Jewish Community Relations Council, organized in 1950, with Sam Scheiner as its first director. When Scheiner left to work at the newly opened Mt. Sinai Hospital, Irwin Gladstein and the Anti-Defamation League's Monroe Schlactus served briefly as JCRC's directors until Scheiner returned to supervise the Minneapolis office of what had now become the Jewish Community Relations Council/Anti-Defamation League of Minnesota and the Dakotas. Meanwhile, in 1938, representatives from Minneapolis, St. Paul, and 17 smaller cities had organized the Minnesota Jewish Council, the first independent statewide community relations group in the United States. The Council hired a photographer to take pictures of people attending meetings of the Silver Shirts, and humorous articles written by *Minneapolis Journal* reporter Eric Sevareid, together with the Council's photographs, held the Silver Shirts up to public ridicule, and many people stopped attending their meetings.

Although it was 1946 when Carey McWilliams wrote his article for a national magazine, *Common Ground,* saying that "In almost every walk of life, an 'iron curtain' separates Jews from non-Jews in Minneapolis . . . One might even say, with a measure of justification, that Minneapolis is the capital of anti-Semitism in the United States," things had already begun to change, and have continued to do so.

When he was campaigning for mayor of Minneapolis in 1945, for example, Hubert Humphrey outlined a five-point program to offset the growth of racial prejudice in Minneapolis. and when he won the election he soon sparked a nationwide movement, as well as local change, by organizing a Fair Employment Practices Commission to identify discrimination and recommend ways to eliminate it. A 1947 survey of Minneapolis hospitals and the Hennepin County Medical Society documented ongoing discriminating against "doctors of the Jewish faith," but by 1951, when the Jewish community opened Mt. Sinai Hospital, Asbury and St. Mary's Hospitals were already permitting Jewish doctors to admit patients, and other hospitals soon began to include Jews on their staff. In 1948, AAA eliminated the country club access that was included with membership and began accepting Jews as members, as did the Minneapolis Club and the Minneapolis Athletic Club. In 1961, Minneapolis elected a Jewish mayor, Arthur Naftalin, who served four terms until 1967, and members of the Jewish community were also becoming leaders in the general community. Dr. Fred Lyon chaired Minneapolis's Human Relations Committee, for example, and Joel Glotter was appointed to serve on the St. Louis Park Citizens Advisory Committee.

Many members of the community also began to join organizations that had previously refused to admit Jews as members. Joseph Seltzer, for example, broke into the Freemasons via his fundraising and charitable efforts at a time when few Minneapolis Jews could gain admittance, and in 1967, he was elected Grand Master of the Freemasons of Minnesota, which had almost 7,500 members at the time, and he traveled to England to represent Minnesota at the installation of the Duke of Kent as world leader of their ancient fraternal order. The State of Israel had more than 60 registered Freemason lodges in the 1970s; in a show of interfaith unity and tolerance, their organization's symbol combined the Masons' traditional cross with the Star of David and the Crescent of Islam, and in 1967, Israeli Masons elected their first Arab leader.

Now, as we move into the 21st century, members of the Jewish community have become increasingly prominent as directors or presidents of formerly Protestant preserves, and visible antisemitism is almost non-existent. The University of Minnesota has a Jewish president, Mark Yudof. The Minneapolis Institute of Art has a Jewish director, Evan Maurer. Minnesota has elected two Jewish senators, Rudy Boschwitz and Paul Wellstone, who is completing his second term. Other members of the Jewish community are teachers, principals, and professors at public and private schools, colleges, and universities, and play leading roles in cultural, social, and public service organizations, state and local politics, law and accounting firms, and corporate life.

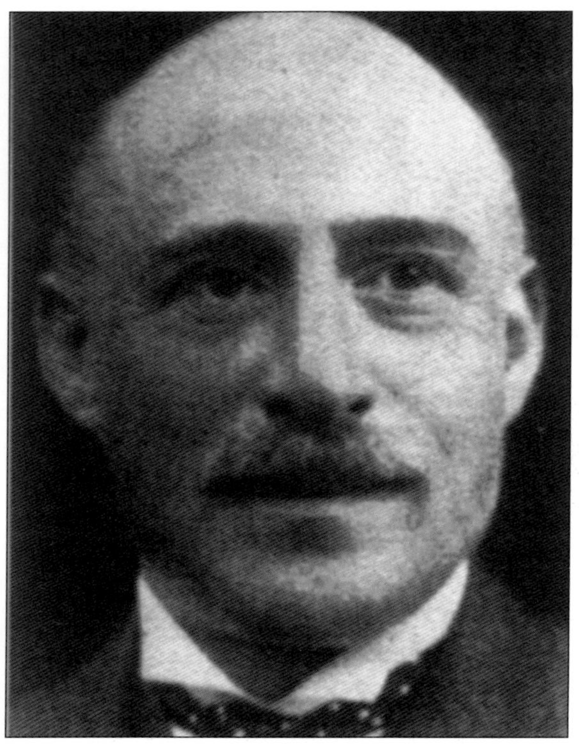

Emanuel Cohen was a lawyer and community leader who was born in Pennsylvania and had come to Minneapolis in the early 1880s. He was the first Jew to be accepted as a member of the elitist Minneapolis Club, and in 1919, he authored a bill and lobbied successfully for its passage by the Minnesota State legislature, which outlawed the restrictive covenants in real estate that were being used largely against Jews. His wife, Nina, was a founding member of the Minneapolis chapter of the National Council of Jewish Women. (Courtesy of IDENTITY, Jewish Community Center of Greater Minneapolis.)

1922 PERSONNEL
MINNEAPOLIS PUBLIC SCHOOLS

No Supervisory personnel of Jewish faiths [sic]

Name	Job	School
Samuel I. Sigal	Page	
Edna C. Levine	Invoice Clerk	
No principals of High Schools		
Mary C. Moses	History Teacher	North High
Esther Friedlander	Latin Teacher	South High
M. J. Shapiro	Physician	Seward Jr. High
Madelaine A. Leavitt	Teacher	Everett
Jennie H. Cohen	Nurse	Greeley
Leo H. Sharp	Visiting Teacher	Greeley
George Cutts	Teacher	Harrison
Sophie Sachs	Teacher	Lowell School
Phyllis M. Fink	Teacher	McKinley
Charlotte R. Goldman	Clerk	Schiller
Samuel Becker	Janitor	Blaine
Goldie Deisner	Teacher	Grant
Sophia R. Haveson	Music	Simmons School

A survey of the Minneapolis public schools' 1,831 employees in 1922 showed only nine teachers, a doctor and a nurse, a janitor, three clerks, and no "supervisory" personnel of the "Jewish faith." (Research by Tom Lewin.)

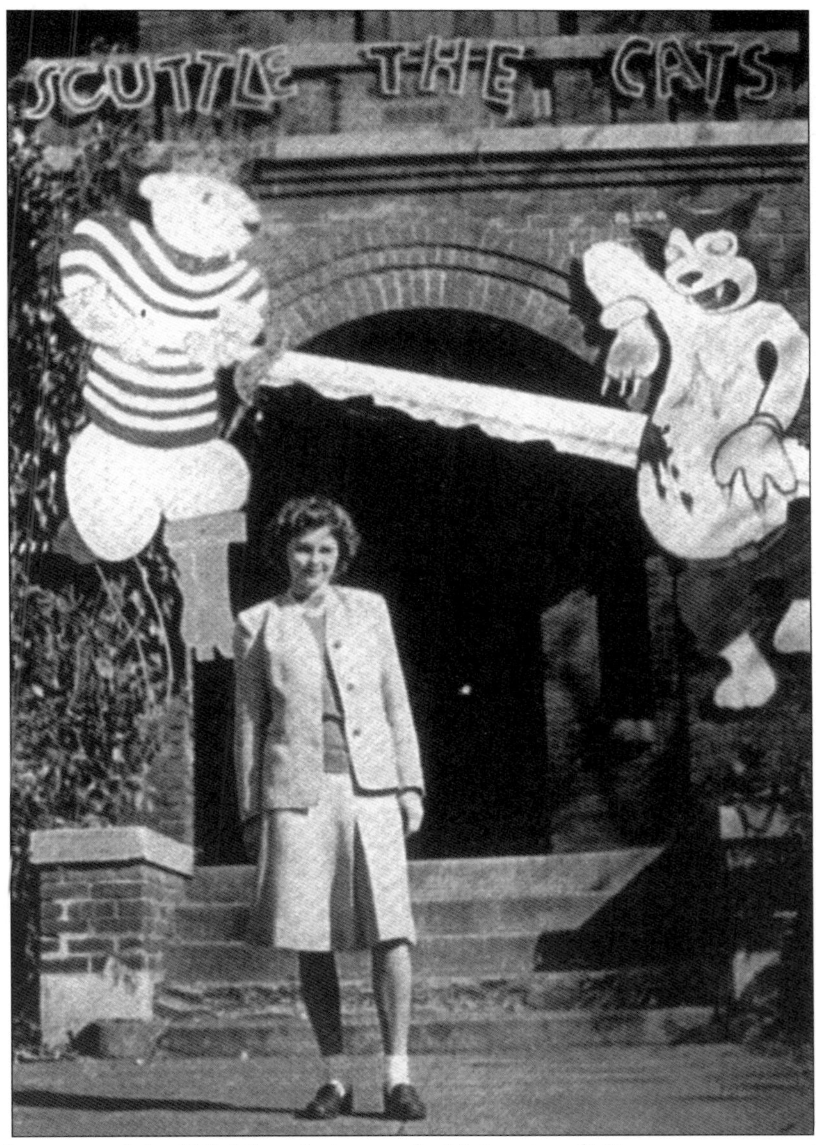

B'nai B'rith supported the Hillel Foundation on the University of Minnesota campus, where most fraternities and sororities, and other student organizations as well, would not accept Jewish members. Jewish students had to wait five years for the university to give them permission in 1940 to establish Hillel, which quickly became a popular place to socialize and study for Jewish students, most of whom lived at home and took the streetcar to school every day. Law School Senior Ben Chernov was Hillel's first president, and as Jewish students rejoiced on campus, Filis Yager wrote in an article for the first edition of their newsletter, the *Hillel Herald*, that it was "indeed miraculous that in the black year of 1940 . . . when three-fourths of the 'civilized' world has blood on its hands and hate in its soul . . . a tiny group of Jews in a corner of America has been invited to organize itself and speak out officially and proudly to its neighbors." Hillel's first office was above a bible school in Dinkytown, but in less than five years they had a building to call their own. Pictured is university student Helen Broude in front of the original Hillel House at Fifteenth and University Avenue, across the street from Folwell Hall. (Courtesy of Hillel Foundation.)

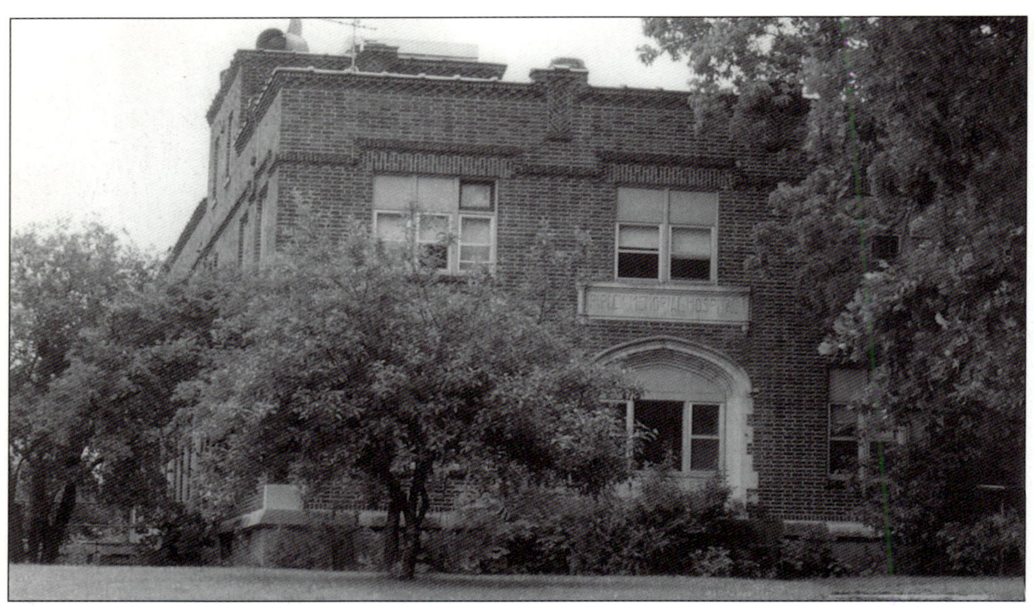

Maternity Hospital, on Glenwood and Penn Avenues North, was built in the 1890s, and was originally known as Ripley Memorial Hospital. For many years, it was one of the few hospitals in the city that accepted Jewish doctors and their patients. During the 1980s, it was converted to a seniors' residence and nursing home. (Photograph by Tom Lewin.)

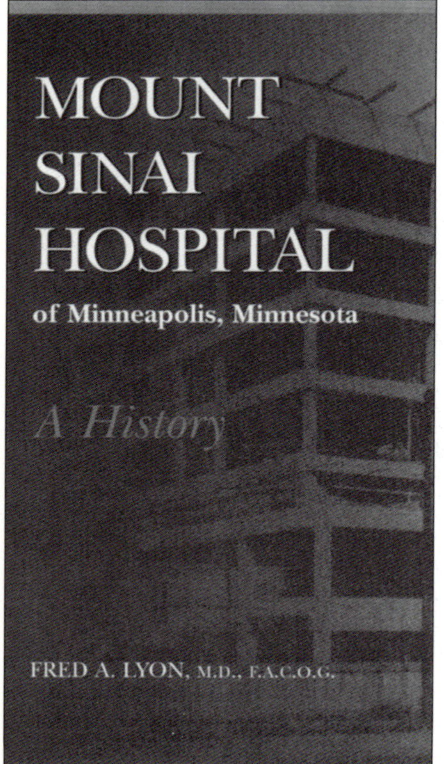

(*left*) Dr. Fred Lyon says that "without Mount Sinai, I would probably not have been able to provide hospital care to my patients . . . Then Mt. Sinai granted admitting privileges to both Jewish and non-Jewish physicians, and soon other Minneapolis hospitals followed suit, opened their doors, and accepted Jewish doctors on their staffs." (Courtesy of Dr. Fred Lyon.)

MATERNITY HOSPITAL
300 Queen Avenue North
MINNEAPOLIS 5, MINNESOTA

Date December 23, 1953 195

In Account with

Mrs. Rhoda (David) Jacobs
4740 Chowen Ave. So
Minneapolis, Minnesota

1 day false labor (12/8/53)	13	00
5 " hospital confinement @ 14.50	72	50
5 days nursery care @ 5.50	27	50
delivery room	25	00
anesthetic	15	00
laboratory charges	10	00
drugs	9	50
dressings	5	00
	177	50

(*above*) Many Jewish obstetricians delivered babies at Maternity Hospital. (Courtesy of Rhoda Lewin.)

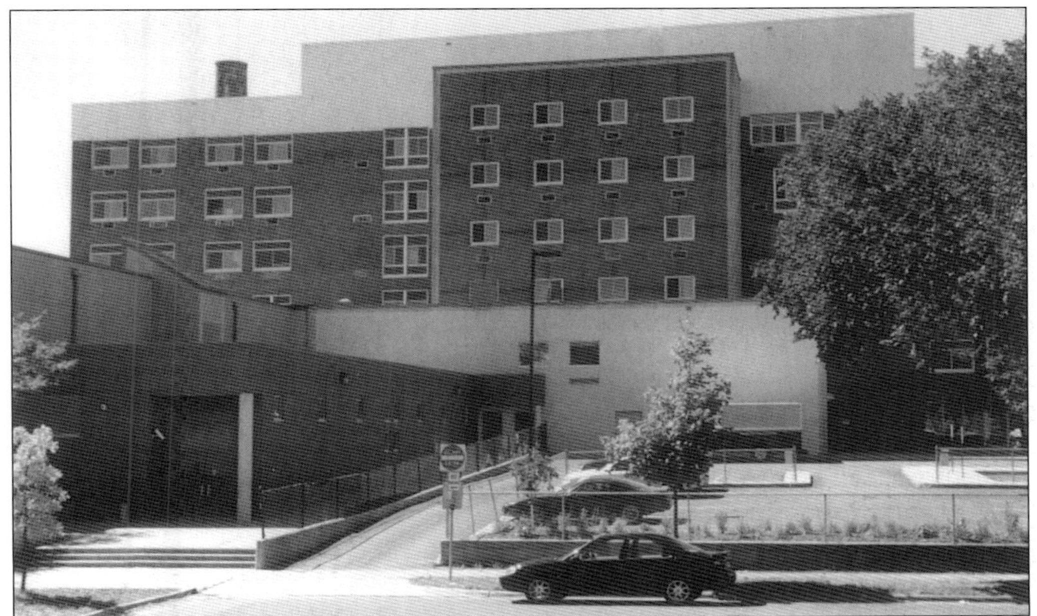

Mt. Sinai Hospital opened in 1951. As antisemitism waned, however, Jewish doctors were integrated into the general medical community, and Mt. Sinai closed in 1991. The remodeled building is now home to the Phillips Eye Care Institute, medical offices, and the Four Winds Community School. (Photograph by Tom Lewin.)

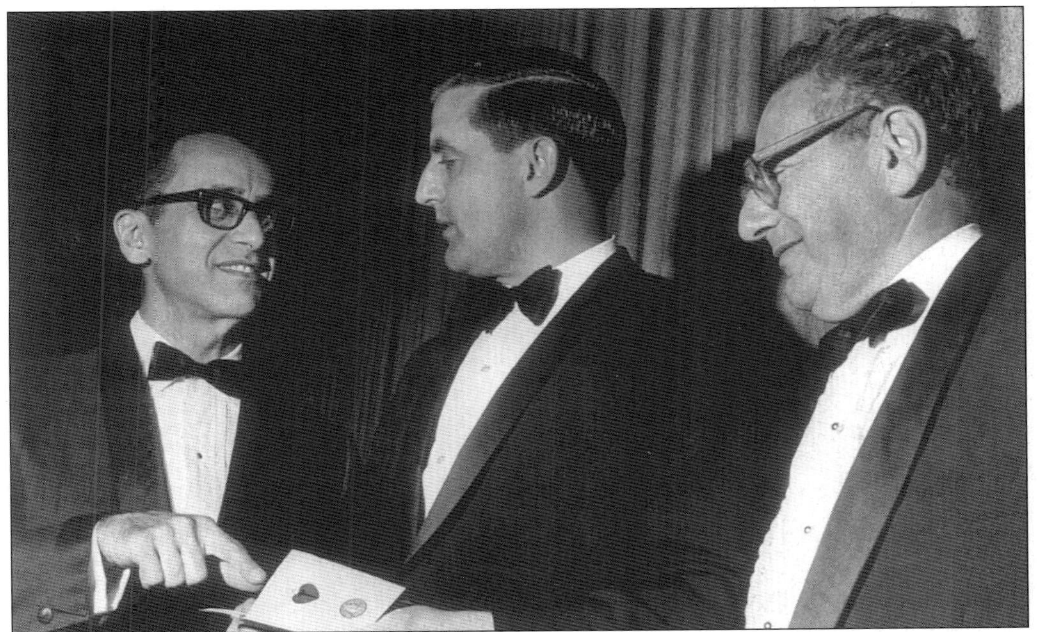

Senator Walter Mondale, pictured here with two Jewish past presidents of the Minnesota Heart Association, Dr. Milton Hurwitz (left) of St. Paul and Dr. Reuben Berman (right) of Minneapolis, was a featured speaker at the annual meeting of the Association in 1968. (Courtesy of Dr. Reuben Berman.)

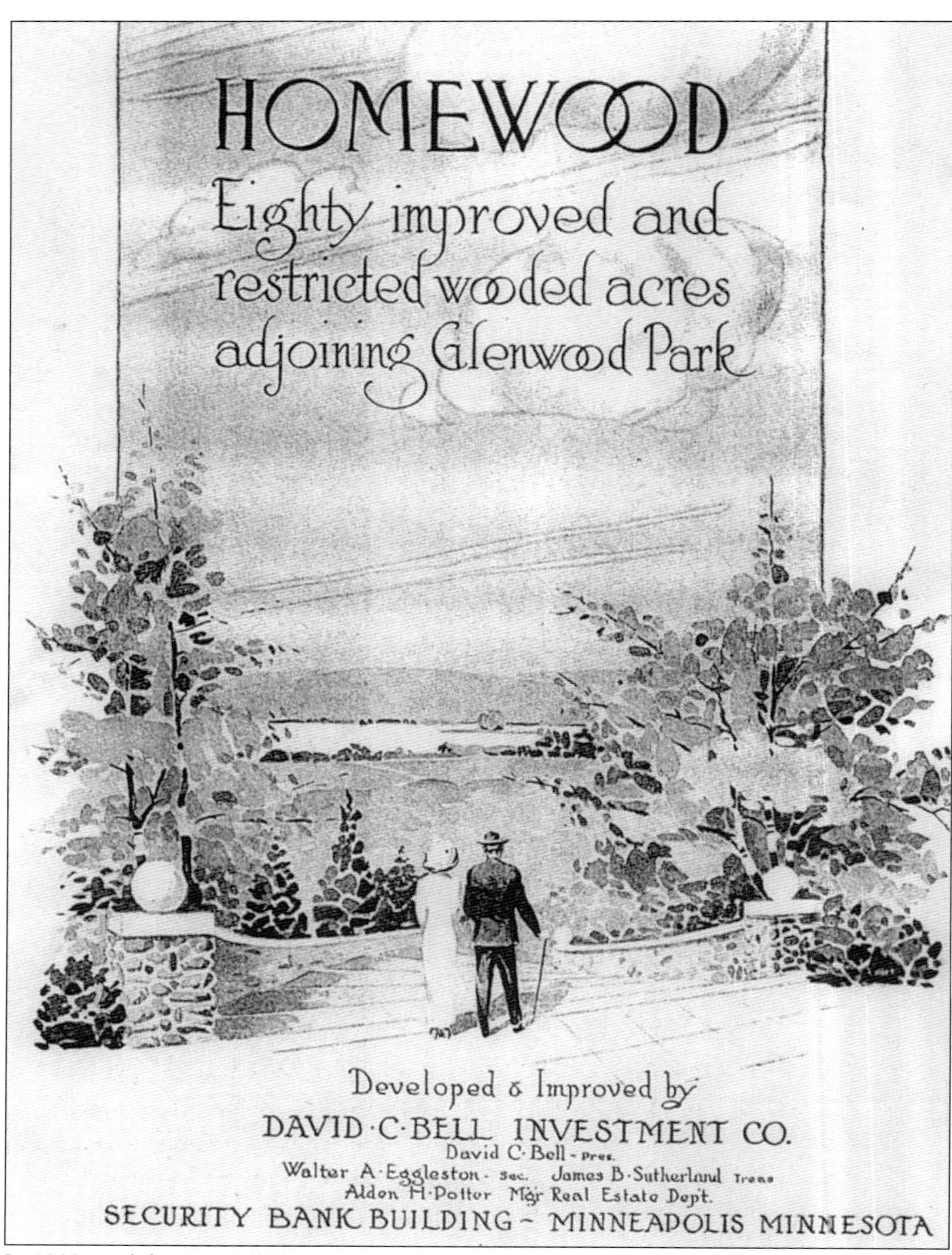

In 1908, a subdivision called Homewood was platted just beyond Penn Avenue. Covenants said that houses had to be on a lot and a half, there could be no unusual additions or outbuildings, and that no blacks or Jews could live there. David C. Bell Investment Co.'s 1920s sales brochure touted Homewood as a neighborhood of 80 "improved and restricted" building sites where buyers' children would have "healthy and well-bred children like themselves for companions." (Courtesy of Beverly Roberts' Homewood Markers Project and Hennepin History Museum.)

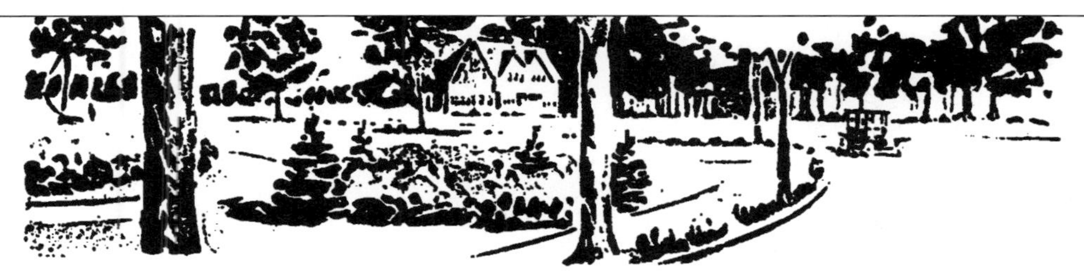

H O M E W O O D

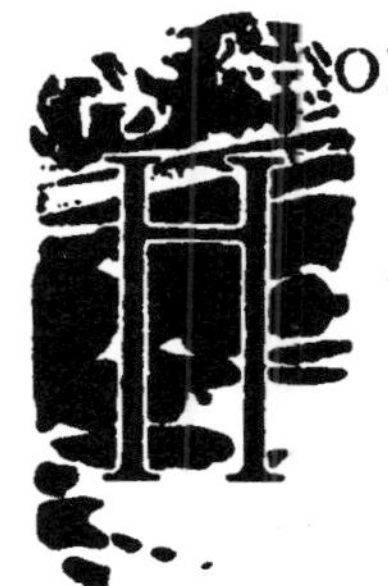

HOMEWOOD was not designed for millionaires or the so-called idle rich, but for the class of progressive business and professional men who prefer to locate their homes among other homes of character and refinement, without paying a fortune for a residence site on which to build, and where the restrictions serve as a protection against undesirable neighbors and unsightly improvements.

Homewood consists of eighty wooded acres adjoining Glenwood Park. At least thirty miles of boulevards connect this park with other parks of the city and with a famous chain of seven beautiful lakes, all of which are being surrounded by boulevards. No finer drive can be found in America.

Homewood is now being improved.

All special improvements, including macadam for streets, are in or are being put in.

This beautiful Homewood district lies within as easy reach of the city's business center as the Lake of the Isles District. A fifteen-minute ride by trolley, or only six minutes by automobile (*on paved streets all the way*) will take you from the city's busy center to the quiet restful life in beautiful Homewood. It is a Parked Residential district covered with sturdy oak trees, giving shade to its beautiful homes and winding streets.

The brochure also promised potential buyers that Homewood was "not designed for millionaires or the so-called idle rich, but for the class of progressive business and professional men who prefer to locate their homes among other homes of character and refinement, without paying a fortune for a residence site on which to build, and where the restrictions serve as a protection against undesirable neighbors." (Courtesy of Hennepin History Museum.)

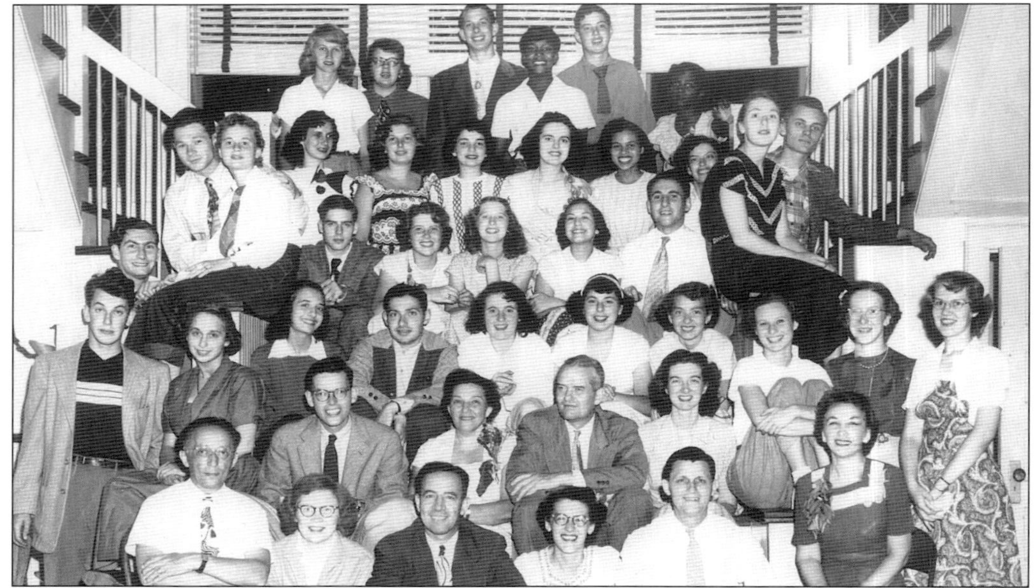

Beth El Synagogue's Young People's League was organized in 1926, the year the congregation moved into its new synagogue building on Fourteenth and Penn Avenues North. Rabbi David Aronson (seated, left, in the front row) and his wife, Bertha (seated at the far right), encouraged interfaith activities like Thanksgiving services and camping trips with neighborhood churches. In 1942, these "happy campers" met to finalize details for their Interfaith Summer Camp. (Courtesy of Bonnie Heller.)

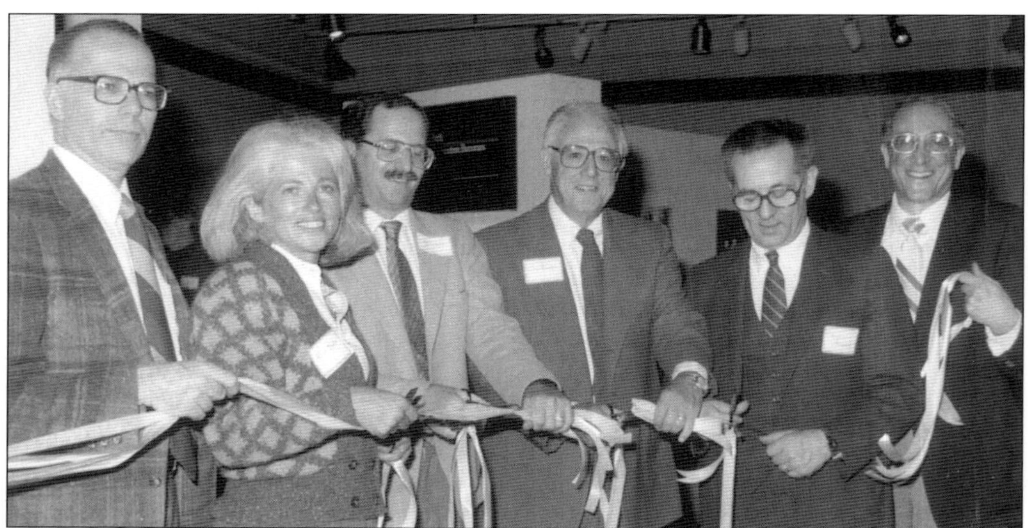

As Executive Director of the Jewish Community Relations Council/Anti-Defamation League of Minnesota and the Dakotas, Mort Ryweck worked to search out and combat antisemitism. He lead the way in arranging for a "Jewish Life in America" exhibit at the Minnesota Historical Society in 1986. Shown at opening night, from left to right, are: Ryweck, MHS Board Member Sylvia Kaplan, St. Paul United Jewish Fund and Council Executive Director Kim Marsh, UJFC President Gerry Hirschhorn, Minneapolis Federation for Jewish Service Executive Director Herman Markowitz, and former State Legislator Robert Latz. (Courtesy of Mort Ryweck.)

Four

Our Synagogues and Religious Schools, and our Jewish Community Organizations

Jews have always believed that community is an extension of family, and they organize agencies to help their less fortunate brethren, in part because every Jew knows that the wheel of fortune continually turns and that they, too, might someday need good deeds and charity, which are summed up in the word *tsedakah*, which means "social justice."

In 1894, German Jewish women organized a Minneapolis chapter of the National Council of Jewish Women to play Lady Bountiful to "the unfortunates"—the new immigrants from Eastern Europe. They started a sewing school for young girls, a vocational school, and a literary and social club, all on the North Side.

B'nai B'rith was also an almost exclusively German-Jewish men's group, and in 1900, East European Jews on the North Side started their own lodge, B'rith Abraham. A $4 annual membership bought $300 in life insurance as well as dances, picnics, and social events. Within seven years, they had seven chapters with 1,500 members—but then B'nai B'rith began inviting B'rith Abraham members to join in their battle against antisemitism, and by 1920, most of them were members of B'nai B'rith instead.

A Jewish Aid Association organized in 1903, with two representatives from every local congregation and lodge, raised almost $15,000 that first year—no small sum in those days—and hired Anna Fox, a trained social worker, at a salary of $1,200 a year to supervise their employment, housing, health, and child welfare services, and to set up a Sheltering Home committee for orphans and the destitute. In 1918, they joined the Minneapolis Community Fund, now the United Way, and after several name changes—they became the Jewish Family Welfare Association in 1924, and the Jewish Family Service Association in 1943—they are known today as the Jewish Family and Children's Service.

Worried about their children succumbing to "the lure of the streets or the secular world," East European Jewish immigrants started the Hebrew Free School in 1894, in a vacant butcher shop at 613 Fifth Street North. It was an after-school program for boys only and had only one teacher, but by 1908, they rented a larger space at Kenesseth Israel synagogue, and in 1913, they changed their name and became the Talmud Torah of Minneapolis—perhaps because in 1907 Ruby Dannenbaum, writing in Chicago's nationally-distributed Jewish newspaper, the *Reform Advocate*, had warned that only the Talmud Torah could keep their children from deserting Judaism. The school now had more than 100 students and a curriculum that included English classes for new immigrants and Hebrew classes that began with the ABC's and worked up to the Bible, Jewish literature and history, and the Talmud. Soon they began admitting girls as students too, and as enrollment continued to grow, the Ladies Auxiliary, organized in 1912, led the fundraising campaign to build a school on Eighth and Fremont in 1915—where they finally held their mortgage burning ceremony in 1943! Although the Orthodox community now has its own school, Torah Academy, Talmud Torah is known worldwide for its quality education and the many graduates who have gone on to become rabbis.

Sam Schwartz attended Talmud Torah from 1924–1933, and remembered it as "almost a home away from home." He and his friends went downtown after school to sell candy in factories and offices to earn money—about 40¢ a day—to help support their families, and then they'd take the streetcar to the Talmud Torah for classes and meetings of their Hebrew-speaking club, Barkai, and to work on *Habarak* (*The Lightning*), a Hebrew-language magazine they published every four to six weeks. They also attended Sunday meetings of the students' Zionist Club and Saturday morning services at Talmud Torah, where even third graders conducted their own services, entirely in Hebrew, with older boys like Joe King, Kenneth Goldblum, and Abraham Zemach acting as cantors. At age 13, he met 11-year-old Goldie Leader at rehearsals for their annual Chanukah celebration, and they were married eight years later.

Meanwhile, there were so many small synagogues flourishing on the North Side that people identified them by their locations—the Lyndale *shul*, the Bryant *shul*, the Emerson *shul*. Ukrainian and Bessarabian immigrants built their own *shul* at Seventh and Washington Avenues in 1894, and Lithuanians met to worship in a loft at Second Street and Sixth Avenue North, where Kenesseth Israel also met until 1895.

By 1907, there were three Orthodox synagogues on the North Side—Anshe Tavrig, Beth Aaron, and Agudas Achim—in addition to Kenesseth Israel and Mikro Kodesh, which had begun as Anshei Israel in 1901. Rabbi Wasser had a little *shulkele* in his home at 915 Elwood, and B'rith Abraham and Bichur Cholim were meeting in rented space or members' homes. Their congregations continued to grow, however, and in 1914, Kenesseth Israel built a synagogue on Sixth and Lyndale. Two years later there was a rift in the congregation, and several members left and built Sharei Zedeck, also known as the *greene shul*, at 726 Bryant. Their building was demolished by WPA workers when Sumner Field Housing was built, and they moved into their new synagogue at 1119 Morgan in 1936, the same year that Mikro Kodesh spent $125,000 to build their new synagogue at 1004 Oliver Avenue North. In 1926, Tifereth B'nai Jacob was still at 801 Elwood, and Agudas Achim, also known as Ahavath Achim, was at 1110 Morgan. The North Side's first Conservative congregation, Beth El, began meeting at the Talmud Torah in 1921, and hired their first Rabbi, David Aronson, in 1924. He served as their Rabbi for 35 years, until Kassel Abelson, who had come to Beth El in 1948 as Assistant Rabbi and then left to be a Chaplain in the U.S. Air Force from 1951–1957, was installed as Beth El's spiritual leader.

By now, Talmud Torah's Social Service department was conducting Americanization classes and sponsoring clinics, athletic teams, sewing and dancing classes, study circles, and social events. In 1922, Dr. Gordon told community leaders, "It's time to find the ways and means to rent a new building, or to enlarge this one," and within two years, the 15,000 Jews living on the North Side had a community center—a mansion at 909 Elwood Avenue that was named for its donor, Emanuel Cohen. The building had space for clubrooms, a gymnasium, an auditorium, and a back-yard pool. Dutchy Strauss coached their baseball team and a sandlot football team that played at Glenwood Park. Music programs now included a Rhythm Band and a piano teacher. In 1930, they started a nursery school with fees of 60¢ a week, and the children wore caps and gowns when it was time to "graduate" and start kindergarten. There was also a Stay-at-Home Camp; the children would meet at the Center and then walk to Folwell or North Commons Park, or go by bus to Glenwood Park.

As the Center continued to grow, they moved next door to more spacious quarters at 915 Elwood, and then, in 1939, both homes were razed to build the new Emanuel Cohen Center. The Ladies' Auxiliary sponsored raffles, dances, and other events, and raised $10,000 of the $60,000 they needed. On July 8, 1945, two months after V-E Day, Minneapolis Mayor Hubert

H. Humphrey joined Center President Sam Finkelstein to raise the flag on the Center's new flagpole, which is still on the front lawn at 1701 Oak Park Avenue North and has a bronze plaque on its black-and-rose-colored marble base that says, "Dedicated to the men and women of the Emanuel Cohen Center who gallantly served in the armed forces of our country."

By the 1930s, Minneapolis also had several activist Zionist groups who dedicated their time and money to helping the persecuted Jews in Europe and supporting the new agricultural settlements in Palestine. The Jewish labor movement was divided into two camps—anti-Zionist Communists and Socialists, with organizations that included the Bund and Workmen's Circle, and pro-Zionist groups like Poale Zion, Pioneer Women, and Farband No. 75, which owned a house at 1010 Knox Avenue North where they ran a loan association and gave scholarships to students.

In 1930, when the Minneapolis Federation for Jewish Service held its first campaign, the 94 Jewish groups asking for support included many out-of-town agencies—tuberculosis hospitals, orphan homes, Hebrew Union College, two theological seminaries, Jewish schools in Europe, and the United Palestine Appeal. Unfortunately, however, the Great Depression had begun. Businesses were beginning to fail, mortgages were in default, and peoples' investments were going down the drain. As the Depression worsened, one out of four American workers was unemployed, dentists had no patients, most doctors couldn't make a living, and many Americans couldn't even afford to buy clothing or enough food for their families. The Federation raised $55,000 of its $65,000 goal in 1930, but by 1933, pledges dipped under $19,000. It wasn't until 1938 that the Federation was able to surpass its 1930 total, in part because the Depression was waning, but also because their focus had shifted to local needs served by agencies like Mt. Sinai Hospital, the Jewish Community Center, a Jewish Vocational Workshop for the Handicapped, an Israel Programs Committee, nursing homes and seniors' residences, a new suburban Talmud Torah, and many other facilities and services.

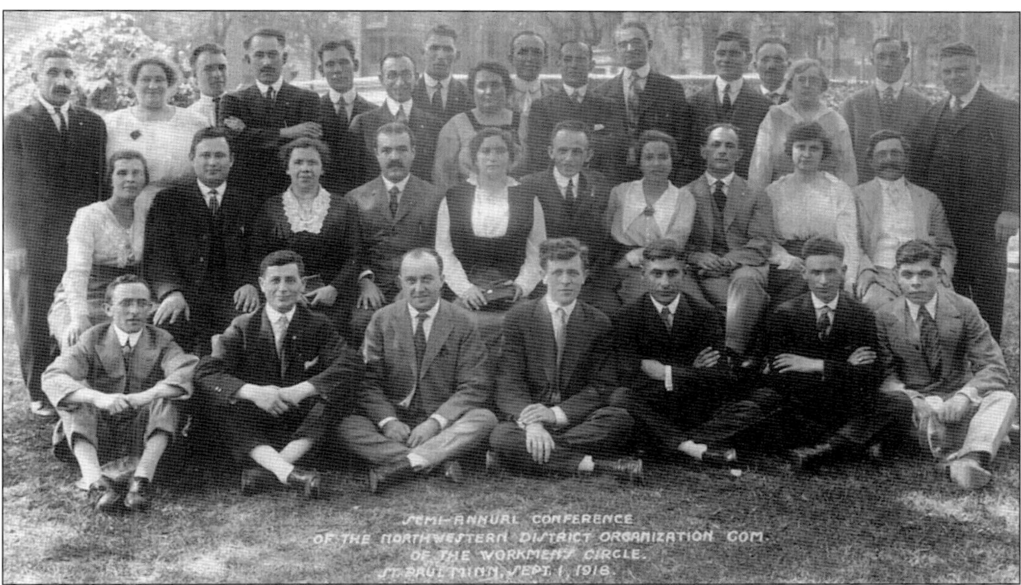

Beginning in 1910, Workmen's Circle provided medical and insurance benefits to members, organized a Yiddish language school and library, staged Yiddish plays in the Finnish Hall on Glenwood Avenue, and sponsored visiting Yiddish lecturers. In 1915, they built the Labor Lyceum in North Minneapolis as a social center, and in 1916, they participated in the political campaign that elected the only Socialist mayor in Minneapolis history, Thomas Van Lear. By the end of the 1940s, however, the group was no longer active. (Courtesy of Jewish Historical Society of the Upper Midwest.)

CONSTITUTION AND BY-LAWS

OF

Associated Jewish Charities ot Minneapolis

Article I. Name.

The name of this corporation shall be Associated Jewish Charities of Minneapolis.

Article II. Object.

The purpose of this corporation shall be as defined in the Articles of Incorporation.

Article III. Membership.

1. Any person who shall pay at least Ten ($10) Dollars per year to the corporation shall be a member thereof for the fiscal year for which such payment is made with a right to vote at all regular and special meetings of the members of said Association.

2. Contributions shall be payable in advance, either annually or in semi-annual or quarterly installments.

3. Six months' delinquency is cessation of membership.

4. The following organizations and activities shall be beneficiaries of the association:

1. Hebrew Ladies' Benevolent Society.
2. Sisters of Peace.
3. The Jewish Free Dispensary.
4. The Jewish Loan Society.
5. The B'nai B'rith Free Employment Bureau.
6. The Sheltering Home.
7. Jewish Orphan Asylum, Cleveland, Ohio.
8. The National Jewish Hospital for Consumptives, Denver, Colorado.
9. Jewish Consumptive Relief Society, Denver, Colorado.

In 1909, nine groups joined together to organize the Associated Jewish Charities of Minneapolis. Membership cost $10 per year, and people were also expected to make donations . . . and to increase them every year! (Courtesy of Jewish Family and Children's Service.)

A complete report of the financial condition, as well as the financial transactions of this organization during the year, and a complete report by each committee of the Association will be made at the time of the Annual Meeting. For the present it is enough to say, that we are compelled to strain every resource to meet the heavy demands which are being made upon us by our many activities.

With the exception of the Superintendent, who receives a salary, the work of the Association has been done and is being done by volunteers, whose time is valuable, but who are willing to give and are enthusiastically giving to the Association all the time at their disposal. We ask the co-operation of every man and woman interested in the success of our enterprise to come to the assistance of these volunteers, by making it unnecessary to personally call for the subscriptions for 1911. In the rear of this publication, will be found a number of subscription blanks, which may be used for every member of your family, who desire to enlist in the membership of this Association, who are not enlisted as yet, as well as to renew your own subscription. Kindly fill them out at your earliest opportunity, and mail them to Mr. David Simon, President of the Association, at the Palace Building, Nicollet Avenue and Fourth Street, of this city. In filling out these blanks, let us say once more that to the extent our funds are limited, to that extent our scope of work must be limited, and in order to carry out in full the plans and objects of our Association, all contributions should be larger than they were in 1910.

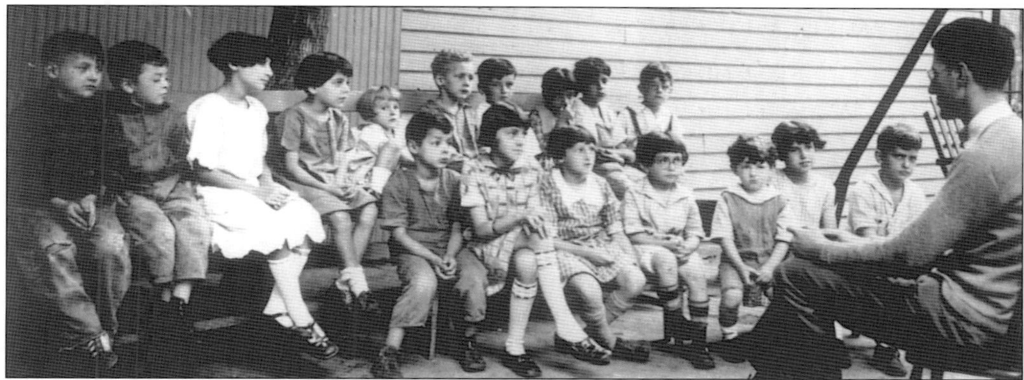

The Jewish Sheltering Home opened at 1704 Oak Park Avenue in 1919. It provided temporary housing and arranged adoptions for children whose parents couldn't support them, were seriously ill, or had died during the influenza epidemic of 1918–1919. (Courtesy of Minnesota Historical Society.)

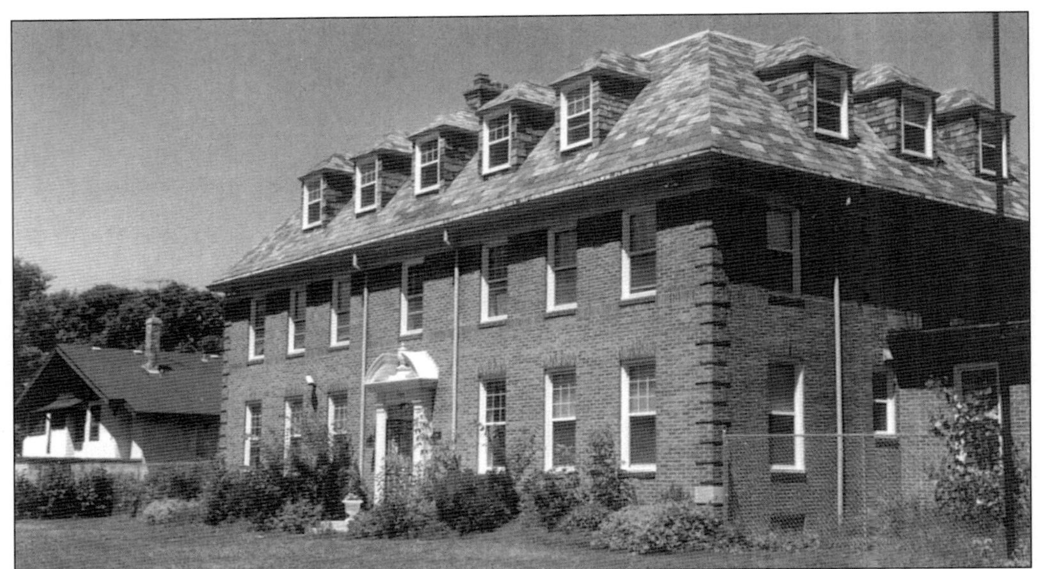

In 1934, the Jewish Sheltering Home moved into this new $20,000 building designed by Liebenberg and Kaplan. Three-year-old Esther Bader and her baby sister, Mary, were living in the home because their parents were ill, and when Esther received a $5 gift from a family friend—an extremely generous gift in those days—she decided to give it to the people who were taking care of her. Superintendent Harry Feller took her to the bank to open an account and deposit her gift, and when the community gathered the following Sunday to lay the cornerstone for their new building, Esther put her bankbook in the cornerstone, where it would draw interest, Feller said, until the building needed to be replaced. (Photo by Tom Lewin.)

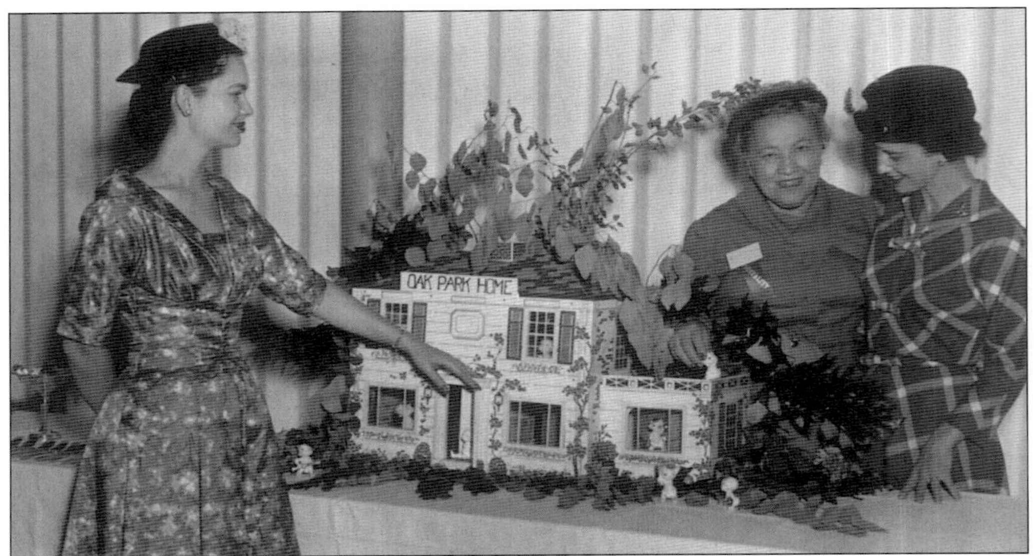

The Oak Park Children's Home Auxiliary also helped with fundraising. Shown at their annual luncheon are Mrs. Ruth Kozberg and Mrs. Maury Applebaum with their guest of honor, Mrs. Orville Freeman, wife of Minnesota's governor. In 1997, the home was purchased by Project Foundation, which provides transitional and/or emergency housing for homeless young people. (Courtesy Jewish Historical Society of the Upper Midwest.)

ספּעשעל מאסס מיטינג

א ספּעשעל מאסס מיטינג, ווערט גערופען פון די מינגעאפּאליס פעדערעשען

זונטאג אבענד, דעם 22טען פעברואר, 8 אוהר

אין תפארת בני יעקב שוהל, 8טע עוועגו און עלוואוד נ.

צו ערקלערען דעם פּובּליקום די גאנצע ארבּייט זייט די פעדערעשען איז גע-גרינדעט, ווי אזוי מען האט דאס געלד צו טיילט צו די פערשידענע אינסטיטו-שענס און ארגאניזעשענס.

אויך די פּלענער ווי מען וועט אנגייהן מיט די ארבּייט אין דעם קאמפּעין פיר דעם צווייטען יאהר, וועלכער פאנגט זיך אן מאנטאג, דעם 2טען מארטש ביז דעם 8טען מארטש.

גוטע רעדנערס וועלען אדרעססירען דעם מיטינג.

בּיטטע קומט אין מאססען מענער און פרויען און בּריינגט אייערע פריינט, עס וועט זיין אַ זעהר אינטערעסאנטע פערזאמלונג.

☛ איינטריט פריי און קיינע קאללעקשענס. ☚

י. ל. בּאָרושאק, טשערמאן

SPECIAL MASS MEETING

THE MINNEAPOLIS FEDERATION FOR JEWISH SERVICE

will hold a Mass Meeting

on Sunday Evening, February 22nd, at 8 o'clock sharp

at the Tifereth B'nai Jacob Synagogue

8th Ave. No. and Elwood

for the purpose of explaining to the public what the Federation has accomplished during its first year of existence, and just how the money was distributed to the various institutions and organizations.

AT THIS MEETING also, plans will be presented for the campaign and drive for 1931, which will commence March 2nd and continue until March 8th.

Good speakers will address the meeting. There will be no charge and no collection made. YOU ARE CORDIALLY INVITED TO COME AND BRING YOUR FRIENDS!

I. L. BORUSHAK, Chairman

The Great Depression was already underway when the Minneapolis Federation for Jewish Service was incorporated on April 15, 1930. The Federation closed out its first year with a "Special Mass Meeting" to tell the community what it had accomplished, and to launch its second fund campaign. (Courtesy Jewish Historical Society of the Upper Midwest.)

Chanukah Entertainment

By the Pupils

SATURDAY, DECEMBER 12TH, 1925,

AT EIGHT P. M.

PROGRAM

Lighting of Candles - - - - - - - *Sam Mirviss and Choir*

Hannoros Halolu - - - - - - - - - - - - *Choir*

"Rock of My Salvation" - - - - - - - *Choir and Audience*

"There Flickers a Light"—Recitation - - - *Ethel Lois Weisberg*

Palestinian Dance—

Pearl Abramowitz, Vivian Bearman, Cecelia Friedell, Anna Gershman, Marcella Goldstein, Rose Hadroff, Sylvia Hershkowitz, Edith Idlekope, Bernice Kelner, Hannah Levy, Belle Levin, Pauline Levins, Lenore Levitch, Esther Nadel, Bonnie Saposnick, Beverly Silverman, Lillian Turchick, Ruth Werner, Rose Yokel

The Dramatic Club "Barkai" presents

"ZERUBABEL"

Hebrew Play in Five Acts by S. Gelb

Belshatzar, King of Babylon - - - - - - *Monroe Levins*

Zerubabel, a Jewish Royal Prince - - - - - - *Joseph King*

Daniel, the Prophet - - - - - - - - - *Hymen Ratner*

Abiah, Daniel's Attendant - - - - - - - *Sam Levitt*

Nabal, An Apostate Jew - - - - - - - - *Morris Cohen*

Tamar, His Daughter - - - - *Rena Rosenberg, Rosalind Shure*

Gaal, a Renegade Jew - - - - - - - - - *Bernard Gordon*

Ashpenaz, Babylonian General - - - - - - *Philip Weiner*

Nebushazban, a Magician - - - - - - - - *Israel Chodosh*

Joshua, Jewish High Priest - - - - - - - *Arnold Grais*

Jews — Soldiers

Musical numbers by

Pauline Brill, Edith Jaffa, Cecelia, Emma and *Anita Levitt*

Each year Talmud Torah students who were members of the Barkai drama club staged a Chanukah program. In addition to "Zerubabel," a Hebrew play in five acts by faculty member S. Gelb, their 1925 program included a Palestinian dance, candle-lighting, a recitation by Ethel Lois Weisberg, and musical numbers by Pauline Brill, Edith Jaffa, and Cecilia, Emma and Anita Levitt. (Courtesy of Pacey Beers.)

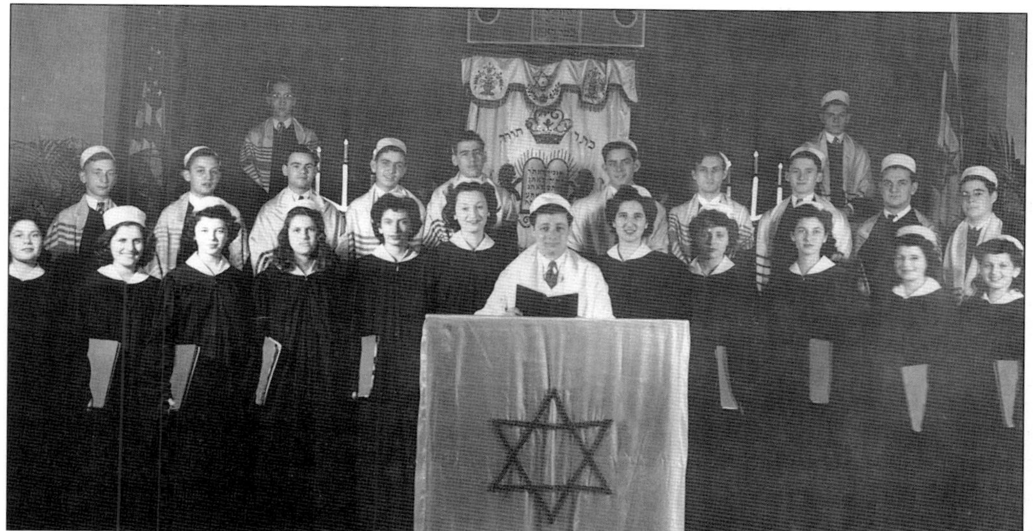

During the Depression and into the '40s, Talmud Torah offered High Holiday services with "no charges, no tickets, and no collection" for community members who could not afford to join a synagogue. There was no Rabbi presiding over the services, and community members gave the sermons. The Talmud Torah Choir also sang at *Shabbat* services in the '40s, with Jerry Hinitz (at the Bima) and Pacey Beers (third from left, back row), taking turns as cantor. At rear, left, is Farrell Stiegler, who directed the choir. The choir members practiced all summer, Beers said, and wore robes they borrowed from North High School, which now had a Jewish principal, Henry Bank. (Courtesy of Pacey Beers.)

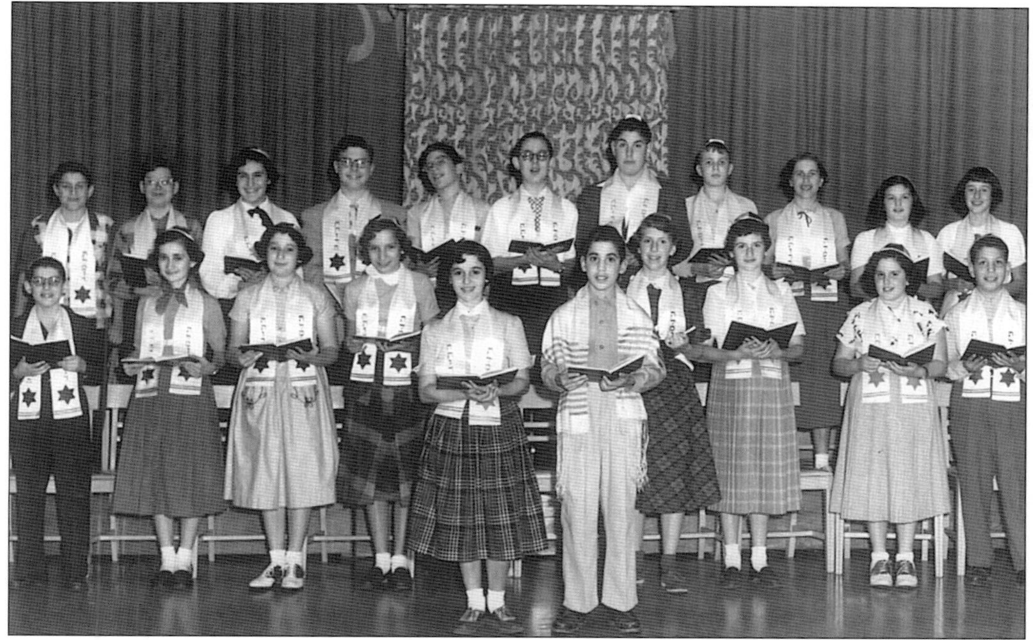

At last—a woman cantor! On September 28, 1953, two students—a boy and a girl—shared the cantorial duties at Talmud Torah's *Shabbat* services. (Courtesy of Jewish Historical Society of the Upper Midwest.)

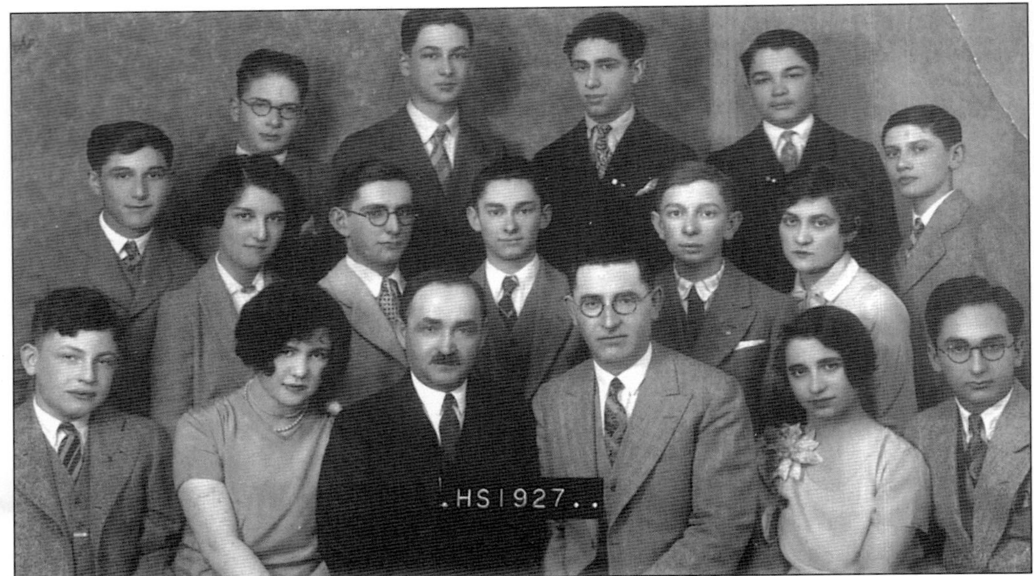

Talmud Torah's 1927 High School graduating class included the following students, from left to right: (front row) Benjamin Avin, Rosalind Shure, faculty members Avin and Heilicher, Bess Dworsky, and Sam Levitt; (middle row) Hilda Bassin, Arnold Grais, Bernard Gordon, Harry Guttman, and Freda Ebin; (back row) Julius Katz, Kenneth Goldblum, (?) Ostrin, Moishe Cohen, Simon Lax, and Hy Applebaum. (Courtesy of Sandra Heims Shapiro.)

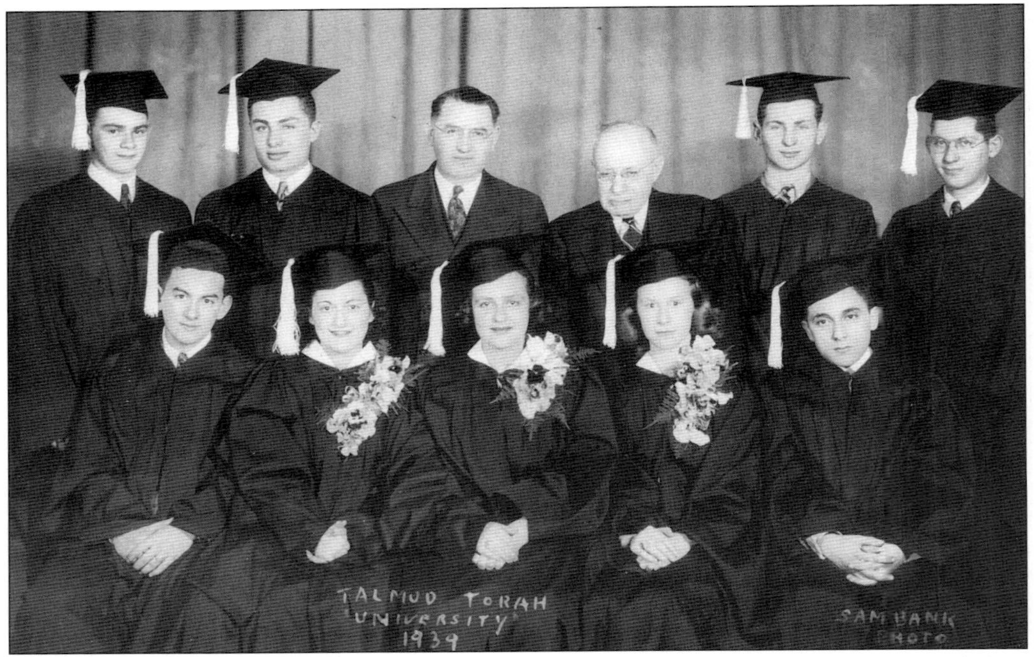

Graduates of Talmud Torah's "University" class in 1939 included the following, from left to right: (front row) Arthur Kruger, Miriam Charney, Claire Zeesman Katz, and Jerry Hinitz; (back row) Pacey Beers, Henry Rappaport, Menahem Heilicher, Talmud Torah Principal Dr. George Gordon, Moshe Goldblum, and Alvin Freedland. (Courtesy of Pacey Beers.)

תלמוד התורה דמיניאפולים

The Talmud Torah of Minneapolis

Fremont and Eighth Avenues North
TELEPHONE HYLAND 2161

DR. GEO. J. GORDON
Educational Director

OFFICERS:

CARL LIFSON	PRESIDENT
L. H. FRISCH	1ST VICE PRESIDENT
DR. D. PINK	2ND VICE PRESIDENT
JOHN Z. GELMAN	TREASURER
DR. N. N. COHEN	SECRETARY
F. ARONSON	FINANCIAL SECRETARY

BRANCHES:
BETH EL SYNAGOGUE
14TH & PENN AVE. N. - CHERRY 2019
ADATH JESHURUN SYNAGOGUE
34TH & DUPONT AVE. SO. - REGENT 1151

June 16, 1938

Dear Harry:

The Board of Directors of the Talmud Torah, the Faculty and the Student Body congratulate you on this momentous occastion in your life.

Do not fall into the vulgar idea that mind is a warehouse and education but a process of stuffing it full of goods. "Education is a companion which no misfortune can depress, no enemy alienate, no despotism enslave. At home, a friend; abroad, an introduction; in solitude, a solace; and in society, an ornament. Without it, what is man? A splendid slave and reasoning savage."

Whatever life may hold in store for you, do not forget the "rock whence you have been hewn". Jewish knowledge, attitudes, ideas and ideals may be the only comforter in your future life that you will need most.

Many years of your life have been spent in the Talmud Torah. You have received much information; you have established different attitudes--please do not cast that off as one would cast off an outworn garment.

We hope that you will be successful and prosperous in every undertaking in the future.

Sincerely yours,

YOUR ALMA MATER

By Geo. J. Gordon.

GJG:FA

Dr. George Gordon, who gave up his medical practice to become Education Director at the Talmud Torah, wrote congratulatory "letters with a message" to graduating seniors. (Courtesy of Talmud Torah.)

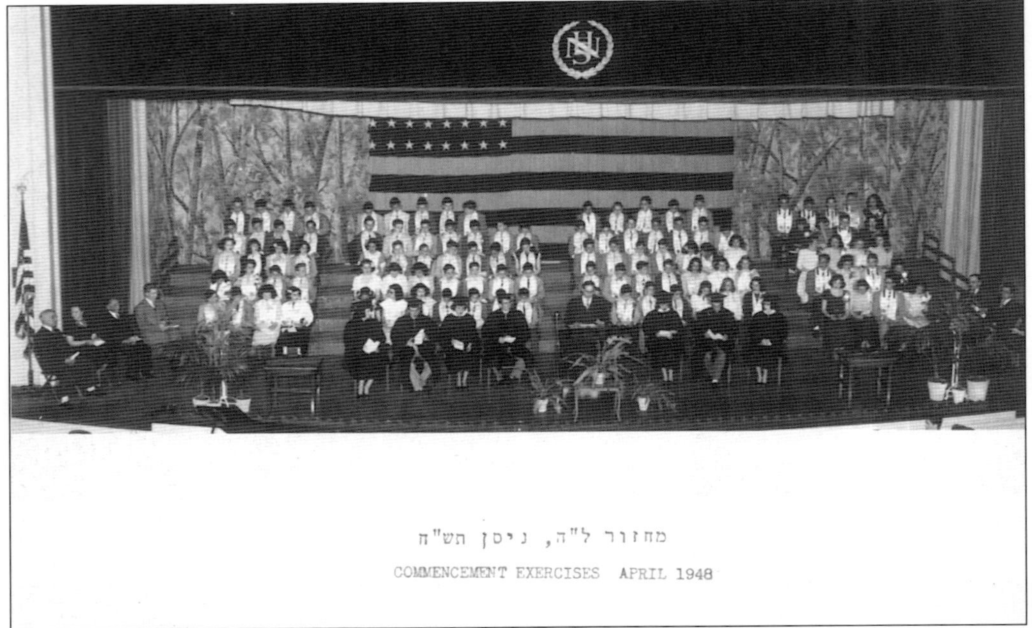

As enrollment continued to grow at the Talmud Torah, graduation ceremonies had to be held at larger sites like the Gymal Doled club in downtown Minneapolis, or at neighborhood schools. Commencement exercises for the class of 1948 were held at North High School. (Courtesy of Jewish Historical Society of the Upper Midwest.)

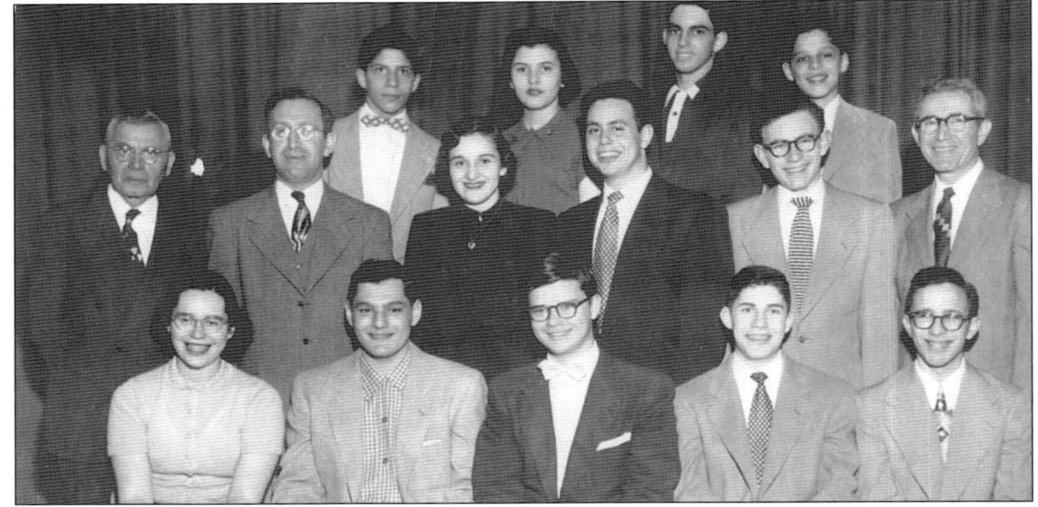

Talmud Torah High Schoolers, and their teachers, were almost all smiles as they posed for their graduation photo. Shown here, from left to right, are the following: (front row) Elinor Soll, Arnold Kaplan, Hanan Rosenstein, Peter Edelman, and Leo Wolf; (middle row) Solomon Zemach, Melvin Bailis, Diana Knight, Stanford Rosen, Ronny Kaiser, and L.I. Kaiser; (back row) Irwin Weisman, Sandra Heims, Laurence Rivkin, and Jeremy Berman. (Courtesy of Sandra Heims Shapiro.)

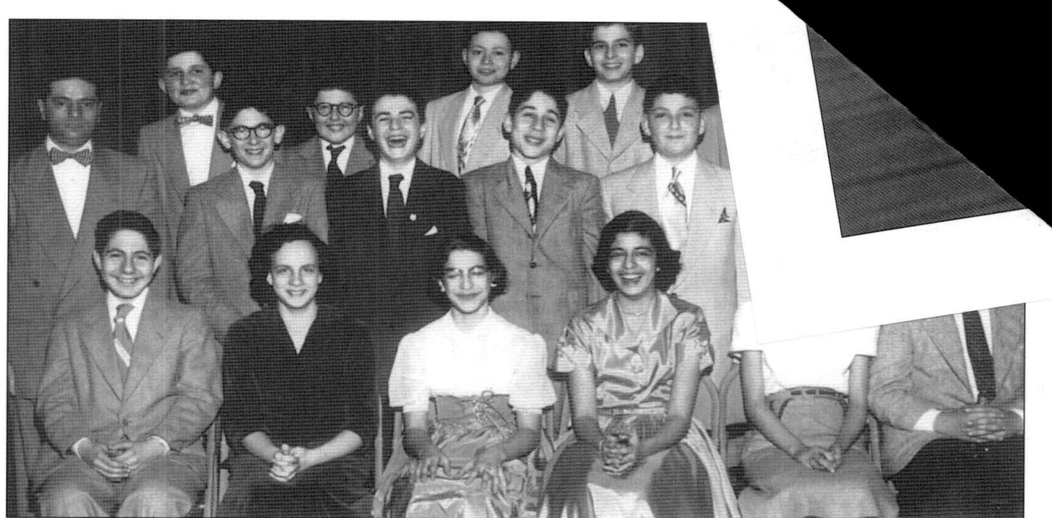

These High School graduates were one of the four graduating classes at the Talmud Torah in 1953. (Courtesy of American Jewish World.)

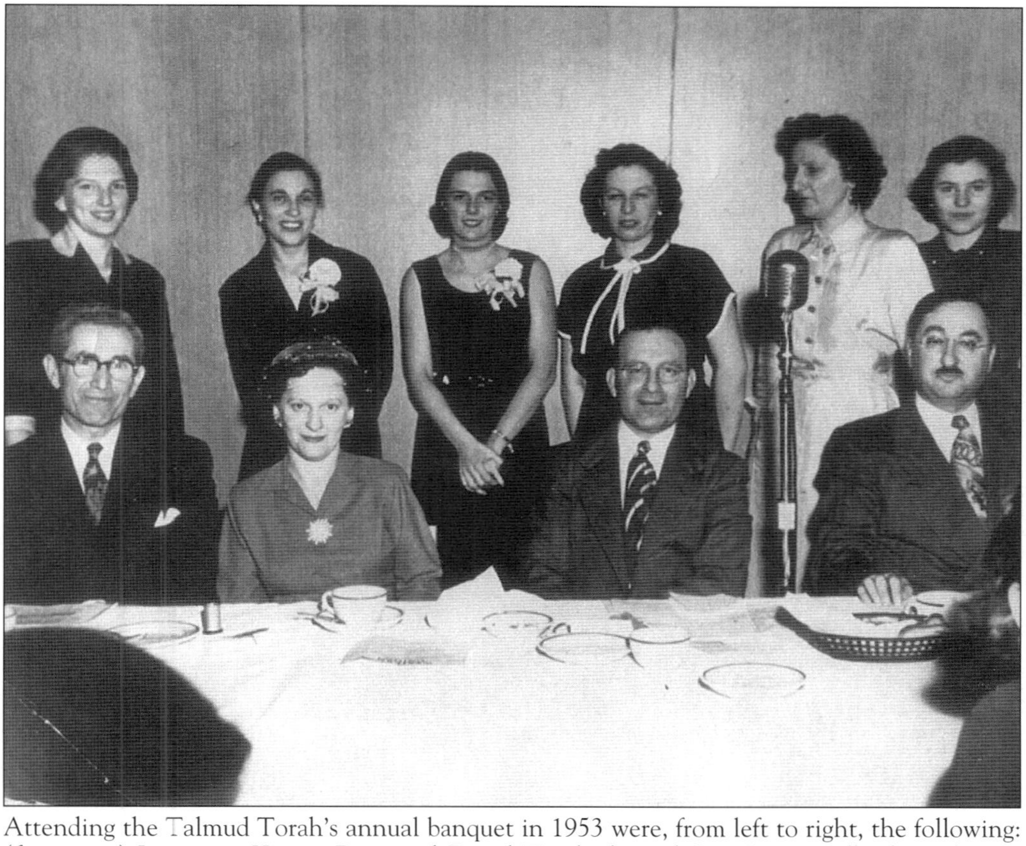

Attending the Talmud Torah's annual banquet in 1953 were, from left to right, the following: (front row) Lawrence Kaiser, Rose and David Turchick, and Sam Leavitt; (back row) Jean Rosenblum-Barnett, Muriel Schwartz, Sis Bialick Tapper, (?) Pesis, (?) Goldberg, and Sandra Heims Shapiro. (Courtesy of Sandra Heims Shapiro.)

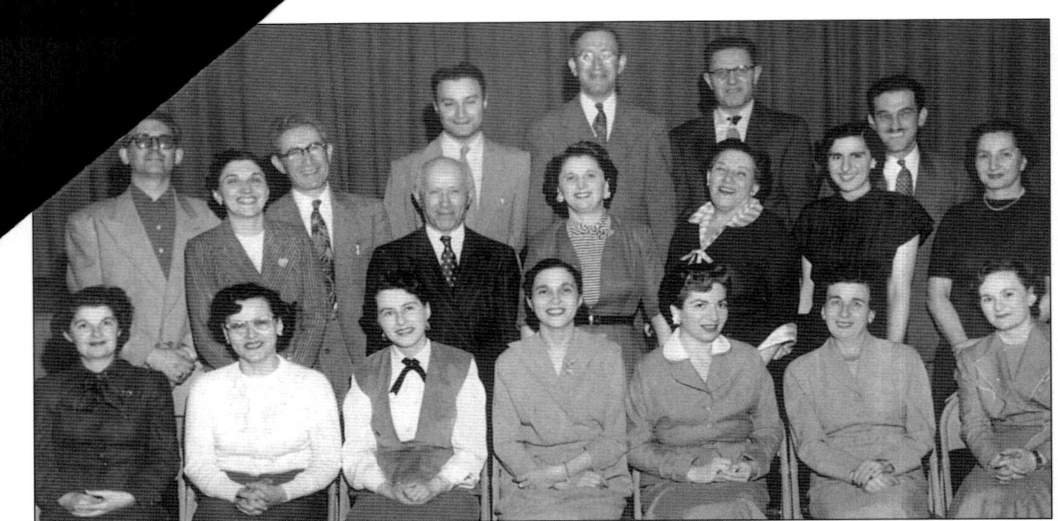

Attending Talmud Torah's Institute of Adult Jewish Studies in 1953 was fun, as well as educational, and it was a popular way to socialize with friends and neighbors on the North Side. (Courtesy of Sandra Heims Shapiro.)

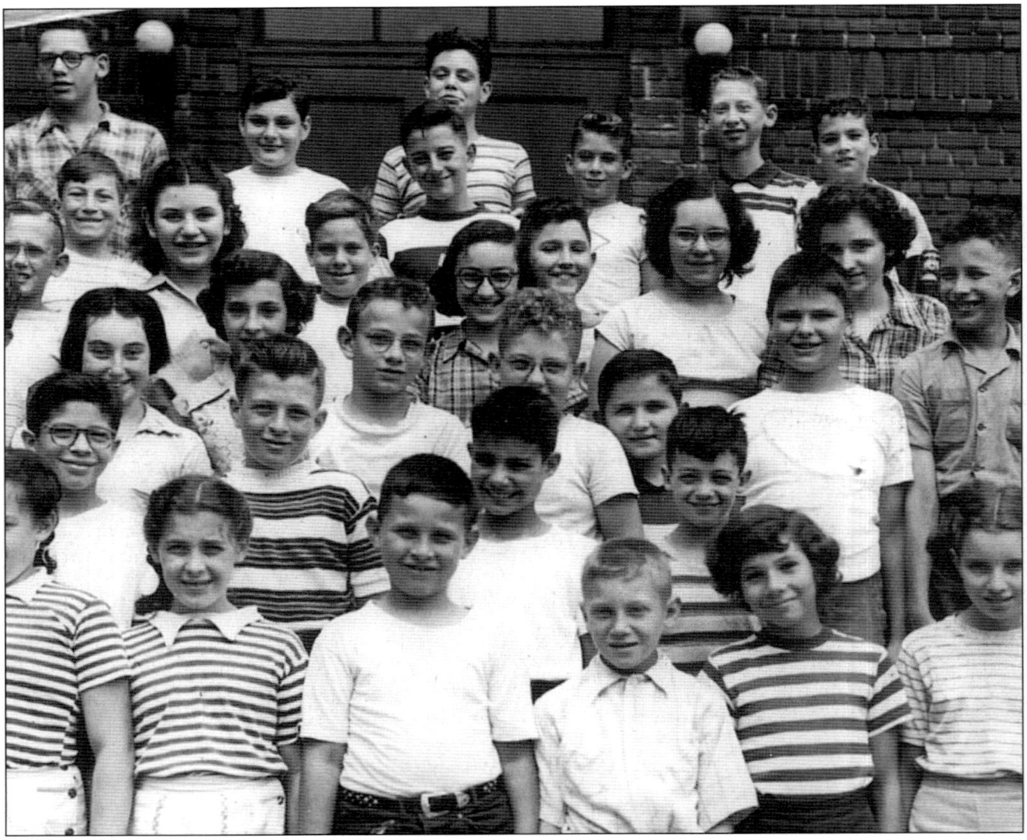

Children's classes at Talmud Torah met after school and on Sunday mornings, for study and for fun, too. (Courtesy of Sandra Heims Shapiro.)

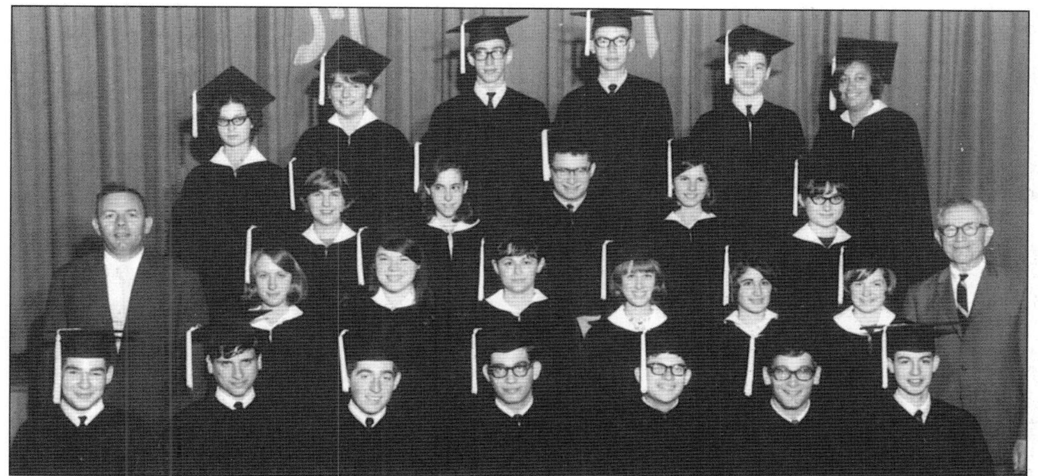

The Talmud Torah graduating class of June 1966, wore caps and gowns. (Courtesy of American Jewish World.)

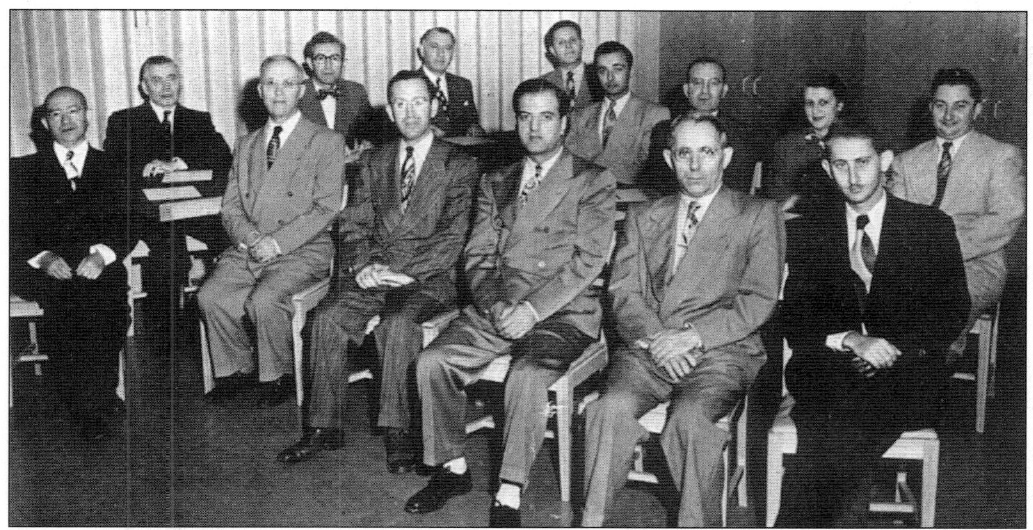

In 1951, the Talmud Torah had 15 full-time and four part-time faculty members. From left to right are the following: (front row) Saul Kahz, Dr. Melvin Bailis, Joseph King, A.M. Senter, and Zev Levin; (back row) Pincus Bernstein, Solomon Zemach, Director L.I. Kaiser, Menahem Heilicher, Dr. Meyer Pilch, Haim Bernstein, David Turchick, and Judith and Meshulam Riklis. Faculty not in the picture included Aaron Kaas, Simcha Gelb, and Louis Kahn. (Courtesy of Helen Broude Tomsky.)

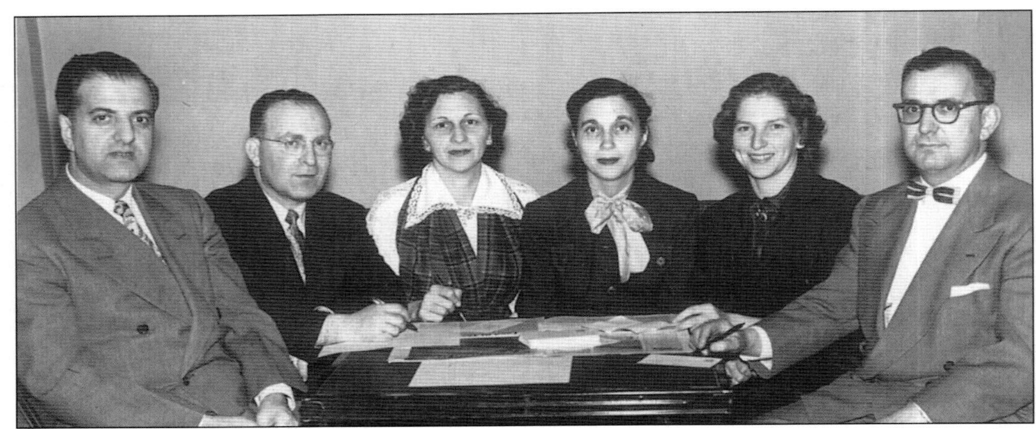

Members of the Talmud Torah Board of Directors (*c.* 1950) included both faculty and members of the community. From left to right are faculty members Joseph King and David Turchick, with four Board members: Mrs. Arthur Rosenfield, Mrs. Jonas Schwartz, Mrs. Eli Barnett, and Arnold Grais. (Courtesy of Jewish Historical Society of the Upper Midwest.)

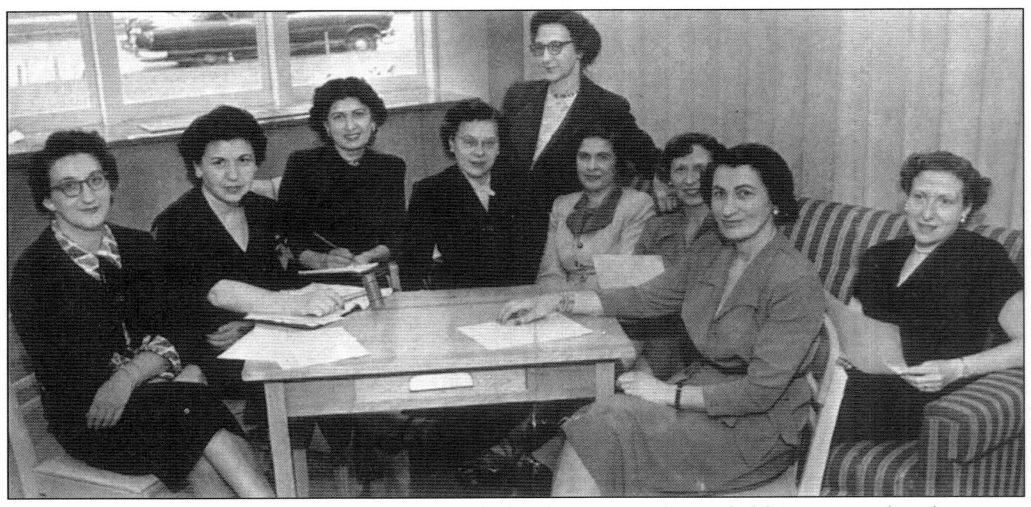

The Talmud Torah Ladies Auxiliary also helped support their children's Jewish education. Members in 1951 included Mmes. David Desnick, Hy Heims, Isadore Ostroviak, Leonard Kool, Jacob Birnberg, Gordon Ackerman, Reuben Silverman, William Schwartz, and Jack Bogdin. (Courtesy of Helen Broude Tomsky.)

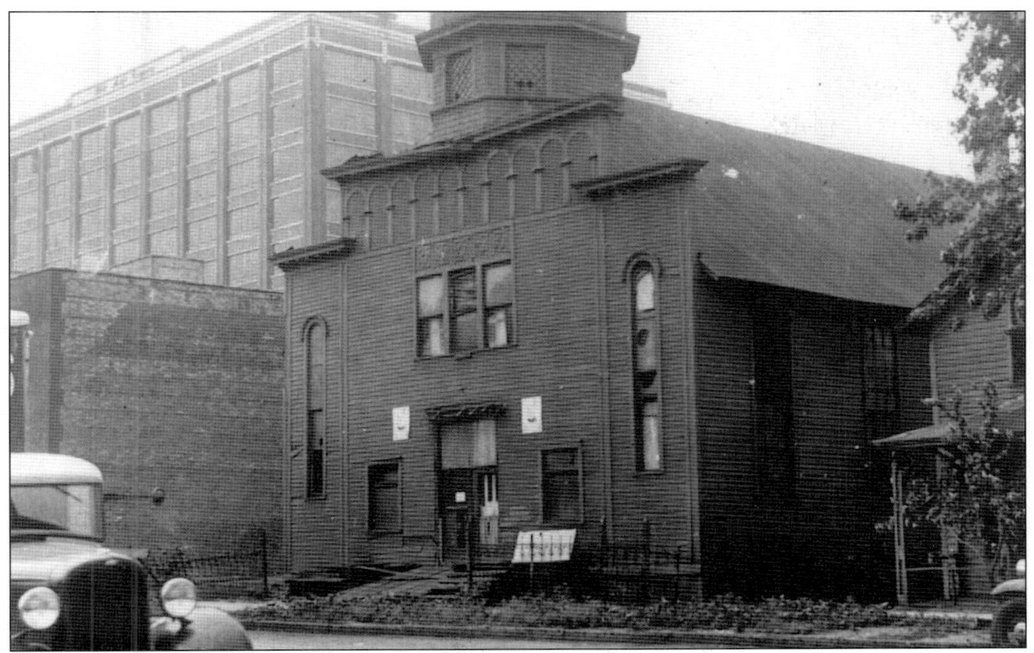

By 1907 Kenesseth Israel, which had built this synagogue at 519 Fourth Street North in 1890, was the largest congregation in North Minneapolis, with 150 members. They had a school, a Sunday School, a House of Refuge program for needy members and newcomers who were permitted to stay for three days and three nights or until they could find employment, and a *Bichur Holim* society that provided doctors and medications to "any worthy patient." (Courtesy of Minnesota Historical Society.)

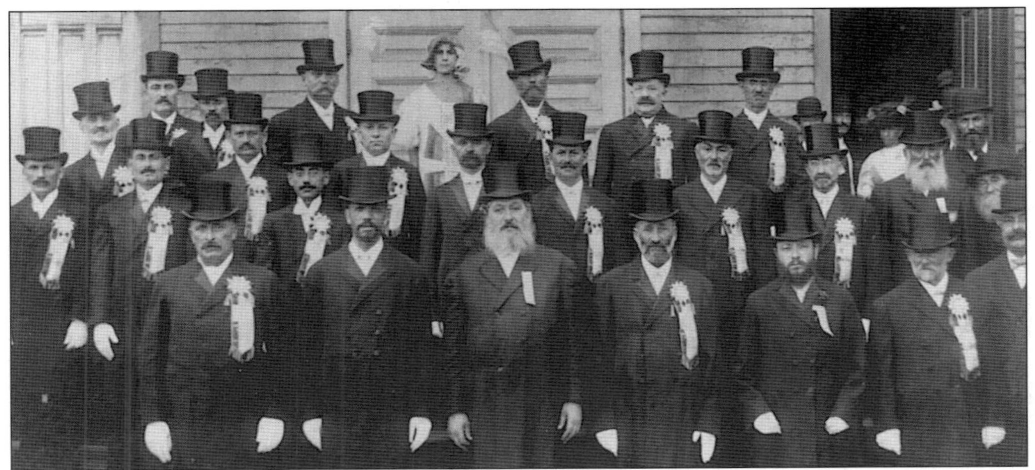

Members of Kenesseth Israel's 1913 building committee, dressed for their annual fundraising event, included, from left to right, (front row) Isaac Schulman, Nathan Lowenthal, Rabbi S.M. Silber, Abe Kaplan, Rev. S. Chazin, Joseph Cohen and B.S. Segal; (middle row) L.B. Levin, Max Davis, Isaac Segal, Joseph Goldfus, I. Kaplan, Moses Dulkin, Nathan Eisenstadt, Morris Borowsky, Selig Kaplan, Nathan Wolpert, J.B. Cohen, and Hirsh Swiller; (back row) Harris Rosenberg, Philip Cohen, Meyer Segal, Abe and Evelyn Witebsky, Hessel Spudeck, Harry Edelman, and Joseph Berenstein. (Courtesy of Jewish Historical Society of the Upper Midwest.)

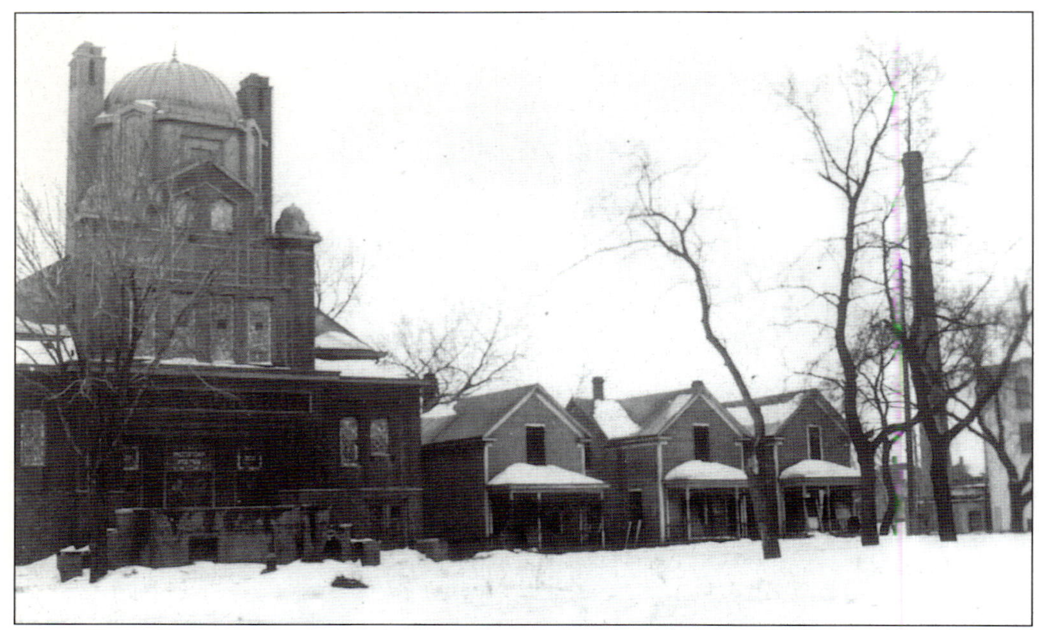

Sharei Zedeck's first synagogue at 726 Bryant Avenue North was razed in 1936 to make way for the Sumner Field Public Housing Project, which in turn was torn down in 1999 to make way for a modern townhouse development. (Courtesy of Minnesota Historical Society.)

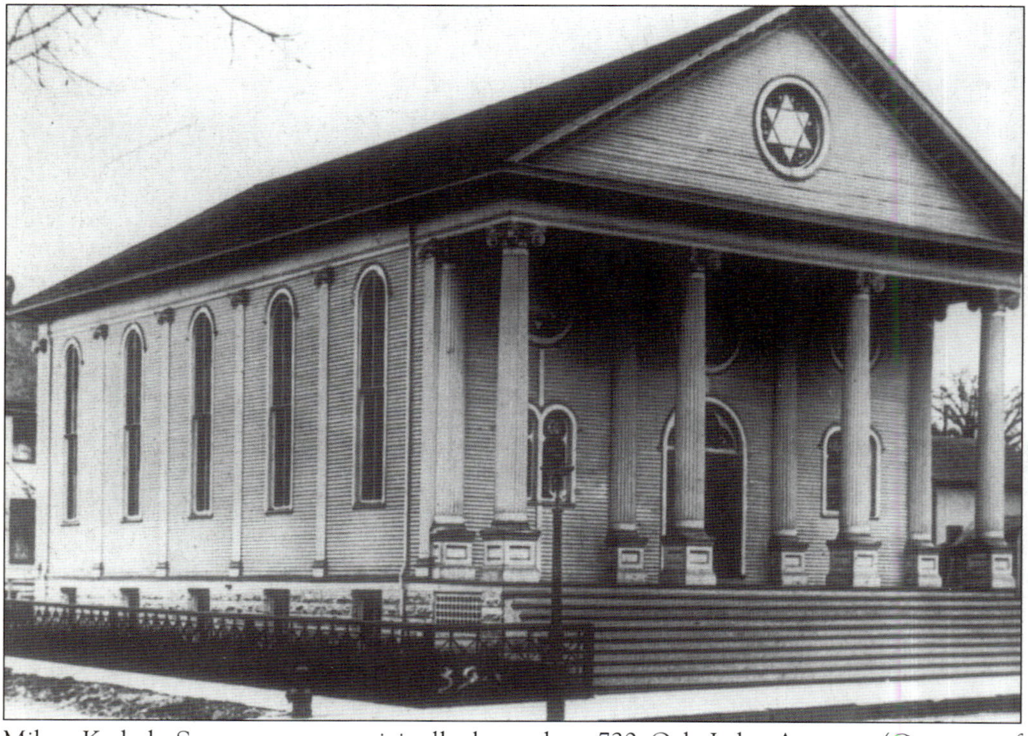

Mikro Kodesh Synagogue was originally located at 720 Oak Lake Avenue. (Courtesy of Minnesota Historical Society.)

In 1922 Beth El members bought a house and lot at Fourteenth and Penn Avenues North for $7,000. Three years later they razed the house to build their synagogue, which was dedicated the following year. The building's cornerstone included the names of Beth El's 25 founding members. (Courtesy of Minnesota Historical Society.)

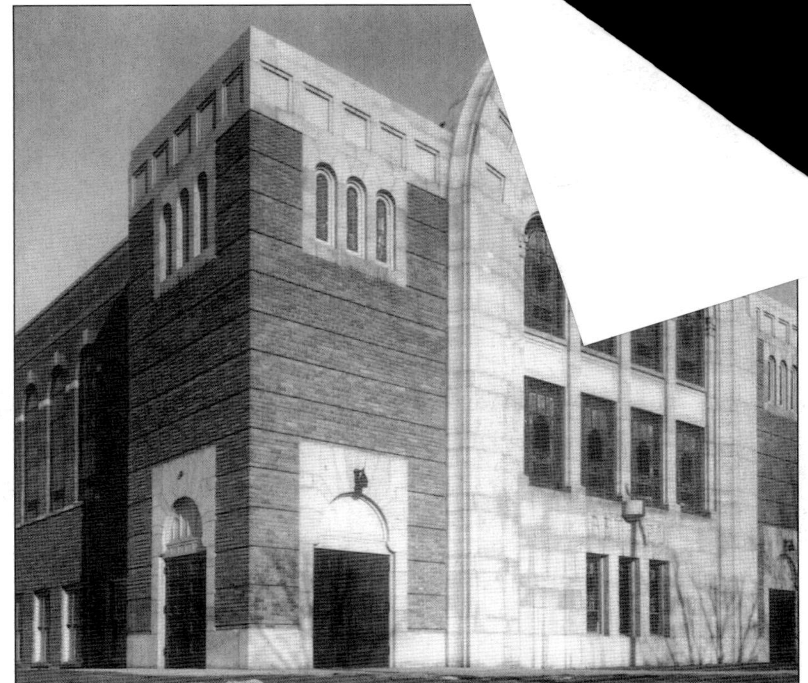

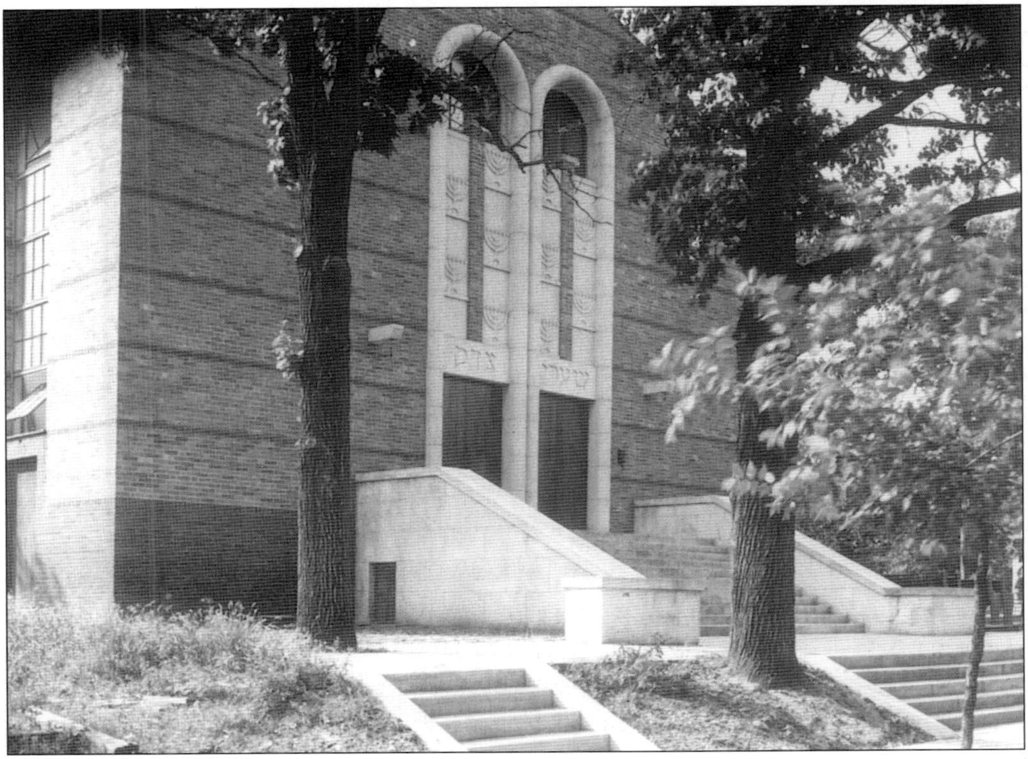

Sharei Zedeck moved to its new building at 1117 Morgan Avenue North in 1936. (Courtesy of Minnesota Historical Society.)

This agreement made and entered into this 28 day of Sep. 1934 by and between the MIKRO KODESH ANSHE SFARD, of the City of Minneapolis, Minn., a religious society duly organized and existing under the laws of Minnesota, through its undersigned Trustees party of the first part and M. Guttman party of the second part Witnesseth:

That said party of the first part in consideration of the covenants and agreements of the said party of the second part hereinafter contained, upon the prompt and full performance of said party of second part of this agreement, and in accordance to the Constitution and By-Laws of this society do hereby agree to sell and convey unto said party of second part by a good and sufficient instrument in writing, subject to ~~said~~ Constitution ~~and By-~~Laws, the following described pew to-wit: The certain pew in the Synagogue at **Oliver and 10th Ave. No** City of Minneapolis, Minn.

Known and designated Mizrach Aisle No. Bench ______ Seat 8. no Main floor. Gallery ______ Bench ______ Seat 48 No.

And said party of the second part in consideration of the premises hereby agrees to pay said party of the first part as and for the purchase price of said pew the sum of 400.00 Dollars in manner and at times following to-wit: and Paid in full.

Jan. ______ 192	$______	July ______ 192	$______
Feb. ______ 192	$______	Aug. ______ 192	$______
Mar. ______ 192	$______	Sept. ______ 192	$______
Apr. ______ 192	$______	Oct. ______ 192	$______
May ______ 192	$______	Nov. ______ 192	$______
June ______ 192	$______	Dec. ______ 192	$______

But should default be made in the payment of said several sums of money or any or either of them, or any part thereof, or in any of the covenant herein to be by said party of the second part kept and performed, or in any violation or breach of the Constitution and By-Laws of said society, by said second party, ~~then this agreement to be null and void at~~ the election of said first party, time being the essence of this agreement, and in case of default by said second party in whole or in part in any of either of the covenants of this agreement to be kept by him or performed, he hereby agrees upon written demand of said first party quietly and peaceably to surrender to said first party said pew and all right, title and interest therein and every part thereof, it being understood until such default that said second party is to have the use and possession of said pew.

All covenants and agreements herein contained shall run with said pew and bind the heirs, successors, administrators and assigns of the respective parties hereto.

It is mutually agreed between the parties hereto that the time of payment shall be an essential part of this contract, and that all covenants and agreements herein contained shall extend to and be obligatory upon the heirs, successors, executors, administrators and assigns of the respective parties.

In witness whereof Both Parties hereto set their hands and seals and the official seal of said society this 28 day of Sep. 1934

Witnesses

______

______ N. Spilberg pres. [SEAL.]

Trustees
A. Sete[illegible] Rec. Secy [SEAL.]
A. Guintman [SEAL.]
Max Schlichtberg [SEAL.]

Mikro Kodesh member M. Guttman paid $400 for lifetime ownership of a pew, which his sons would inherit when he died. (Courtesy of Jewish Historical Society of the Upper Midwest.)

CONTRACT

FOR

PEW

Cong. Mikro Kodesh

Anshe Sfard

Oliver and 10th Ave. No.

and ______

Minneapolis, Minn.

On November 24, 1937, Mikro Kodesh dedicated its new building at 1004 Oliver Avenue North, which it paid for in part by selling pews to members. (Courtesy of Minnesota Historical Society.)

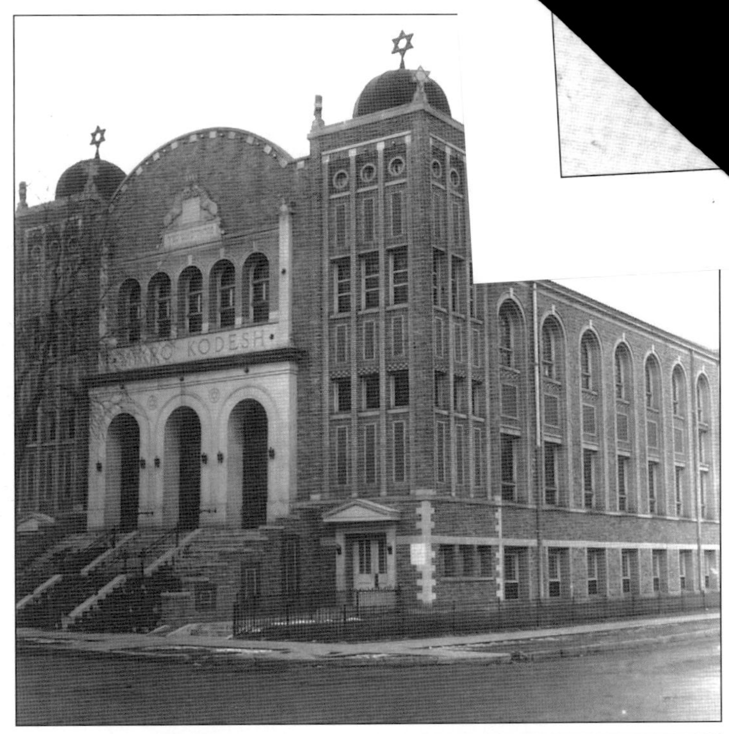

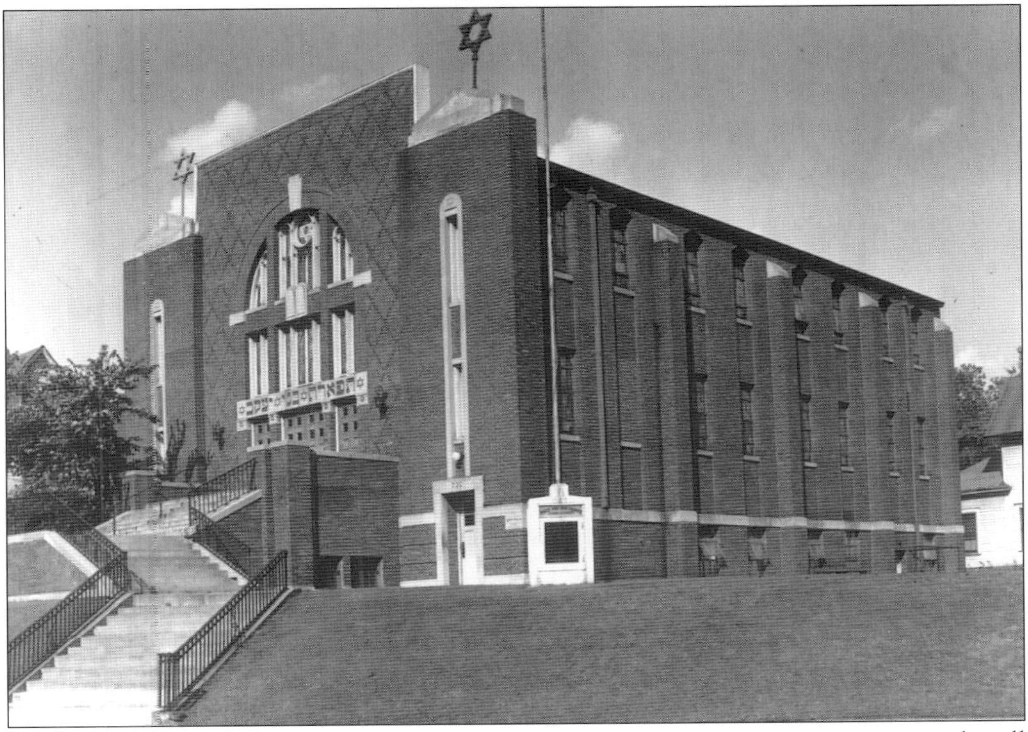

When Tifereth B'nai Jacob built their new synagogue at 810 Elwood in 1948, many people still referred to it as the "Elwood *shul*." (Photo by Tom Lewin.)

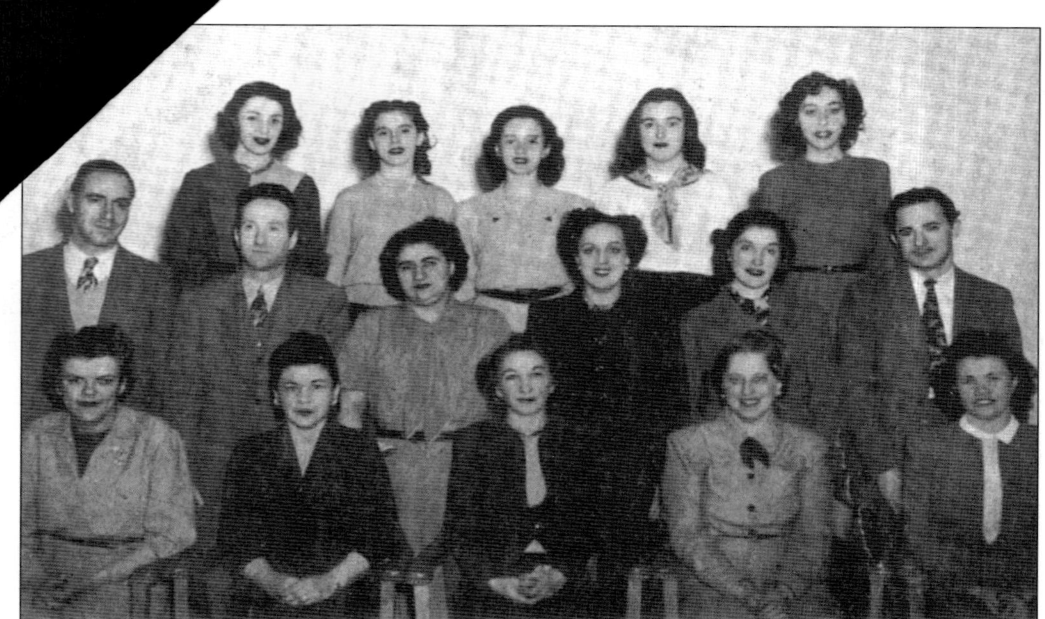

Beth El Religious School staff in the 1940s included, from left to right, the following: (front row) Muriel Steinman, Rosaline Heims, *Rebbitzen* Bertha Aronson, Bessie Kahn, and Florence Rosenberg; (middle row) Dr. Michael Baker, Dr. Jacob Bearman, Rose Goldman, Harriet Cohen, Marilyn Wolkoff, and Lewis Kahn; (back row) Ethel Yarosh, Helen Broude, Hynda Gottstein, Ruth Perwein, and Lily Steinberg. (Courtesy of Sandra Heims Shapiro.).

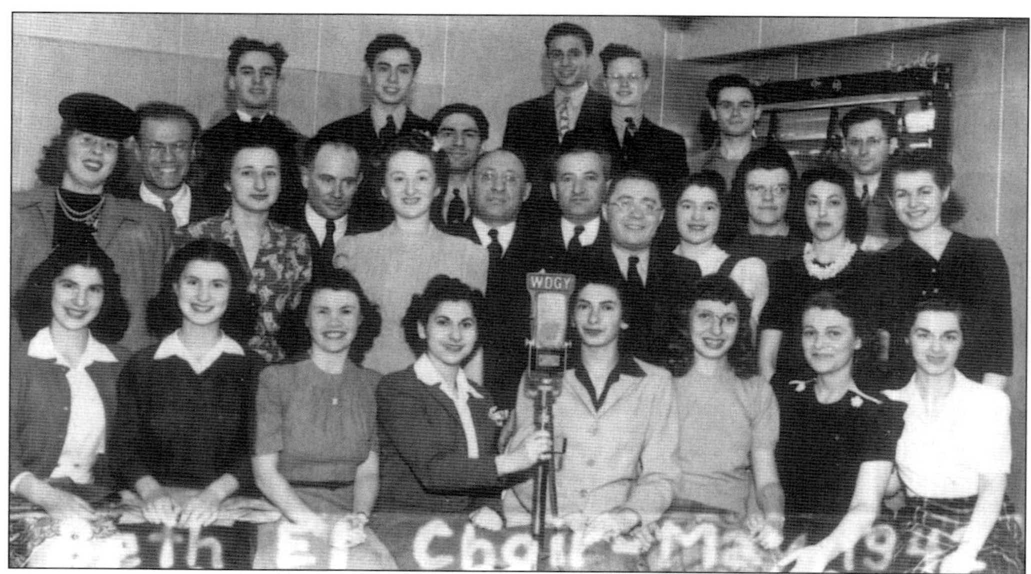

Members of the Beth El choir who went "on the air" at radio station WDGY in 1942 included, from left to right, the following: (front and middle rows, many unidentified) Nate Licht, Sophie Teener, Eddie Gross, Muriel Steinman, Eleanor and Gloria Werner, Florence Rosenberg, Fern Kopman, Helen Bernstein, and Cantor Max Weisberg; (back row) Saul Niefeld, Mort Leifman, Gerson Ribnick, Mervin Tomsky, Pacey Beers, and Leon Sorkin. (Courtesy of Helen Broude Tomsky.)

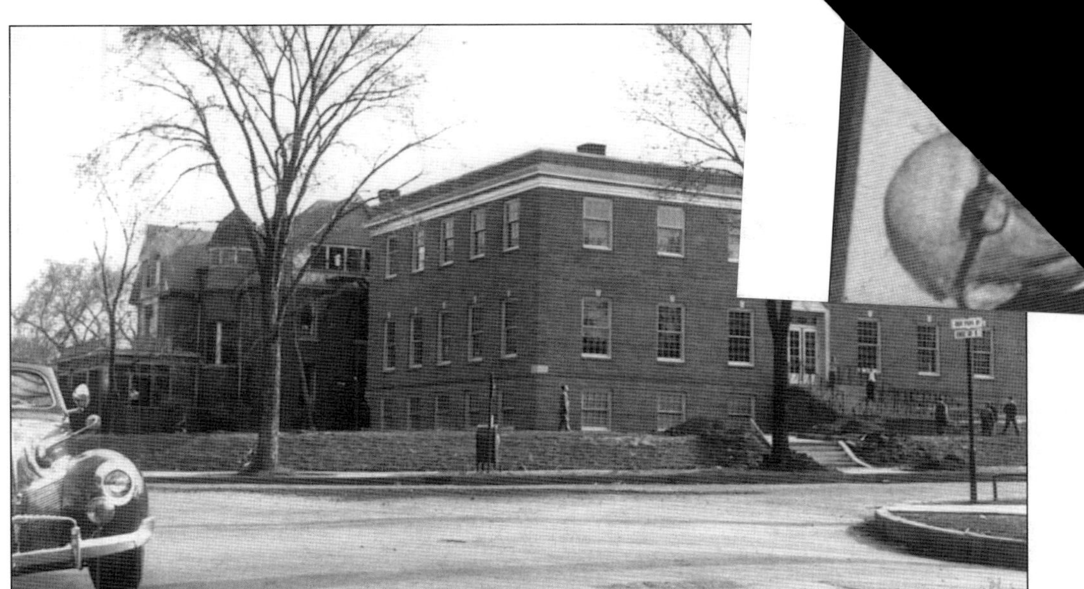

The Emanuel Cohen Center razed a house it had purchased on Oak Park Avenue to build this new $60,000 building, which opened with a week-long celebration in May 1940. To the left is the old Center, a mansion at 909 Elwood originally owned by Emanuel Cohen, who had donated it to the community in 1924 so the Center could have a building to call their own. (Courtesy of Minneapolis Collection, Minneapolis Public Library)

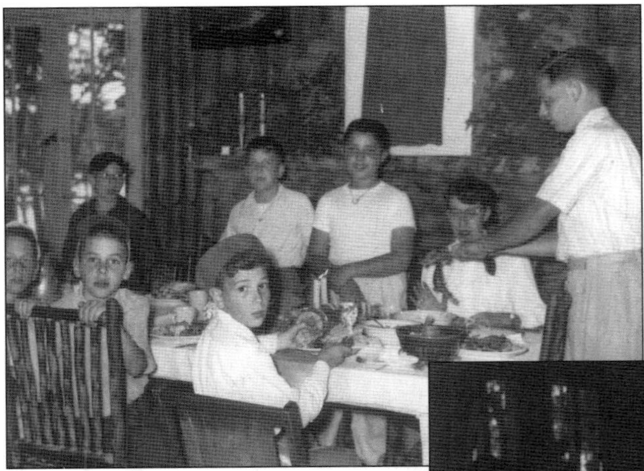

The Emanuel Cohen Center expected about 300 to attend their first children's Oneg Shabbat—but almost 600 boys and girls showed up, and it continued to be a popular event. (Courtesy of American Jewish World.)

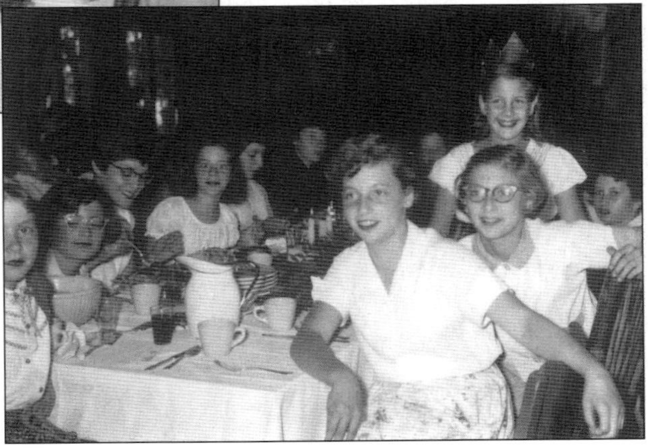

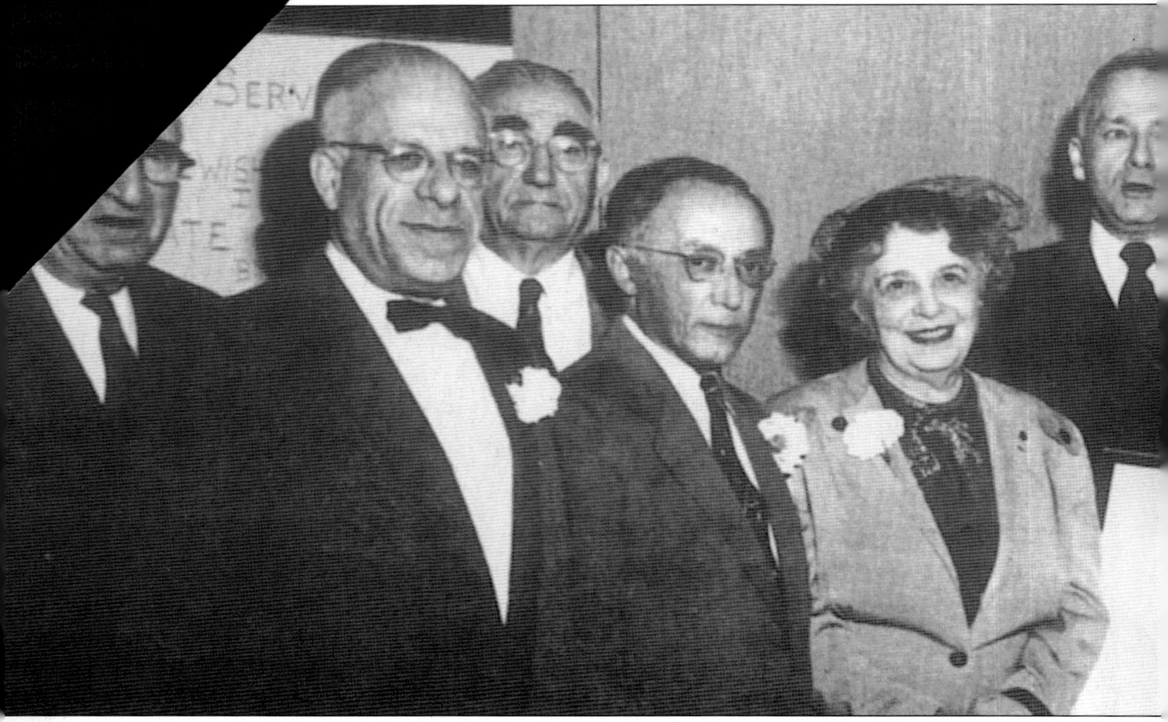

Past members of the Board of Directors of the Minneapolis Federation for Jewish Service met in April 1980, to celebrate the 50th anniversary of Federation's founding. From left to right are John Gelman, Temple Israel Rabbi Albert Minda, Dr. Moses Barron, Beth El Rabbi David

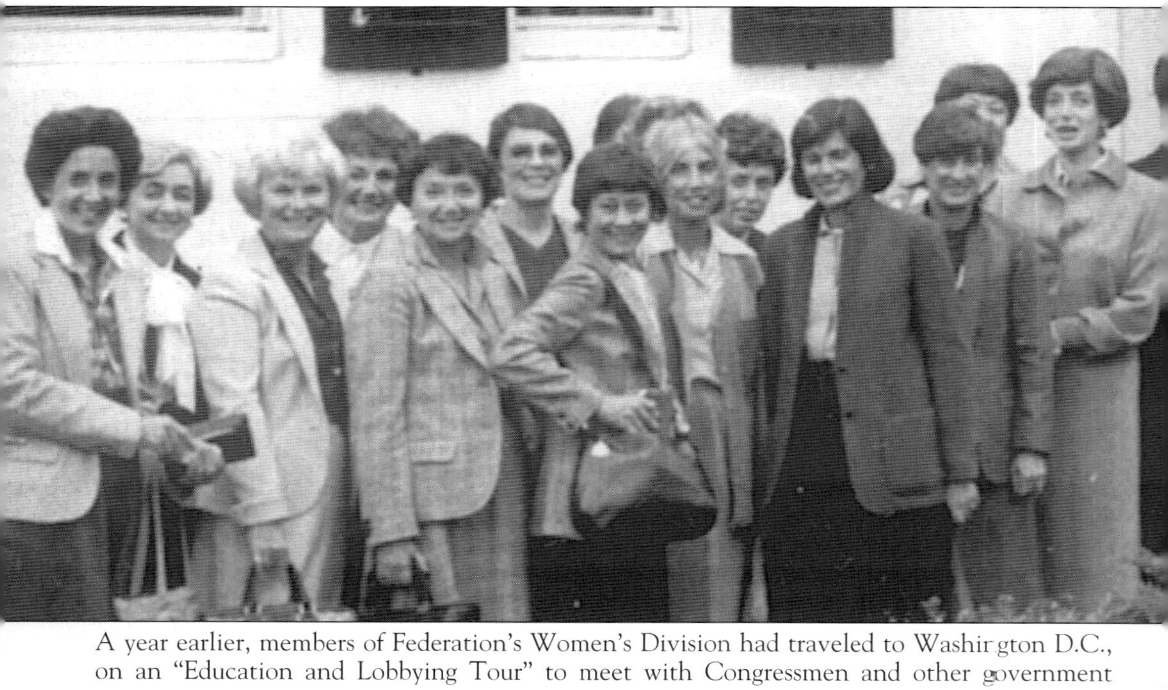

A year earlier, members of Federation's Women's Division had traveled to Washington D.C., on an "Education and Lobbying Tour" to meet with Congressmen and other government

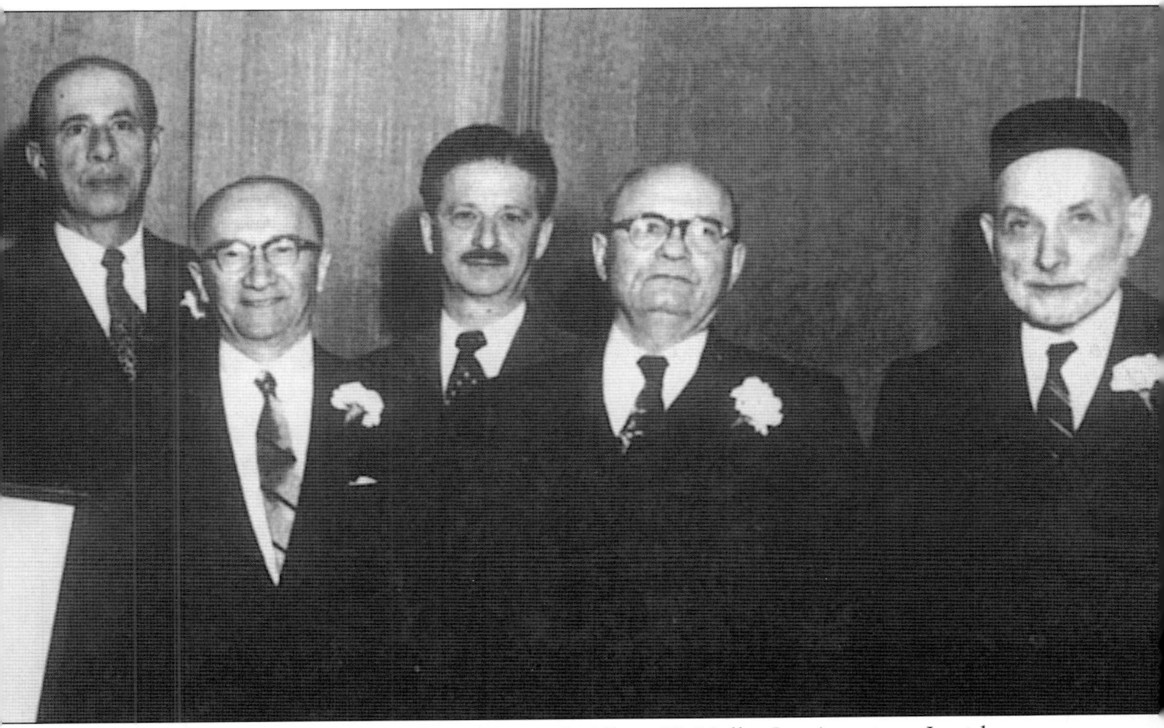

Aronson, Mrs. James Kantrowitz, Amos Deinard, Albert H. Heller Jr., American Jewish World publisher Leo H. Frisch, Benjamin Zalkind, Henry B. Cohen, and Rabbi S.I. Levin. (Courtesy of Minneapolis Federation for Jewish Service.)

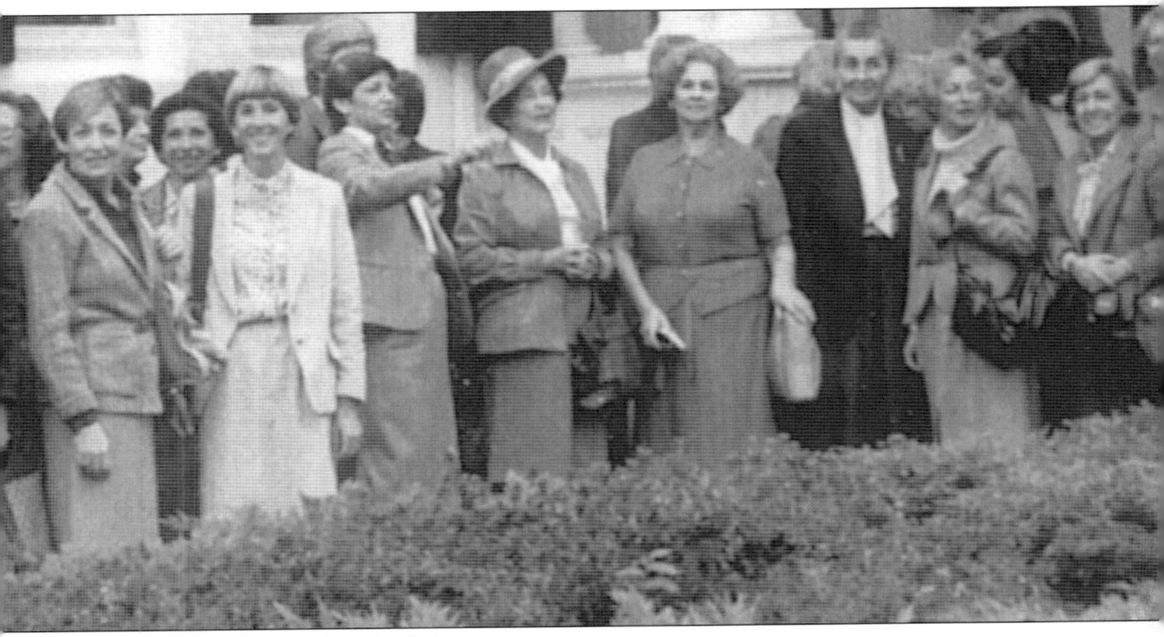

officials. (Courtesy of Helen Wolk.)

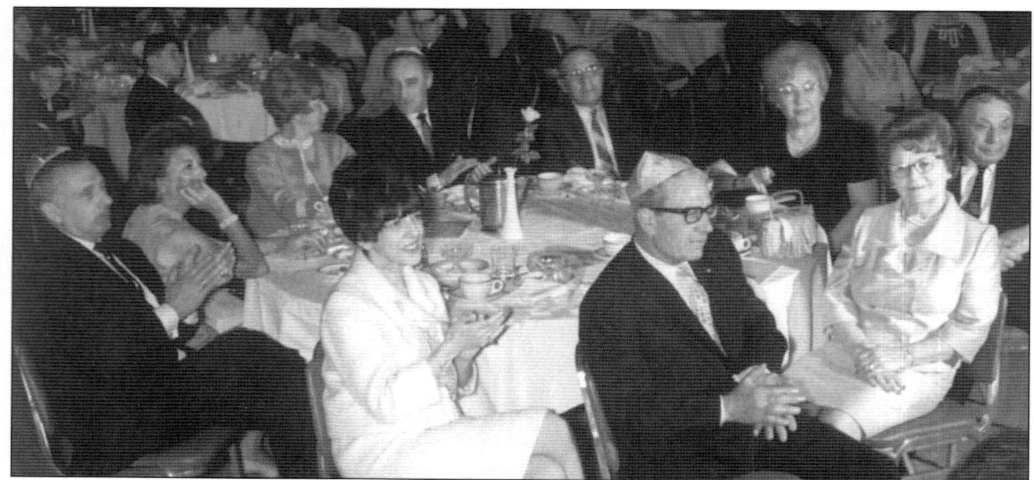

At their annual fundraising banquet on May 29, 1966, members of the Twin Cities Merkos L'Inyonei Chinuch, an Orthodox Jewish organization, honored William and Jennie Guttman for their dedication and hard work in the community. From left to right are Harry and Bessie Schnitzer, Hy and Ann Hymanson, Mike and Idelle Asman, Eve and Joe Ettinger, and William and Goldie Schnitzer. (Courtesy of Marcia Schnitzer Hinitz.)

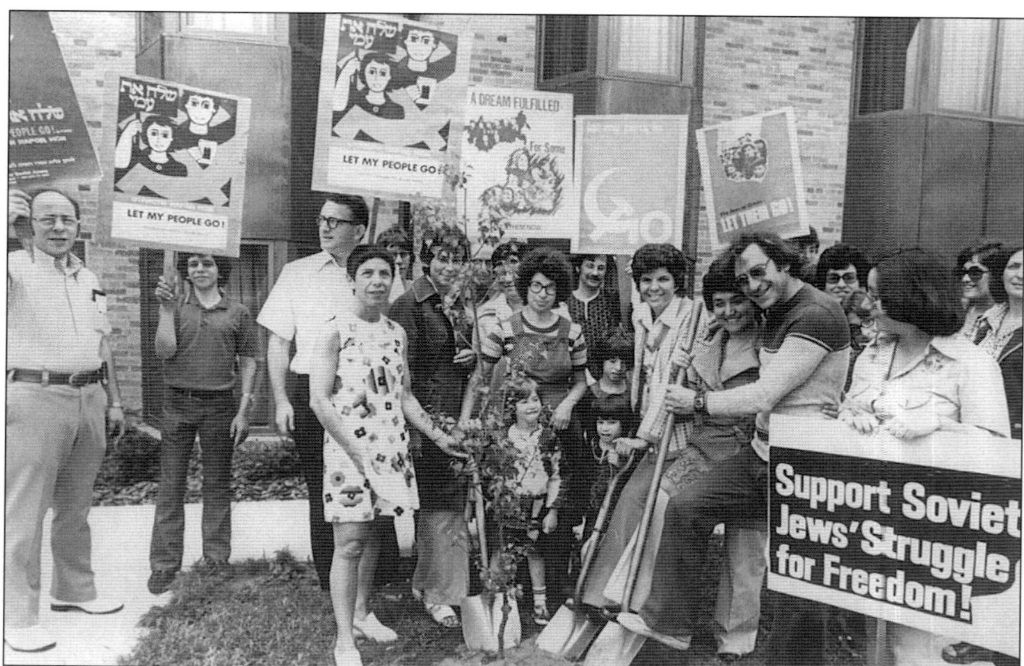

In 1973 community members organized the Soviet Jewry Action Committee to support Jews who wanted to leave the Soviet Union. Sharon Lerner designed the sign they planted in front of every Twin Cities synagogue in 1974, with assistance from Dr. Leonard Greene (left) and his sons Bruce and Jeff, Charles and Janet Frisch, Herb Kohn, Judy Silverman, Sharon and Harry Lerner and their three children, Marsha Yugend, and many others. Dr. Greene and his wife, Carole Sue, also wrote a Soviet Jewry Action newsletter. Later the organization mushroomed into the Minnesota-Dakotas Action Committee for Soviet Jewry. (Courtesy of Harry Lerner.)

Five

SCHOOLS, SPORTS AND SOCIAL LIFE, LOVE AND MARRIAGE

North Side children and their parents socialized with their *landsmen*—the families of other East European immigrants—at meetings, dances, book groups, bridge parties, and other get-togethers at their synagogues and social halls, as well as at each others' homes. They went skating or sledding during the winter, and when summer finally arrived they picnicked and went swimming and sunbathing at Minneapolis's many parks and lakes.

It was an era when it was safe to walk home alone, even at night, and many people did walk or took the streetcar because they couldn't afford to buy a car, or felt they didn't need one. Children walked to school even when it was 20 degrees below zero, although it could be a very long walk if you lived near Glenwood Park, for instance, and went to North High School.

The organizations they belonged to also contributed to their social lives. Synagogue and B'nai B'rith men's and women's groups, and BBYO and BBYW—the B'nai B'rith boys and girls clubs—and women's groups like Hadassah and NCJW, for example, had their own bridge and chess clubs and picnics, dances and other social events. Many long-gone men's groups enjoyed brief popularity, including the Sons of Benjamin, Mendelssohn Camp of Modern Woodmen of America, Woodmen of the World, Knights and Ladies of Security, Loyal Mystic Legion of America, Modern Samaritans, Modern Brotherhood, Supreme Court of Honor, and Free Sons of Israel. In the 1920s the Minneapolis Consistory of the 32nd Degree Masons had more young Jewish members than any other chapter in the United States.

Neighborhood parks were family gathering places. North Commons, for example, which covered nine square blocks between James and Morgan, and 16th and 19th Avenues North, had a skating rink in the winter, a park building where children could take tap-dancing lessons and sign up for other activities, and a baseball diamond on the corner of 16th and Morgan where young men played softball evenings and weekends. The annual Fourth of July and North Side Picnic celebrations also included food booths, a doll buggy parade, fireworks, and other special events. During the summer crowds gathered at the Park Board-sponsored pops concerts on the bandstand on top of the hill to listen to local swing bands and more "serious" groups playing Sousa marches and other popular classics, while salespeople walked through the crowd selling popcorn, candy bars, and bottles of pop, and distributing mimeographed programs and advertising handbills for neighborhood businesses.

Most University of Minnesota students lived at home and took the streetcar to school. They ate lunch, studied, and socialized at Coffman Union or the B'nai B'rith-sponsored Hillel House, where activities included discussion groups, Hebrew classes, a choral group, a debate team, a drama group, and sports teams. The Menorah Society had begun in 1904 as a Jewish literary group, but as the years went by students, faculty, and alumni socialized at Menorah's dances, sleigh rides, banquets, and picnics, as well as study sessions. Scroll and Key was founded in 1916 by a group of Jewish young women who weren't interested in the fraternity or sorority "problem"—as most fraternities and sororities didn't want Jews as members—and in later years there were also two Jewish sororities on campus, Sigma Delta Tau and Alpha Epsilon Phi, and three Jewish fraternities, Sigma Alpha Mu, Phi Epsilon Pi, and Zeta Beta Tau, which had their own sorority and fraternity houses.

The Monarch Club was originally known by the Hebrew name *Moharos*. It began in 1926, when some seven- and eight-year-old boys got together at the Emanuel Cohen Center and started what was supposed to be a cooking club, according to founding member Sheldon Pinck. Their "manager" was Joe Nudell and their athletic director was Dutchy Strauss. The boys helped remodel the building, which was an old mansion donated by philanthropist Emanuel Cohen, turning the bedrooms into meeting rooms and setting up ping pong tables in the attic. They also played sandlot football at North Commons Park, and basketball at the Talmud Torah and then at Lincoln Junior High School. Original members were Sheldon Pinck, Melvin Shink, Walter Landy, Harold Herman, Dr. Irving Herman, Jack Kossof, Sidney Shapiro, and Leon Cook, and club leaders included Jack Reimer, Hy Rapaport, Harry Rappaport and Si Weisman.

Until the late 1880s, Minneapolis residents who wanted a high school education—not considered a necessity in that era—had to attend Central, the city's only public high school. However, North Side residents decided they needed their own school, and on January 1, 1889, North High School opened its new building at Eighteenth and Emerson Avenues North. By 1896, enrollment was increasing so rapidly that a bigger school was needed, and the "new North" was built at 1719 Freemont Avenue North. In 1966 North ranked fifth among Minnesota's 500 high schools in the number of graduates who went on to doctoral degrees, and ranked 207th among 24,284 schools nationwide. Also, North had one of the strongest chapters in the National Forensic League, its band and choir continually scored "A" ratings in district competitions, and its gymnastic team, which included "stars" like Midwest champion Mickey Nathanson, won the state title 15 times between 1943 and 1965. Jewish students at North High School also organized their own service and social clubs—Menorah Club for the boys, Kadimah for the girls—because they couldn't join clubs like Seton Hi, a Catholic girls' club, or the Christian Fellowship, and although a few did join Blue Triangle, Silver Triangle, or Hi-Y, girls' and boys' clubs sponsored by the YWCA and YMCA, most of them didn't feel comfortable during prayer-time, which was usually how the groups' meetings began.

One of the year's major events for Talmud Torah graduates was their annual dinner dance, which continued until 1995, with proceeds earmarked for Talmud Torah's educational programs. There were usually 700 to 900 people attending what some people referred to as the community's "social event of the season." Ida Sanders recalled that when she was a senior in Bet Hamidrash in 1917, she worked as a waitress at their first "Supper Dance" at the Radisson Hotel that cost only $5 per couple for an event that included a band and a meal composed mostly of kosher cold cuts. Later they moved to the Nicollet Hotel, which would kosher their banquet kitchen for the occasion. During the Depression many people didn't attend, she said, because they couldn't afford the "fancy dress-up clothes." At the 1941 dance, which was held on December 7, they stopped dancing at 9 p.m. and turned on the radio to hear President Roosevelt saying "This is a day that will live in infamy" as he described the Japanese attack on Pearl Harbor. "Everything's Coming Up Magic" was the theme for the 1991 dance, and by now tickets cost $85 per couple, but included a raffle for prizes like a microwave oven, a coin-operated jukebox donated by the Heilicher family, or a one-year membership in the Northwest Tennis and Swim Club.

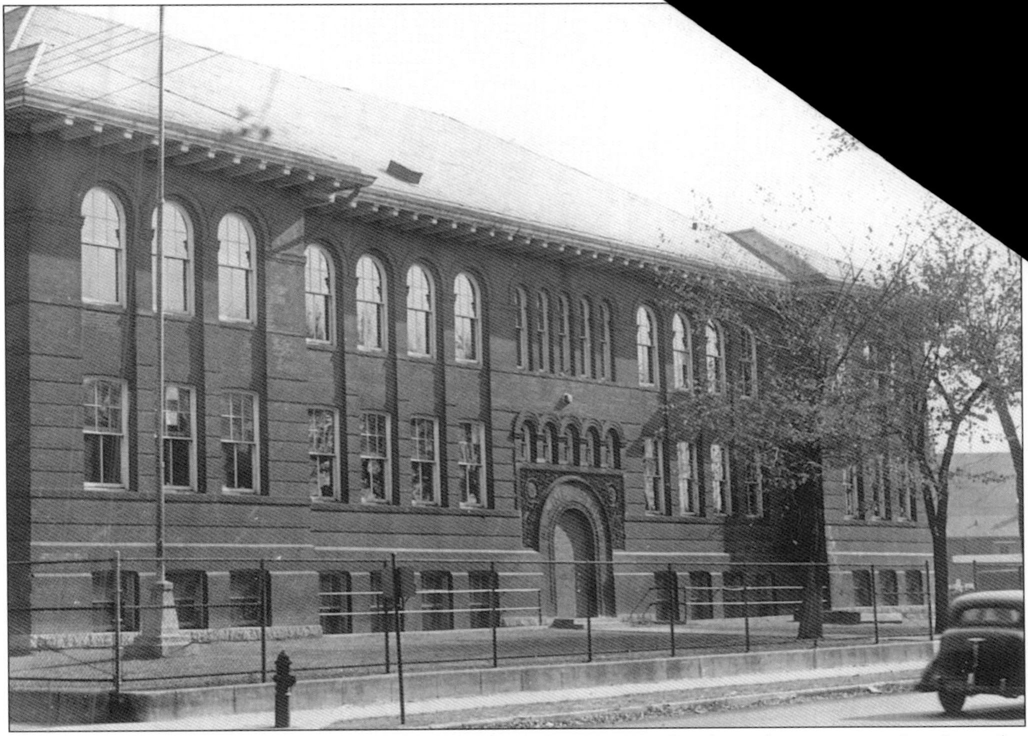

Blaine School, at 12th Avenue North and Third Street, was the first elementary school on the North Side. Built in 1893, it had 13 classrooms, two kindergarten rooms, one bathroom, a kitchen and a dining room, a library, and a nurse's office that was called a "medical inspection room." (Courtesy of Minneapolis Public Schools.)

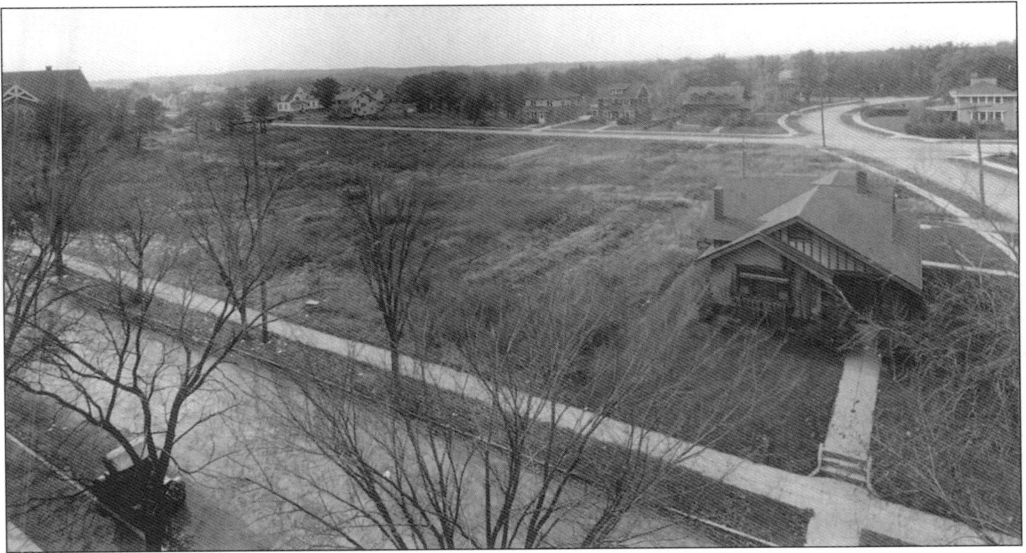

When construction began in 1905 for Lincoln Elementary School, which later became John Hay Elementary School, the area surrounding 10th and Penn Avenue North was farmland. (Courtesy of Minneapolis Public Schools.)

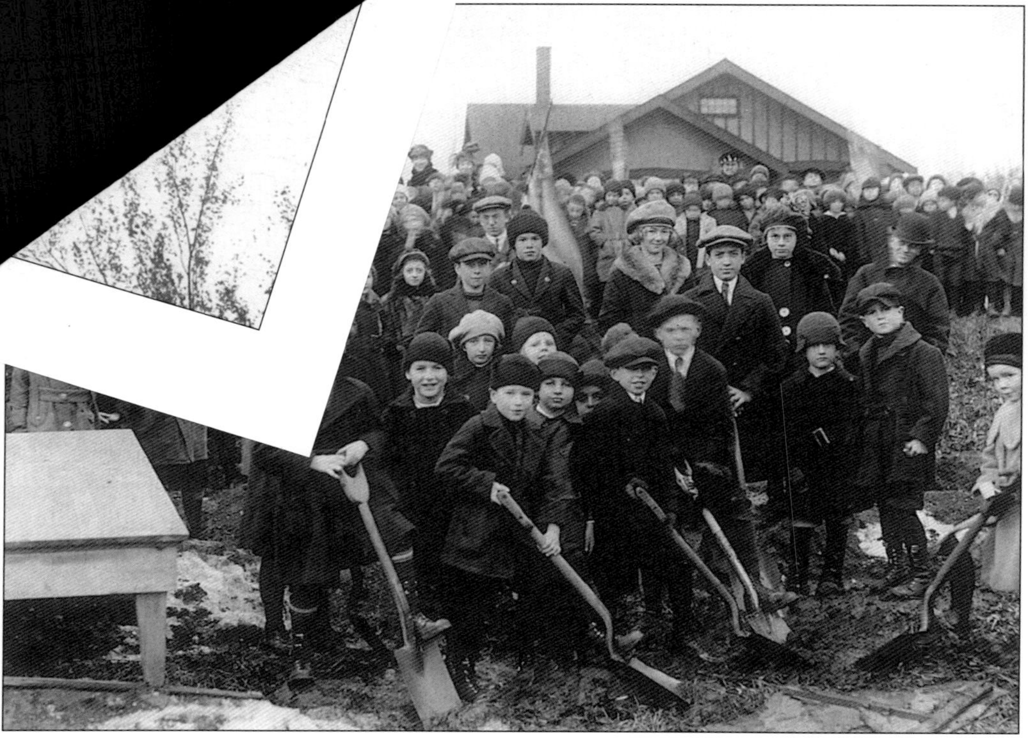

Community leaders and neighborhood families gathered for the Lincoln School groundbreaking ceremony. (Courtesy of Minneapolis Public Schools.)

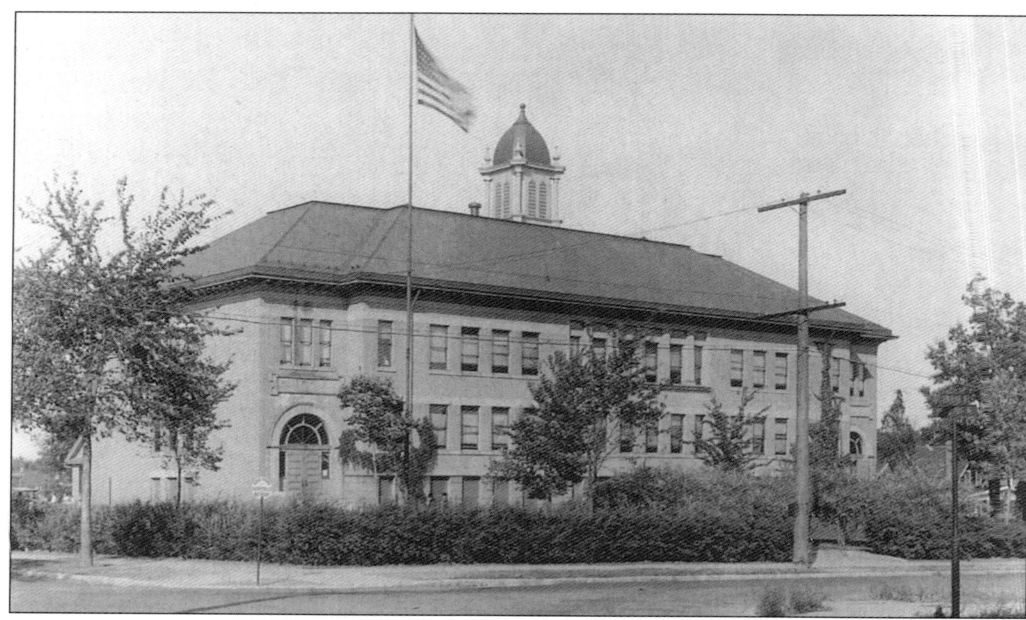

On December 12, 1922, Lincoln Elementary School became John Hay Elementary School. In 1925, the house next to the school, which the city had purchased in 1909, was razed to make room for a building addition. (Courtesy of Minneapolis Public Schools.)

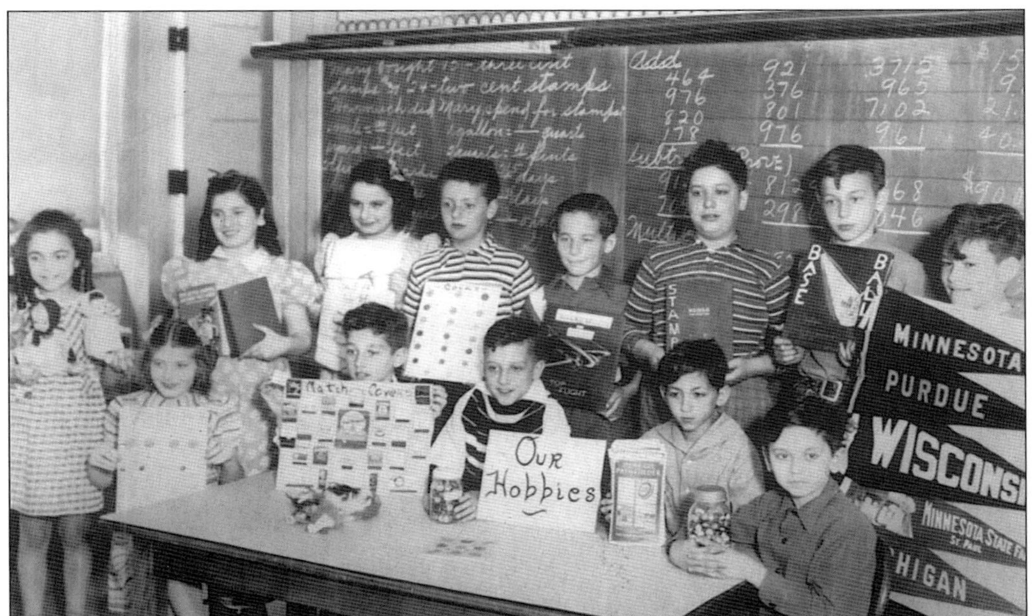

In 1939, these fourth graders at John Hay Elementary School—where classes were half empty on the Jewish holidays—showed off their hobbies as part of a class assignment, including reading books, playing with dolls, collecting stamps and other items, and attending sporting events or listening to them on the radio. (Courtesy of Jewish Historical Society of the Upper Midwest.)

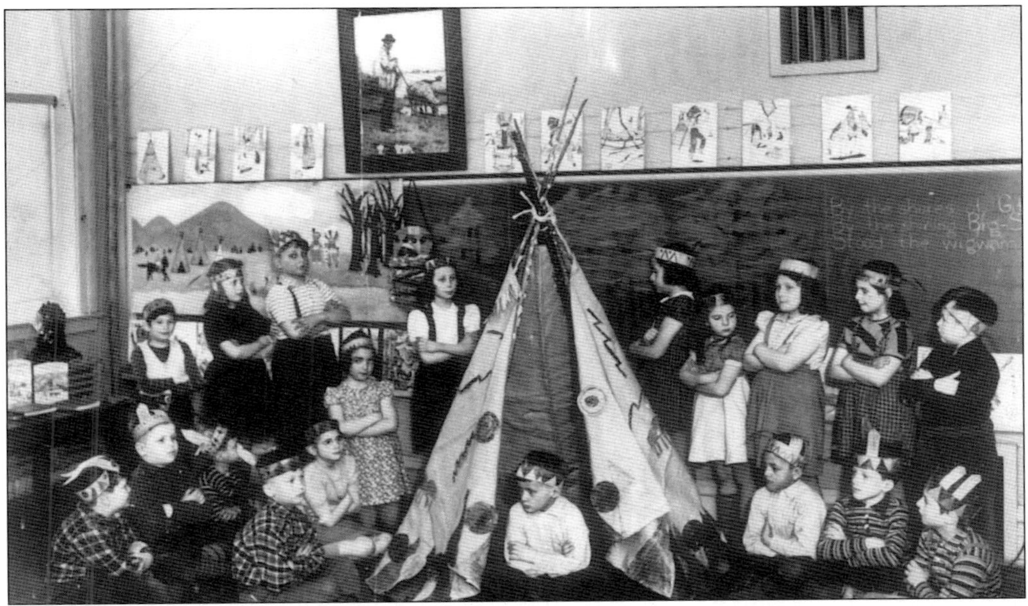

Third graders at John Hay Elementary School also learned about Native American Indian culture. They set up tents, designed and made their own headdresses, and folded their arms and assumed serious expressions to be "in character" for their Indian Pow-Wow, which would conclude with appropriate songs and dances. (Courtesy of Harry Lerner.)

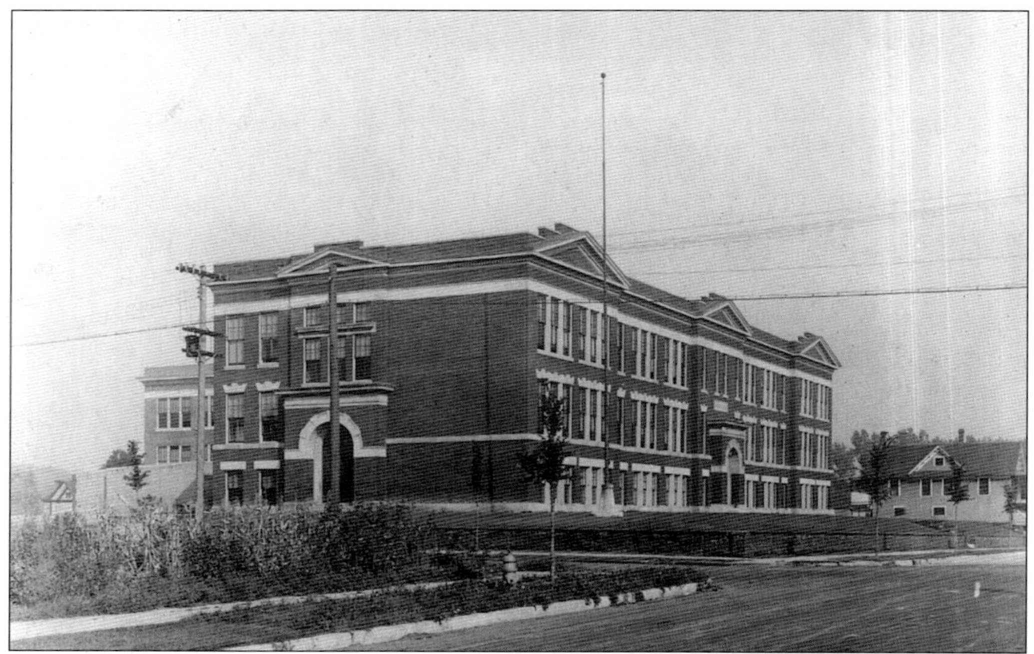

Willard School at Queen and 16th Avenue North was built in 1910, with an addition in 1920. It had 21 classrooms, two kindergarten rooms, and an auditorium-gymnasium, as well as a library and a community kitchen. (Courtesy of Minneapolis Public Schools.)

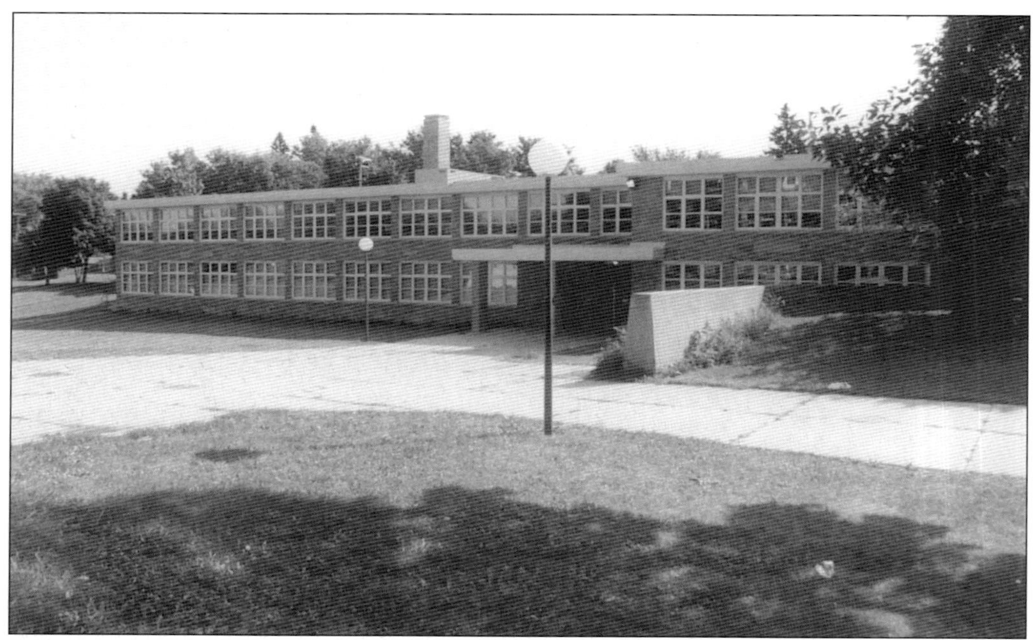

The Talmud Torah Building at 1616 Queen Avenue North was across the street from Willard School. When Talmud Torah moved to its new building in St. Louis Park they sold the building to the School Board, which converted it into a "gated annex" to Willard. (Photo by Tom Lewin.)

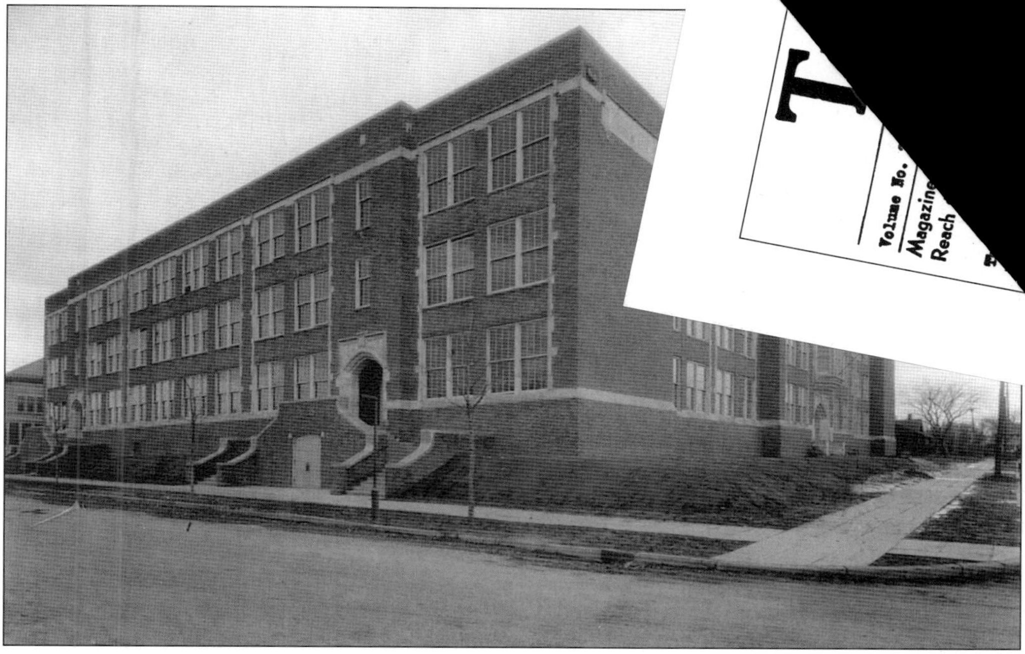

Lincoln Junior High School at Penn and 12th Avenue North was built in 1923. It was located next to John Hay, and had 27 classrooms, an auditorium, a library and study hall, a gymnasium and swimming pool, a music room, and shops where students learned woodworking, electrical work, printing, sheet metal work, mechanical drawing, and blueprints. There were two laboratories for general sciences and agricultural research, and, for girls only, classrooms where they learned cooking, sewing, fitting, and "domestic arts." (Courtesy of Minneapolis Public Schools.)

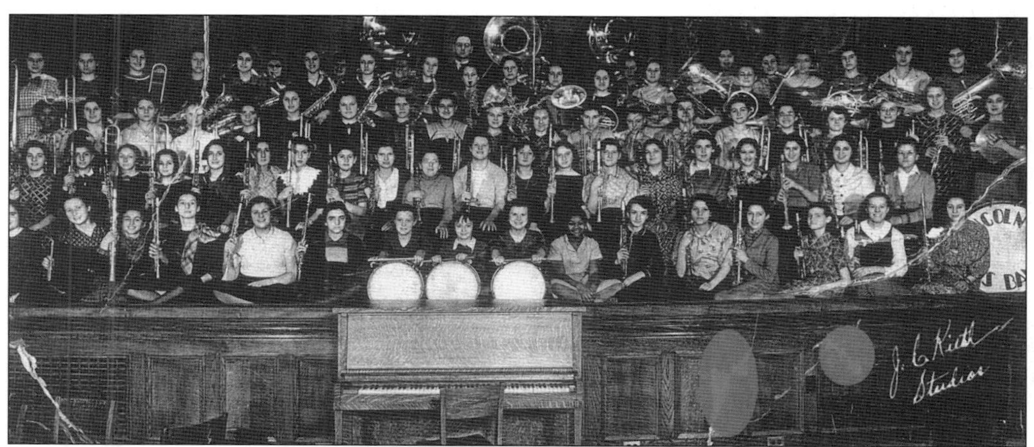

When this picture of the Lincoln Junior High School band was taken in 1935, more than half the students at Lincoln were Jewish. (Courtesy of Tillie Jaffy.)

HE LINCOLN LIFE

9 Lincoln Junior High School, Minneapolis, Minnesota November 9, 1949 No. 2

Subscriptions
$2,596.75

"Anybody wanna buy a magazine?" at's the sentence that has been heard most, throughout Lincoln between October 20 and 31 That sentence represented the magazine subscriptions sales campaign that has been going on here. Our goal was to sell $2,000. in magazine subscriptions.

The profits from the magazine subscriptions drive will be used to purchase a tape recorder, a couple radios, new equipment for the Home Economics rooms and plants and shrubs for our courts.

The top salesmen day by day have been; October 21, James Elvin, Home Room 101; October 24, Mike Weinberg, from 311; October 25, Arnold Kaplan, 101; October 26, Allen Blumenthal, and Elaine Goldman

The entire total from the school is $2,599.75? The ten top salesmen and the three top home room advisors who are to be dinner guests of Mr. Devine will be announced soon.

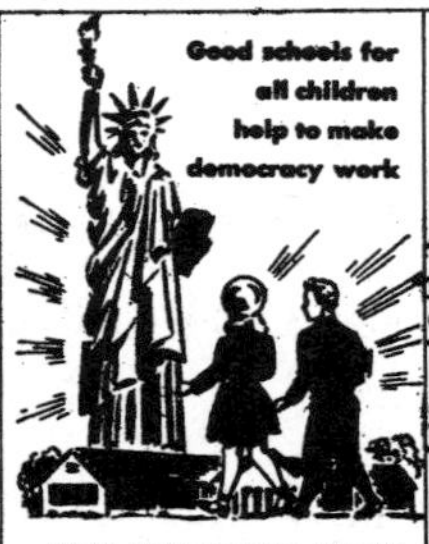

AMERICAN EDUCATION WEEK
PROGRAM HELD NOVEMBER 6 - 12

In recognition of American Education Week, Lincoln will have an auditorium program, tours of the building, and decorations in the show cases. The auditorium program will be presented November 9, during which a short speech will be given by a student about the theme of the program "The meaning of American Education Week."

The common learnings classes will present living pictures of children going to school in other lands. A small group from the music department under the direction the music department under the direction of Mr. Fisher will play.

The movie, "Making the Most of School", will conclude the program.

Parents will be conducted on tours of the school by the Student Council. The tours will take place on Monday and Wednesday at 10:00 and Tuesday and Thursday at 2:00.

The trophy cases will be decorated and posters will be on bulletin boards and stores throughout the community.

STAR AND TRIBUNE INVITE
STAFF TO NEWS CLINIC

Lincoln Staff again has been invited to participate in the High School Newspaper Clinic sponsored each year by the Minneapolis Star and Tribune.

The Clinic will be held Thursday, November 17, at the Radisson Hotel, and will conclude in the Minneapolis Star and Tribune Building.

At the General Session the theme will be "Increasing Reader Interest in High School Papers." A report by George Grim on his trip overseas will also be given.

Students will visit Star and Tribune plant and see behind - the-scene operation of a metropolitan newspaper.

Members from the Lincoln Life staff to attend are Gerald Swates, Marlene Alpert, Ted Orliss, Helen Engel, Art Oleisky, Marcia Engelson Marianne Kaplan, Shell Silverman, Larry Goldberg and one other member yet to be named.

Members from News I are Jack Litewsky, Robert Weiss, Harriet Lebow, Marlene Christensen and Barbara Lessack.

HELP MAKE OUR SCHOOLS STRONG
AMERICAN EDUCATION WEEK
NOVEMBER 6-12

PAGENT TO HONOR
MINNESOTA CENTENNIAL

Lincoln will honor the Minnesota Centennial by presenting a program in the auditorium entitled "Minnesota Centennial - Only Yesterday" on Thursday, November 10.

Three episodes will be presented by eighth and ninth grade Drama Classes under the direction of Miss Flood and Mrs. Seestrom. Episode One will present the period from 17 to 18 century. Episode Two will present the period of the 19 century. Episode Three will present last two decades of 19 century.

Some of the main characters are: Mr. Sibley, Art Oleisky; Governor Ramsey, Ed Gershenovitz; Mr. Gedne, Arnold Silberman; and Little Crew, Marshall Hallfin.

The Glee Club will sing "Long, Long Ago", and "Tenting Tonight" under the direction of Mr. George Belsheim.

The Band will play "Alloueta," "Minnesota, Hail to Thee," and "Oh, Susannah." These will be under the direction of Mr. George E. Fisher.

BOOK WEEK PLAY
TO BE PRESENTED

The eighth grade drama class will present an auditorium in celebration of Book Week.

The Book Review will consist of various short scenes from favorite stories of junior high readers.

Miss Flood is in charge of the program.

BIRDS AND MONKEYS
TO BE AT LINCOLN

The Pamahasika Pets, the greatest bird show on earth, will appear here at the auditorium on November 14. Under the direction of Mr. Raymond V. Roberts the bird show appeared at the Children's Theatre on Enchanted Island in 1933 with a Century of Progress Show.

In the show you will see canaries riding the ferris wheel and merry-go-round, and doing barrel rolls. Among the performances of the macaws, gorgeous creatures from Brazil, and cockatoos, the greatest trained birds in the world, is a dance act in which six beautiful white birds waltz together. The birds' gym class does hair-breadth turns on horizontal bars. One of the birds, Little Billy, mystifies the onlookers by his great intelligence in adding and subtracting.

Given as the finale of the show is the effective battle scene in which the American birds storm the enemy fort and even go so far as to fire a cannon, ending in American victory.

UPHOLD EDUCATION!
Plan to visit your school

Students at Lincoln Junior High published their own newspaper, the *Lincoln Life*, beginning in 1920. Invited to attend the *Star Tribune* News Clinic were staff members Gerald Swatez, Marlene Alpert, Ted Orliss, Helen Engel, Arthur Oleisky, Marcia Engelson, Marianne Kaplan, Shel Silverman and Larry Goldberg, and first-year journalism students Jack Litowsky, Robert Weiss, Harriet Lebow, and Barbara Lessack. (Courtesy of Bobbi Goldfarb.)

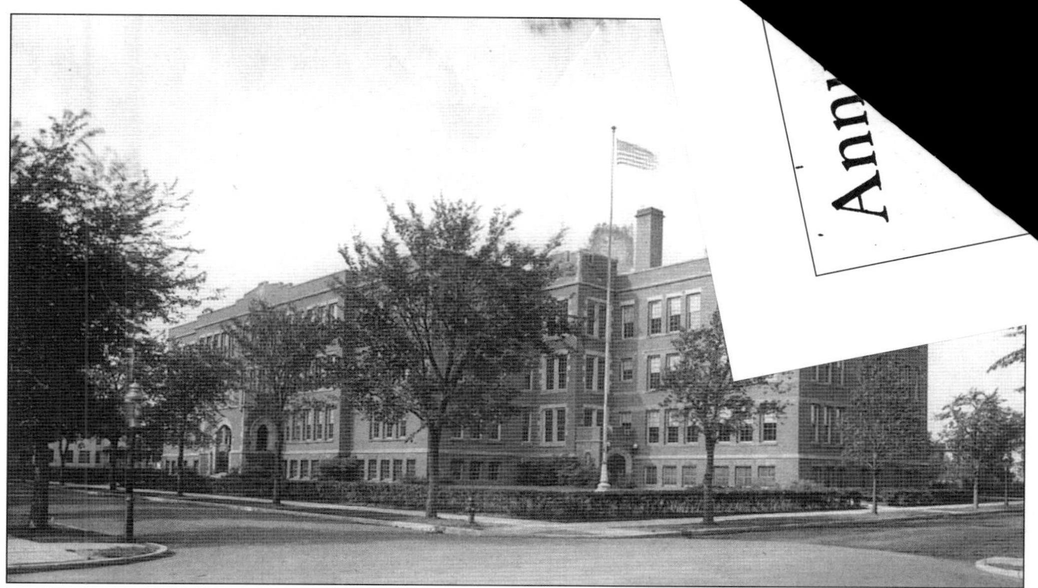

North High School's new building at 17th and Fremont Avenue North was built in 1914. It included 48 classrooms and areas for mechanical and architectural drawing, classes in art, typewriting, stenography, and bookkeeping, and laboratories for stereoptics, chemistry, physics, and botany, as well as a garage where gas engine lectures were held. There were also a music room, two libraries, and machine shops where male students could learn woodturning, painting, forging, machine-work, and other skills. (Courtesy of Minneapolis Public Schools.)

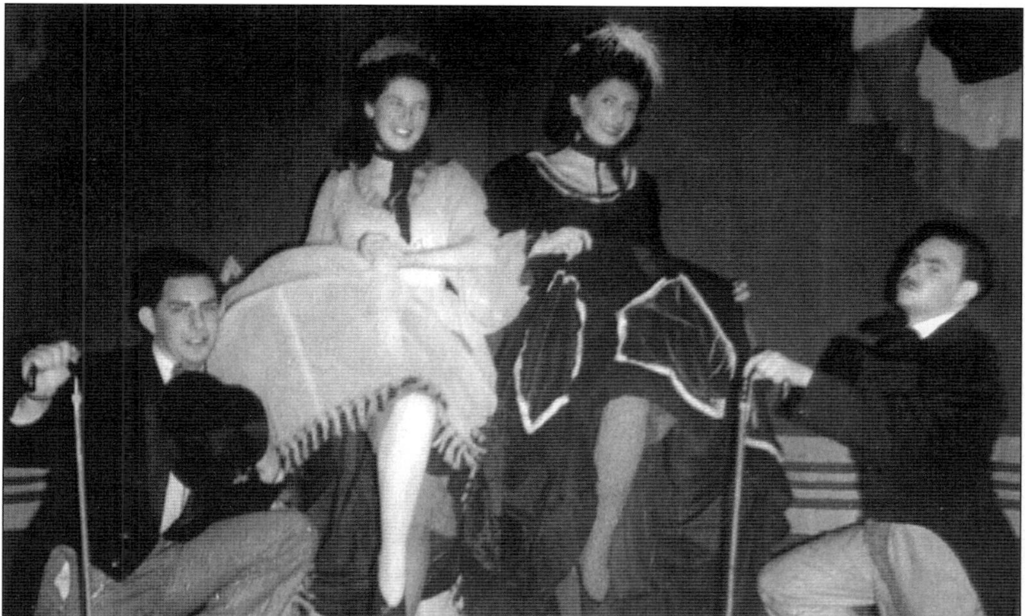

North High School drama students staged plays several times a year. Pacey Beers began his lifetime career in music and theatre in drama class at North High School, where Pacey (right) and Mel Maisel, Riva Hinitz, and (unidentified) starred in this musical. (Courtesy of Pacey Beers.)

...ual Declamatory Contest

NORTH HIGH AUDITORIUM

MAY 29. 1924.

Program

Boys' Quartet - - - - - - - - - - Selected

Lester Brown, Clarence Kloehn, Leslie Klagstad, Vincent Comee

Girls' Contest

1. Herve Riel - - - - - - - - - - - Browning

Hazelle Krumholz

2. The Highwayman - - - - - - - - - Noyes

Evelyn Weisberg

3. The Heart of Eric - - - - - - - - - Peake

Lala Fineman

4. Trip's Disobedience - - - - - - - - - Oswald

Helen Posnick

Instrumental Trio — Traum der Sennerin - - - - Labitzky

Lois Rosoff, Harold Rosoff, Abe Goldberg

Boys' Contest

1. The Soldier Boy - - - - - - - - - - - Long

Nathan Berman

2 The Flag - - - - - - - - - - - - Bruce

Leonard J. Berman

3. Toussaint Louverture - - - - - - - - Phillips

Harold Goldenberg

4. Intervention in Cuba - - - - - - - - Thurston

Abe Bargolis

Tarantelle - - - - - - - - - - - - Drdla

Instrumental Trio

Decision of Judges - - - - - - - - Mr. W. W. Hobbs

Judges

Miss Helen R. Fish, Mr. David London, Mr. Eloi G. Bauers

Jewish students ruled the podium at North High School's annual speech competition in 1924. (Courtesy of Jewish Historical Society of the Upper Midwest.)

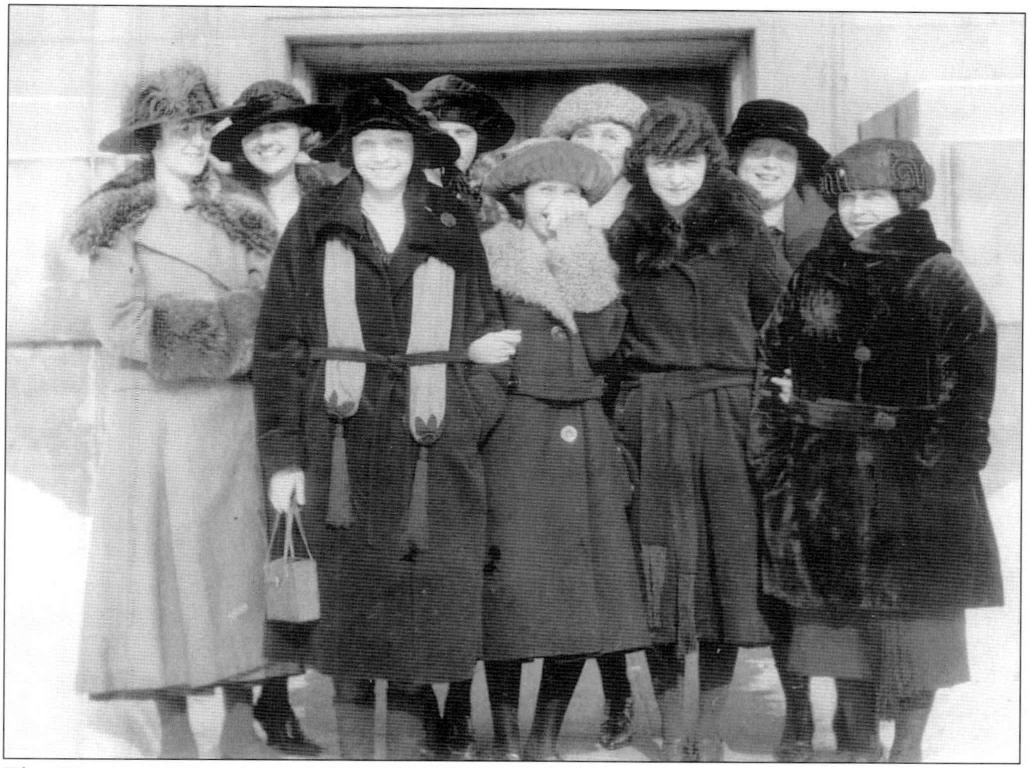

The "Extension Bunch" posed for this photo in front of Vincent Hall on the University of Minnesota campus in the 1920s. They had full-time jobs, but they attended evening and weekend classes at the University. (Courtesy of Florence Greene.)

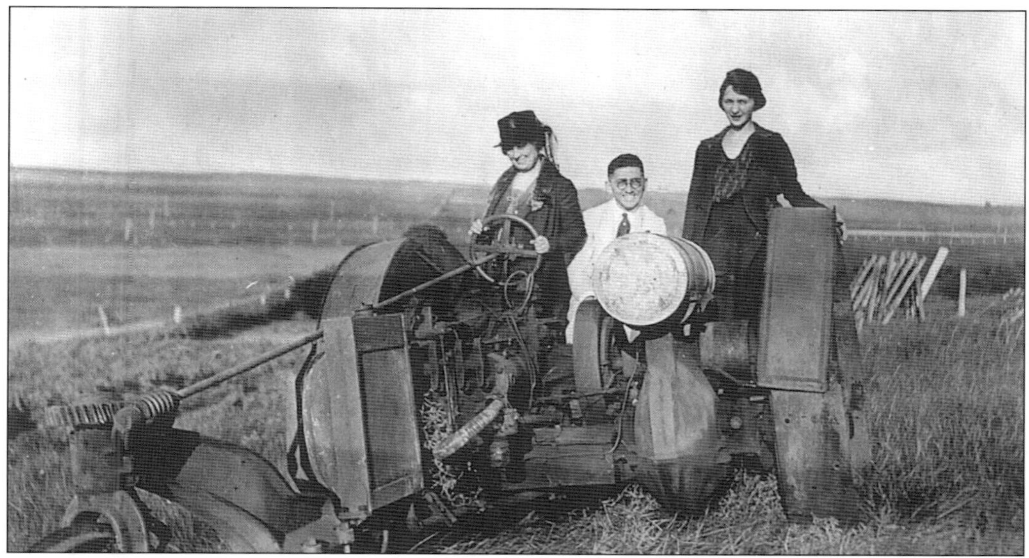

University of Minnesota Law School faculty member George Glick also toured as a Chatauqua speaker. This photo with Mrs. Wales and Miss Randall, members of The Wales Players, was taken in Redfield, South Dakota, in 1920. (Courtesy of Florence Greene.)

Frederick J. Wulling
Dean

The University of Minnesota
College of Pharmacy
Minneapolis

July 5, 1910.

Mr. Samuel J. Broude,
1313 Washington Avenue North,
Minneapolis, Minn.

Dear Mr. Broude: You have earned the following ratings in your junior work:

Botany, 1st semester .... G
Botany, 2nd semester.............. E
Chemical Philosophy.............. P++
Pharmaceutical Chemistry .... E
Metrology & Mathematics 100
Pharmacy.......................... 98
Pharmacy Laboratory.............. E
Pharmacy Record Book .... E
Materia Medica 95
Qualitative Analysis .... P
General Chemistry................ P
Organic Chemistry .... E

Preserve these ratings carefully and bring with you in September.

Very truly yours,

FREDERICK J. WULLING, Dean.

Yours is the best junior record.
Hope you will do as well in the
senior work.
F.J.W.

"Report cards" at the University of Minnesota were very different in the early part of the century. Pharmacy School Dean Frederick Wulling added a personal note to Sam Broude's 1910 grades to tell him, "Yours is the best junior record." (Courtesy of Helen Broude Tomsky.)

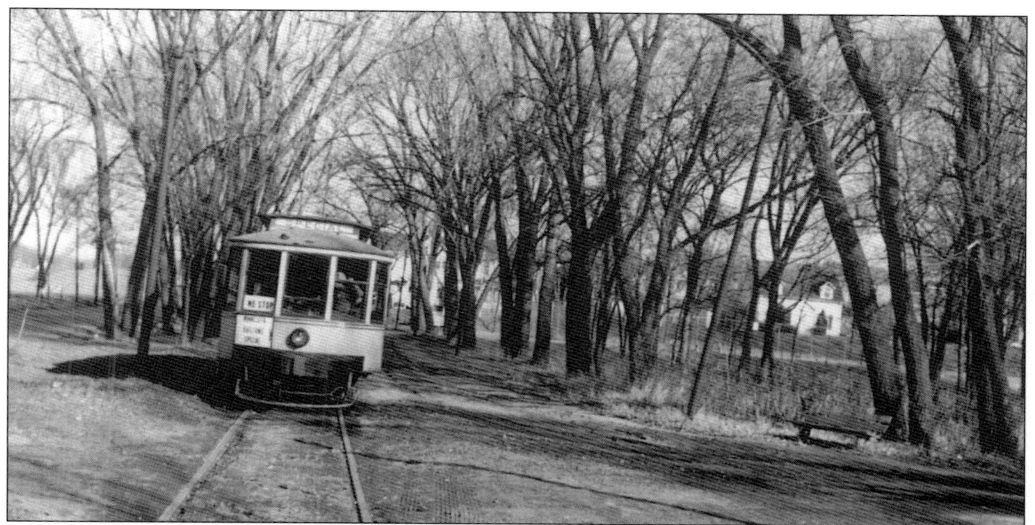

You could take the streetcar all the way to Glenwood Park—the end of the line—to go picnicking or to a party at the Glenwood Chalet, a favorite place for senior proms and other special events. When this picture was taken, Glenwood Park was a grassy woodland. Today it's known as Theodore Wirth Park and has an 18-hole golf course and a par-3 course, wildflower gardens named after community activist Bess Mlnarik, hiking and biking paths, a lake, and a picnic area complete with tables, benches, and barbecues. (Courtesy of Minnesota Transportation Museum.)

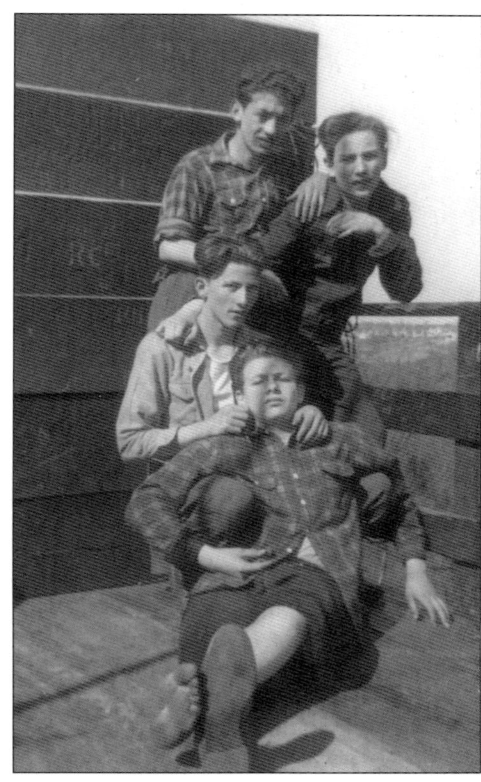

Ski jumps can be more fun in the summer time—or at least Al Chapman, Eddie Silver, Dave Pflaum, and Sheldon Burstein thought so when they "hung out" at Glenwood Park in the 1940s. (Courtesy of Marcia Schnitzer Hinitz.)

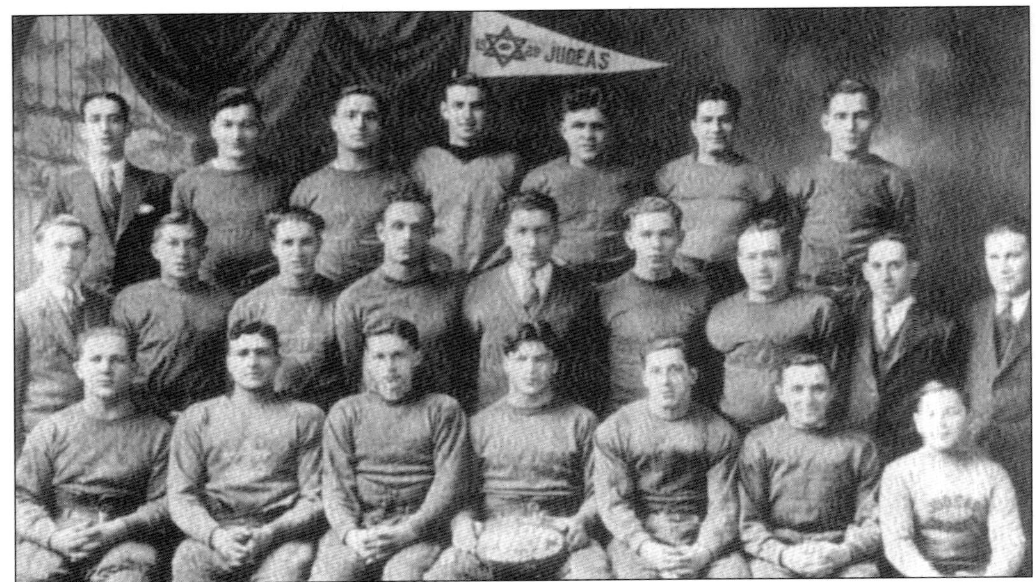

The pennant behind the Judeas, with its football centered on the Star of David, is another indication of how immigrants' children proudly displayed their Jewish identity. The Judeas were sponsored by the Emanuel Cohen Center, but competed with teams sponsored by Christian groups and churches, as well as by other Jewish organizations. They won the "City Champs" trophy in 1929—their fourth consecutive season without a single loss. (Courtesy of IDENTITY magazine, Minneapolis Jewish Community Center.)

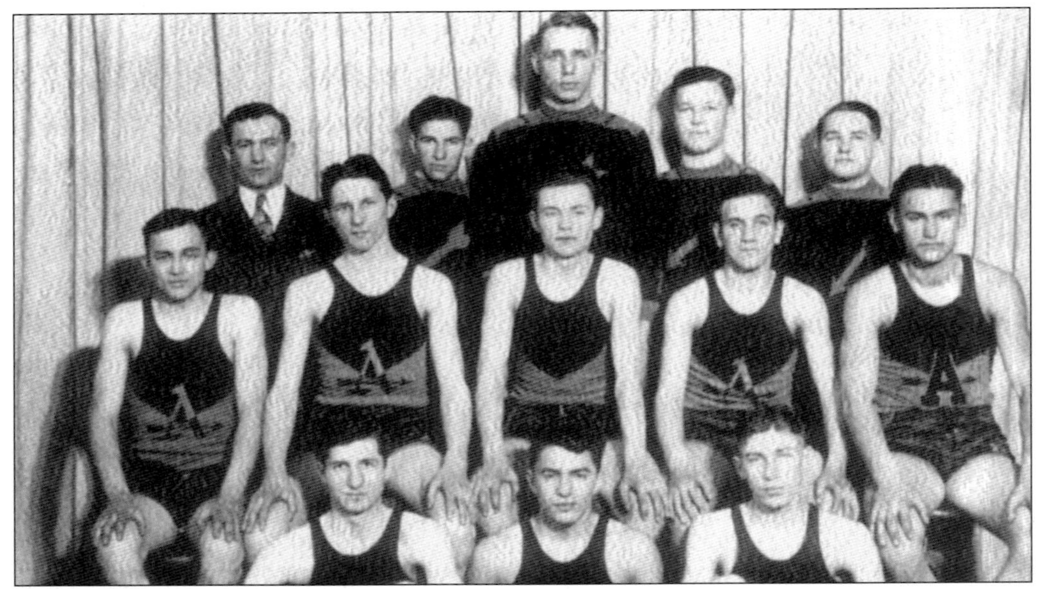

Competition could be tough in the Settlement House Basketball League, but in 193[illegible] the Emanuel Cohen Center's Atlas team won the A.A.U. State Junior Championship. The team was originally sponsored by Gymal Doled, a businessmen's social club founded in 1908 by a group of University of Minnesota graduates. They changed their name to Standard Club in 1945, because they wanted a "less Jewish" name. (Courtesy of IDENTITY magazine, Minneapolis Jewish Community Center.)

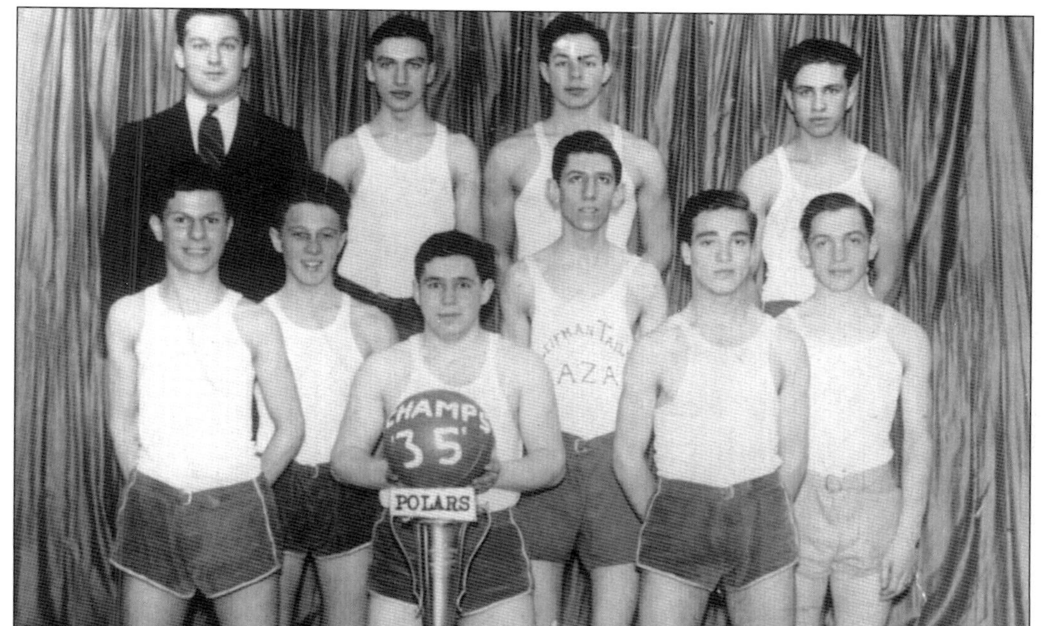

The Polars Club basketball team at the Emanuel Cohen Center shows off the trophy they won in 1939. (Courtesy of Morris Fruen.)

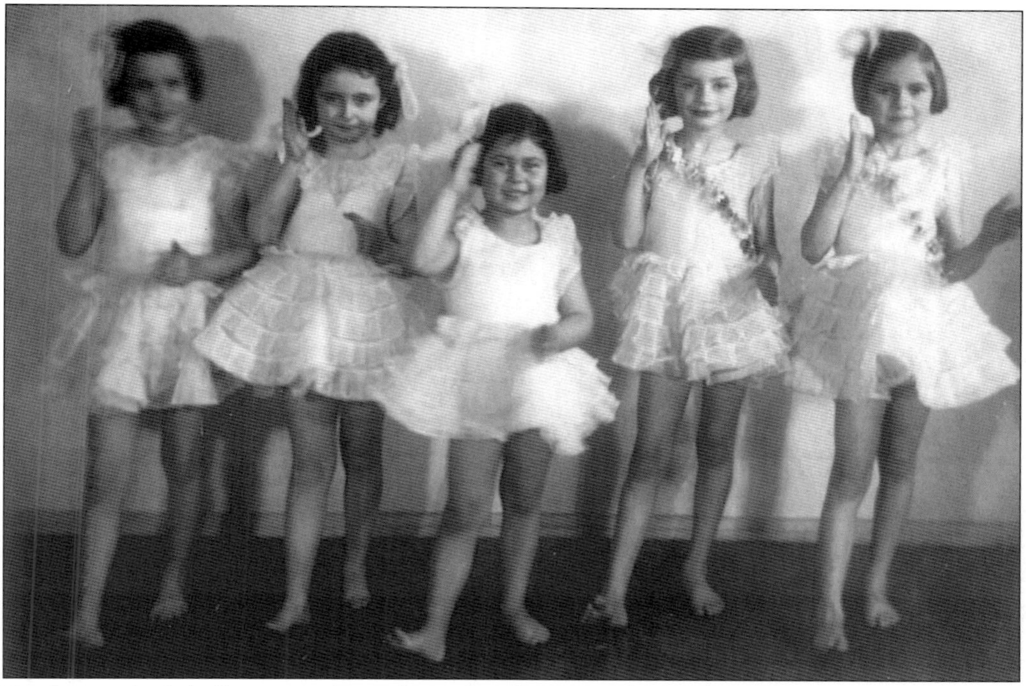

Five happy, little ballerinas-to-be performed at their annual recital in 1934. Many children took private lessons or attended free dancing classes at the Emanuel Cohen Center or at North Commons Park. Shown here from left to right are Cecile Cavalry, Charlene Feinberg, Lois Gilbert, Betty Sue Frank, and Helen Broude. (Courtesy of Helen Broude Tomsky.)

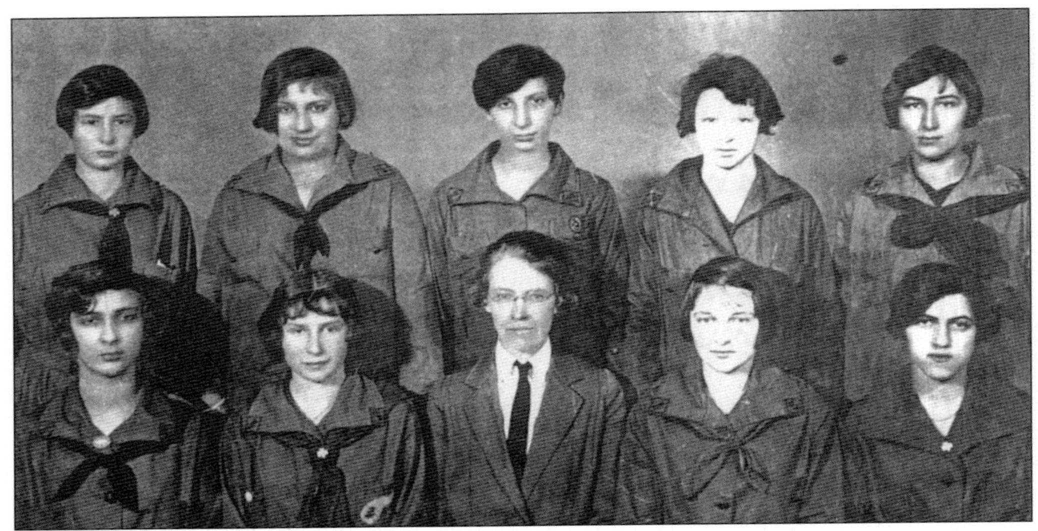

North High School's first Girl Scout troop was organized in 1916. In 1928 Ruth Drum (center, front) lead Troop 4, whose members included Henrietta and Leah Lisovsky, Raleigh Aaronson, Jeanette Rothstein, Beatrice Shuskin, Sylvia Segal, Miriam Stein, Helen Streitman, and Florence Stoller. Henrietta won the coveted Golden Eaglet Award in 1930, but died at age 18 in February of that year, just before the award ceremony. (Courtesy of Ruth Davis.)

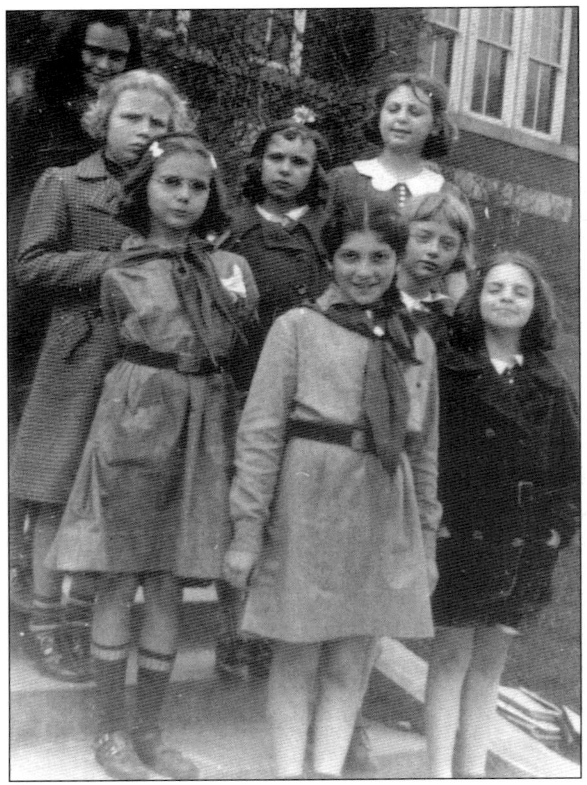

Willard School Girl Scout Troop 177 was lead by Mrs. Margaret Hoffman in the late '30s, when members of the troop included, from left to right, the following: (first row) Millicent Sorokurs and Yetta Wiesman; (second row) Helen Broude and Lois Aasland; (third row) Joyce Randall, Beverly Petrick, and Betty Toberman; (fourth row) Maureen Braman. (Courtesy of Ruth Davis and Helen Broude Tomsky.)

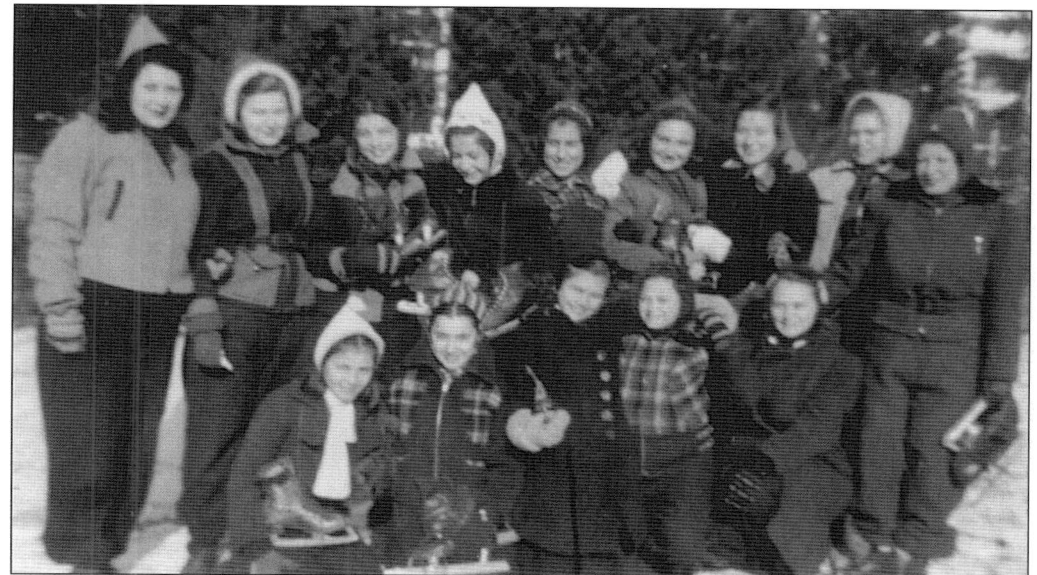

Sonja Tapper led Beth El's Troop 148, organized in the 1930s. Ready to go ice skating at North Commons Park in February 1940, shown here from left to right, are the following: (front row) Lillian Rosen, Joyce Finkelstein, Helen Broude, and two unidentified Scouts; (back row) Mrs. Fein, Susan Levine, Roberta Cohen, Myrle Lebowske, Marilyn Schermer, Myra Brickman, (?) Rauch, and unidentified, with Mrs. Fein on the left and Mrs. Tapper on the right. (Courtesy of Ruth Davis.)

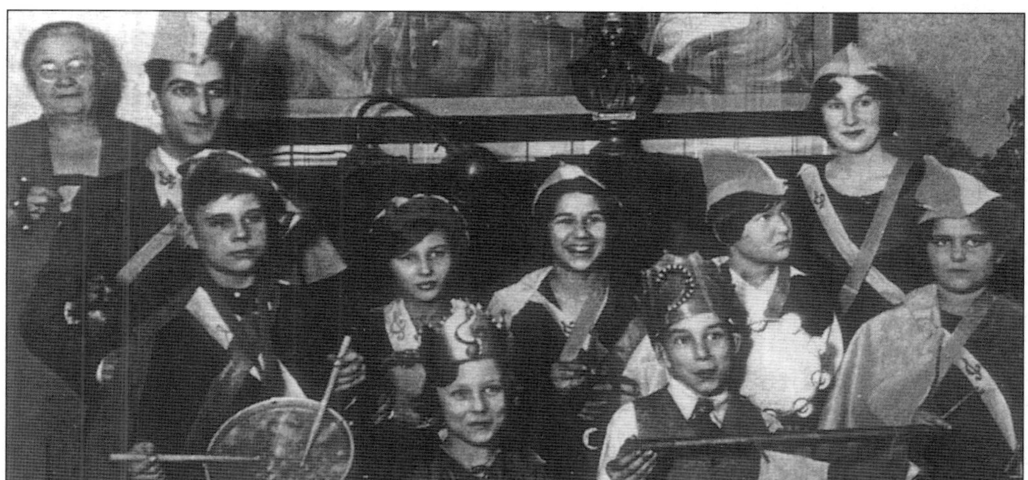

Leah Lisovsky Bernstein (right, rear) was an athlete, artist, dancer, actress, and talented pianist. At North High School she was president of her Girl Scout troop, played on the girls' volleyball, basketball and baseball teams, won a 1927 scholarship to study at the Minneapolis Art Institute and won the All-City Original Composition Contest in 1927, 1928, and 1929. She taught piano, organized a rhythm band in her living room, and painted the mural on the wall "to add color to the room and create a mood for my music studio." Her elderly neighbor, Mrs. Dryer, and North High classmate and violinist Vahe Santoorjian (left rear) also played with the band. (From *Leah: For Freedom… For Love… An Autobiography of Leah Bernstein*, by Leah Lisovsky Bernstein, courtesy of Ruth Davis.)

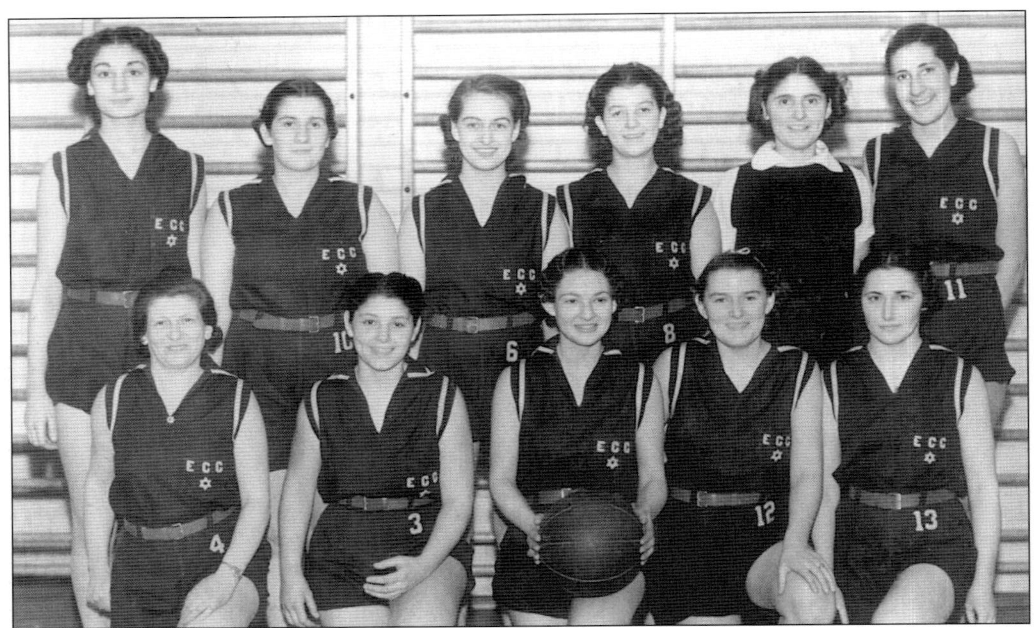

Young women met at the Emanuel Cohen Center on February 16, 1933, to organize a sports and social club. They considered three names—Sparklers, Bar-Kochva, and Auroras—and not surprisingly, Auroras was their unanimous choice. They decided club dues would be 2¢ a week, chose green and white as their club colors, and elected Frances Held, president; Ethel Orenstein, vice president; Inez Kolusky, secretary; June Richie, treasurer; and Mary Silvers, sergeant-at-arms. (Courtesy of Jewish Historical Society of the Upper Midwest.)

AURORA CLUB BRIDGE

at the

Emanuel Cohen Center

909 ELWOOD AVE.

SUNDAY FEB. 24, 1935 AT 2 P. M.

PRIZES ENTERTAINMENT

ADMISSION 10c

The Auroras met at the Center every Sunday to play bridge. (Courtesy of Jewish Historical Society of the Upper Midwest.)

AURORA FALL FROLIC

November 28th, 1934, 8 p. m.

AT THE

TALMUD TORAH

Cor. 8th. & Fremont N.

Admission: 15c Checking Free

Their "Big Four" organizers, Mary Fisher, Marion Shapiro, Marilyn Schwartzman, and Marion Prell raised money by organizing bridge tournaments and their annual Fall Frolic. (Courtesy of Jewish Historical Society of the Upper Midwest.)

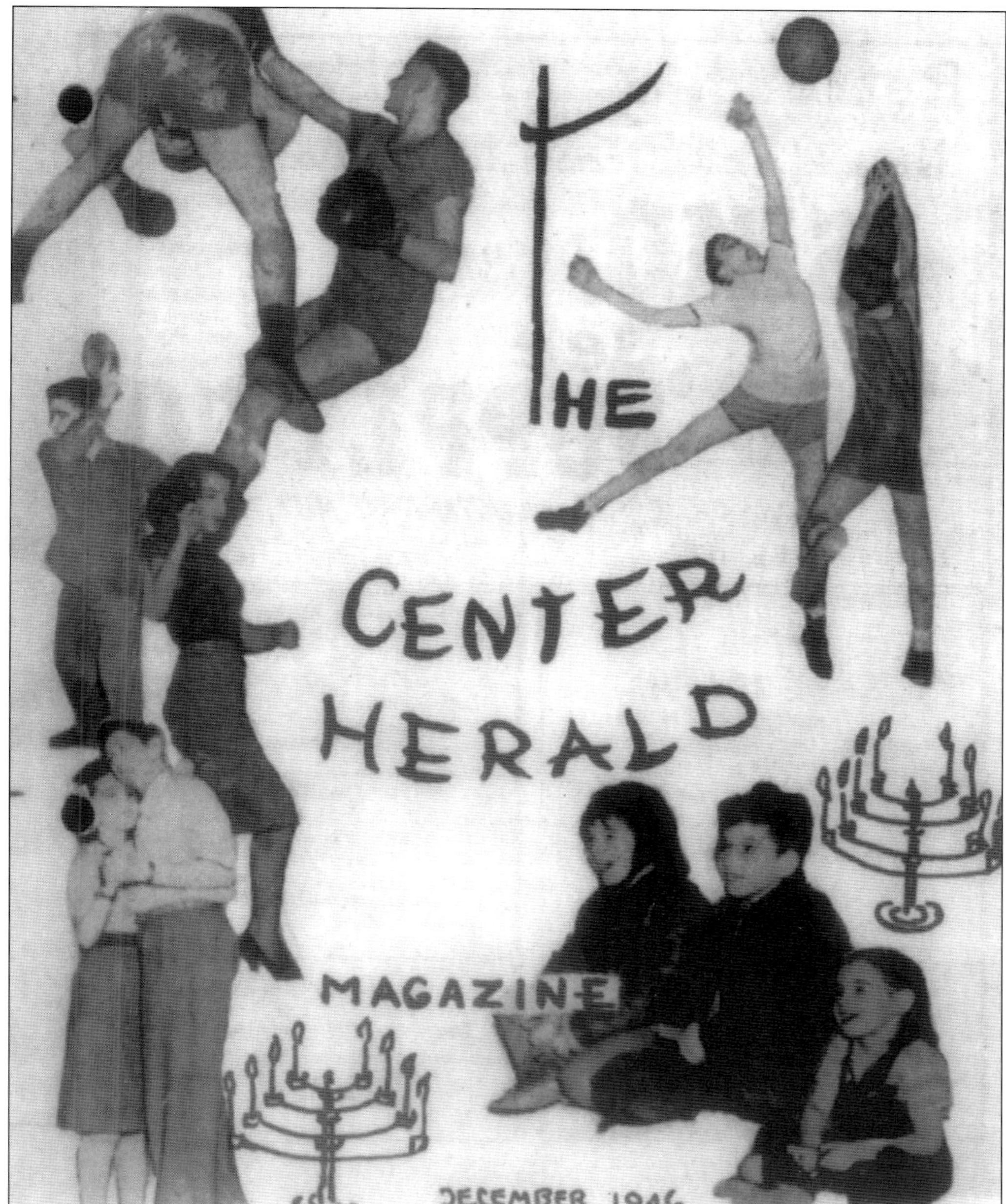

And there was something for everybody at the Jewish Community Center, including sports, dances, story-telling sessions, and holiday celebrations. (Courtesy of Jewish Historical Society of the Upper Midwest.)

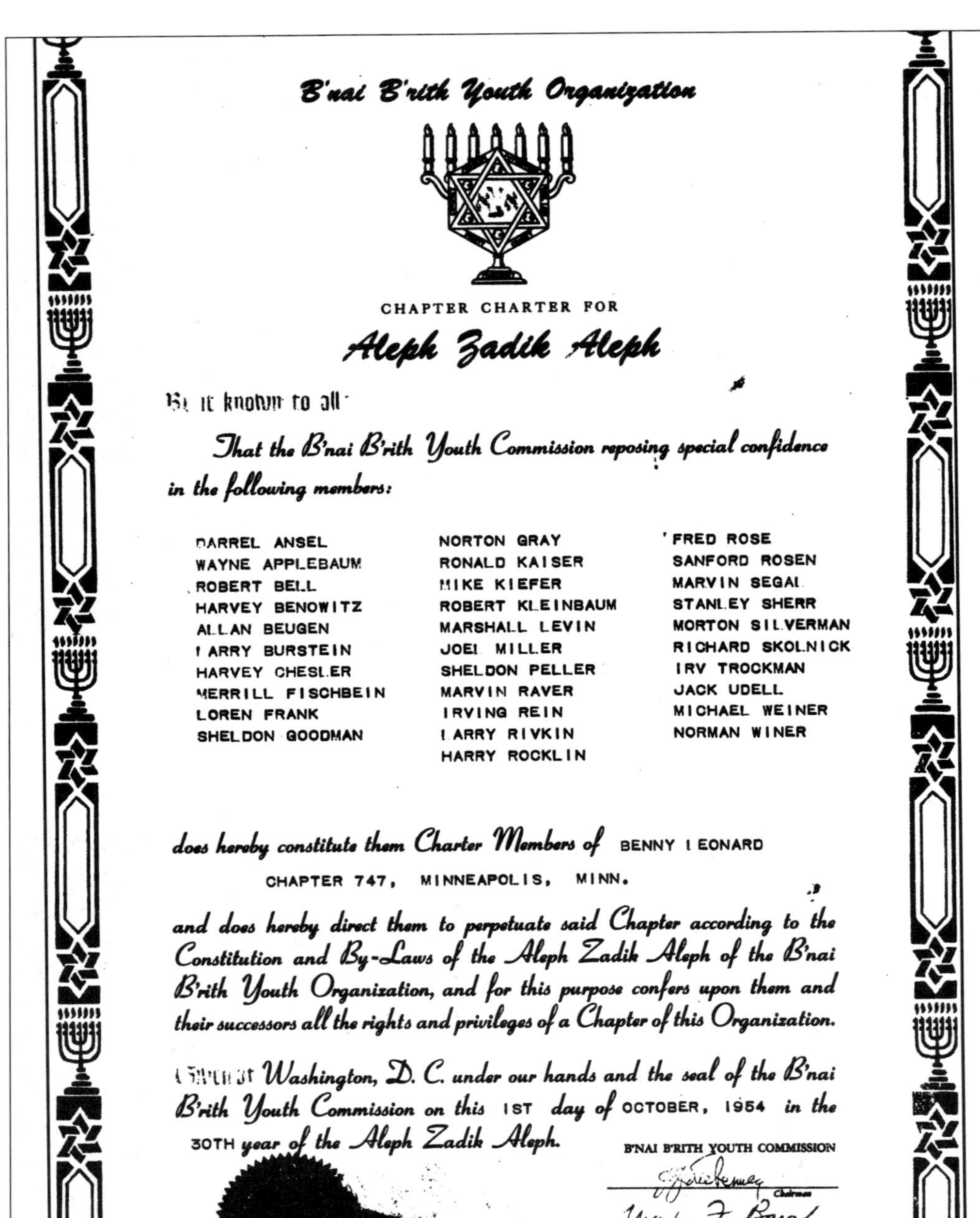
B'nai B'rith Youth Organization

CHAPTER CHARTER FOR

Aleph Zadik Aleph

Be it known to all:

That the B'nai B'rith Youth Commission reposing special confidence in the following members:

DARREL ANSEL
WAYNE APPLEBAUM
ROBERT BELL
HARVEY BENOWITZ
ALLAN BEUGEN
LARRY BURSTEIN
HARVEY CHESLER
MERRILL FISCHBEIN
LOREN FRANK
SHELDON GOODMAN
NORTON GRAY
RONALD KAISER
MIKE KIEFER
ROBERT KLEINBAUM
MARSHALL LEVIN
JOEL MILLER
SHELDON PELLER
MARVIN RAVER
IRVING REIN
LARRY RIVKIN
HARRY ROCKLIN
FRED ROSE
SANFORD ROSEN
MARVIN SEGAL
STANLEY SHERR
MORTON SILVERMAN
RICHARD SKOLNICK
IRV TROCKMAN
JACK UDELL
MICHAEL WEINER
NORMAN WINER

does hereby constitute them Charter Members of BENNY LEONARD CHAPTER 747, MINNEAPOLIS, MINN.

and does hereby direct them to perpetuate said Chapter according to the Constitution and By-Laws of the Aleph Zadik Aleph of the B'nai B'rith Youth Organization, and for this purpose confers upon them and their successors all the rights and privileges of a Chapter of this Organization.

Given at Washington, D. C. under our hands and the seal of the B'nai B'rith Youth Commission on this 1ST day of OCTOBER, 1954 in the 30TH year of the Aleph Zadik Aleph.

B'NAI B'RITH YOUTH COMMISSION

Chairman

Director

Jewish young people organized sports and social clubs like Benny Leonard AZA because they often weren't welcome at local gymnasiums and clubs, and couldn't play on teams sponsored by neighborhood churches. When a charter became available, they grabbed it, and on October 1, 1954, Benny Leonard AZA became Chapter 747 of the North Star Region, District No. 6 of the B'nai B'rith Youth Organization (BBYO), the world's largest Jewish youth group. (Courtesy of Bob Kleinbaum.)

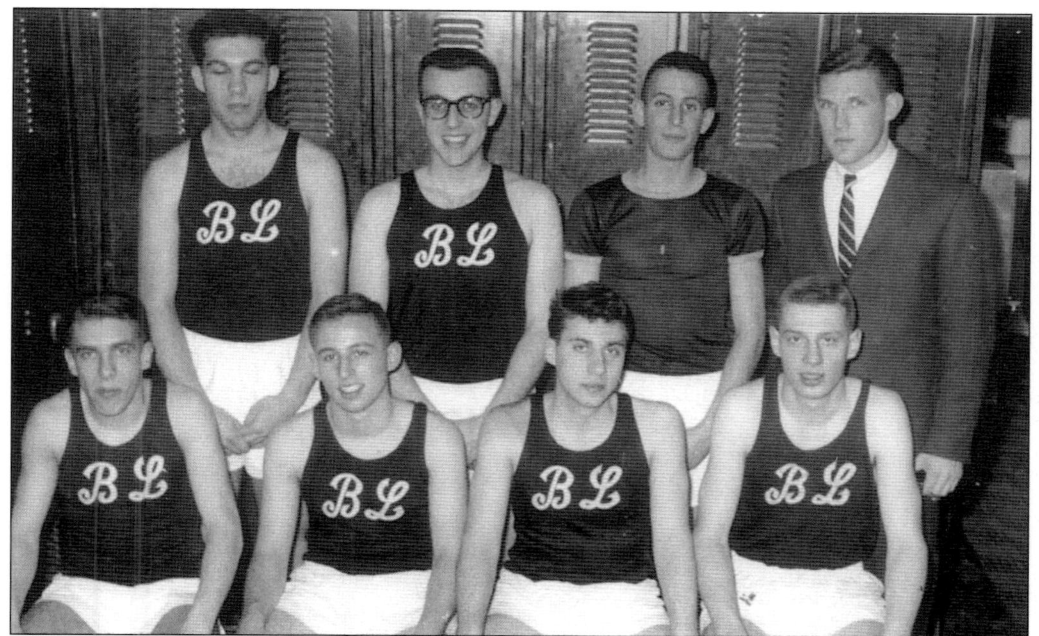

They began as a group of more than 40 childhood chums who grew up together on the North Side and were exceptional athletes in basketball, softball, and football at Lincoln Junior High School. Their basketball team, shown in the locker room at the Emanuel Cohen Center, made it all the way to the national AZA tournament in Chicago in 1955. From left to right are the following: (front row) Harvey Chesler, Shel Peller, Marvin Raver, and Stan Taube; (back row) Joel Miller, Marvin Segal, Norman Ressen, and coach Chick Bronstien. (Courtesy of Merrill Fischbein and Bob Kleinbaum.)

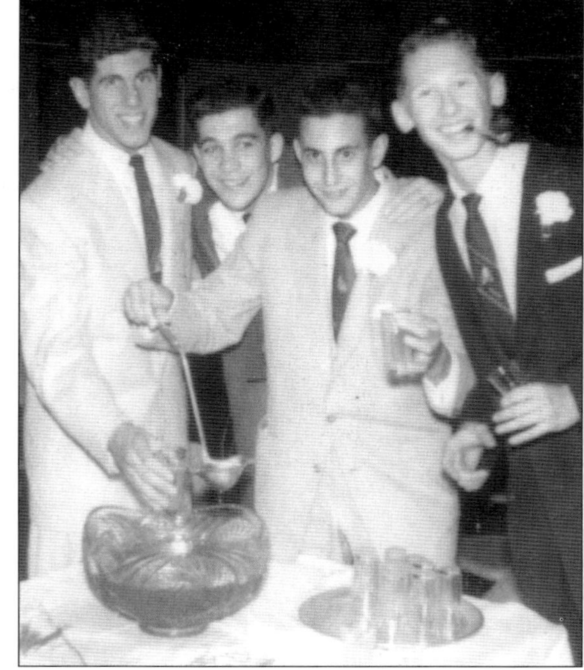

They celebrated with a dinner dance the following week at Brookview Country Club. Sampling the punch, from left to right, are Loren Frank, who co-chaired the event with Harvey Chesler, Larry Burstein, Wayne Applebaum and Mort Silverman, who served as entertainment co-chair with Marv Segal, Norty Gray, and Sandy Rosen. (Courtesy of Bob Kleinbaum.)

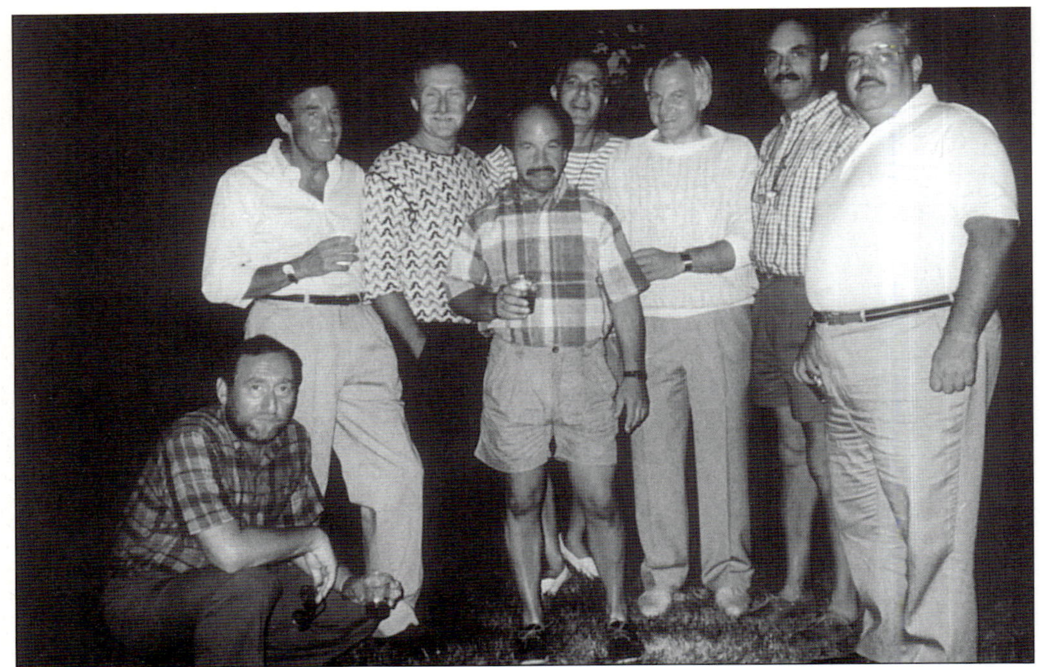

They still meet for lunch on the second Wednesday of every other month at the Golden Valley Country Club, have a wiener roast every summer, and plan a reunion every five years that coincides with the North High School All-Class Reunion. Current members include, from left to right, Norton Gray, Ron Haskovitz, Merrill Fischbein, Sherm Langer, Allan Marcus, Darrell Ansel, Bob Kleinbaum, and Mike Kiefer, plus Wayne Applebaum, Allen Beugen, Gene Scherling, Marv Segal, Mort Silverman, and Fred Rose. (Courtesy of Bob Kleinbaum.)

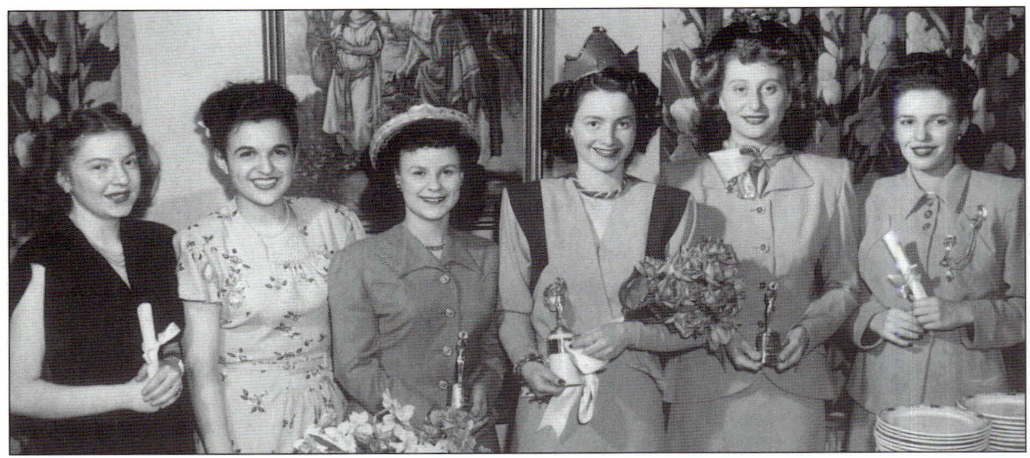

BBYW was a branch of the B'nai B'rith Youth Organization organized to give B'nai B'rith Young Women a transition from girlhood to the time they'd feel they were ready to join their mothers' organization, the Upper Midwest chapter of B'nai B'rith Women, at age 25. Ione Furman Stiegler was president of BBYW for two years in the 1940s, and is still a member of B'nai B'rith Women. Winners for points earned in service to the community at their annual luncheon were, from left to right, Sally Leafman, Estelle Isenberg, Ockie Beers, Rita Katzman, Ione Furman, and Shirley Milstein. (Courtesy of Ione Furman Stiegler.)

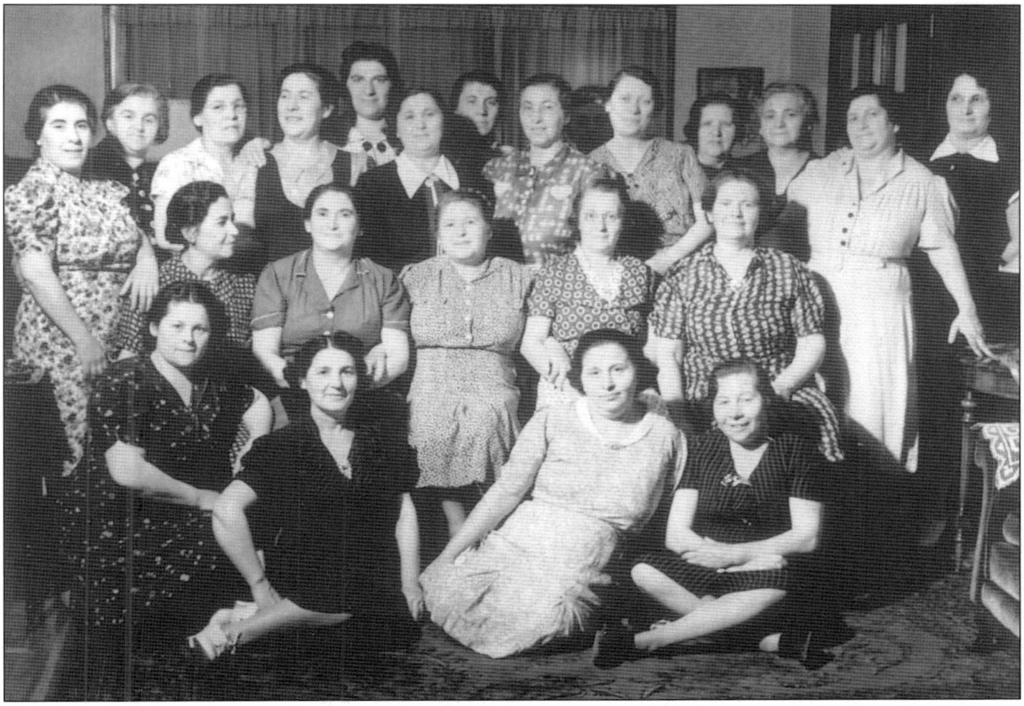

In the 1930s and 1940s Lena Schwartz Lerner (second from left, front row) and her friends met regularly at each others' North Side homes for conversation and refreshments. They called their group the Ladies' Cultural League. (Courtesy of Harry Lerner.)

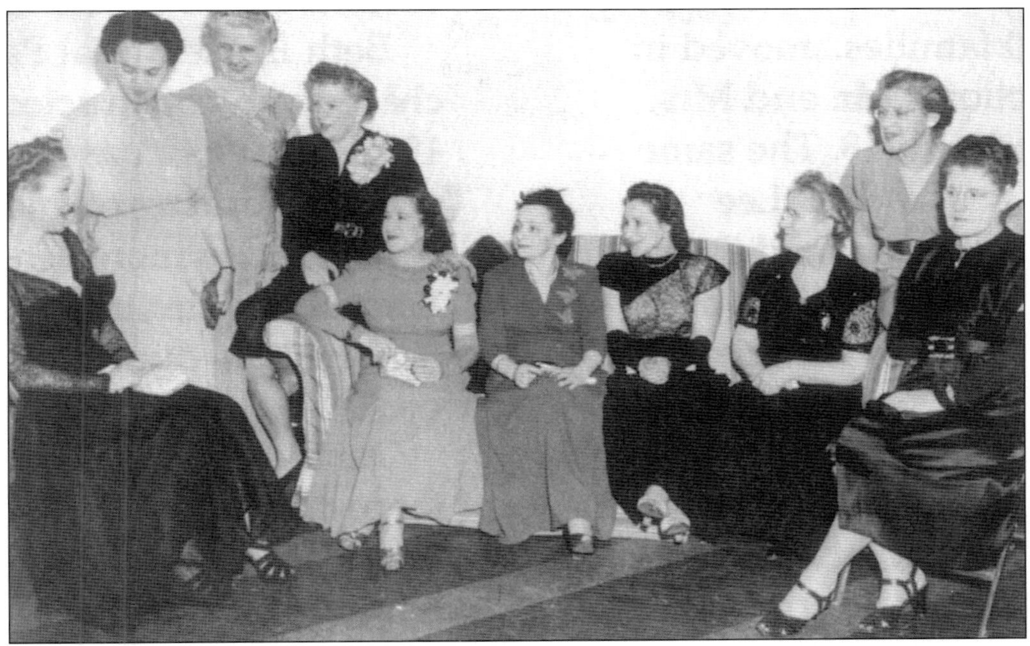

Beth El Women's League members dressed in formal attire for their annual dinner dance. (Courtesy of Jewish Historical Society of the Upper Midwest.)

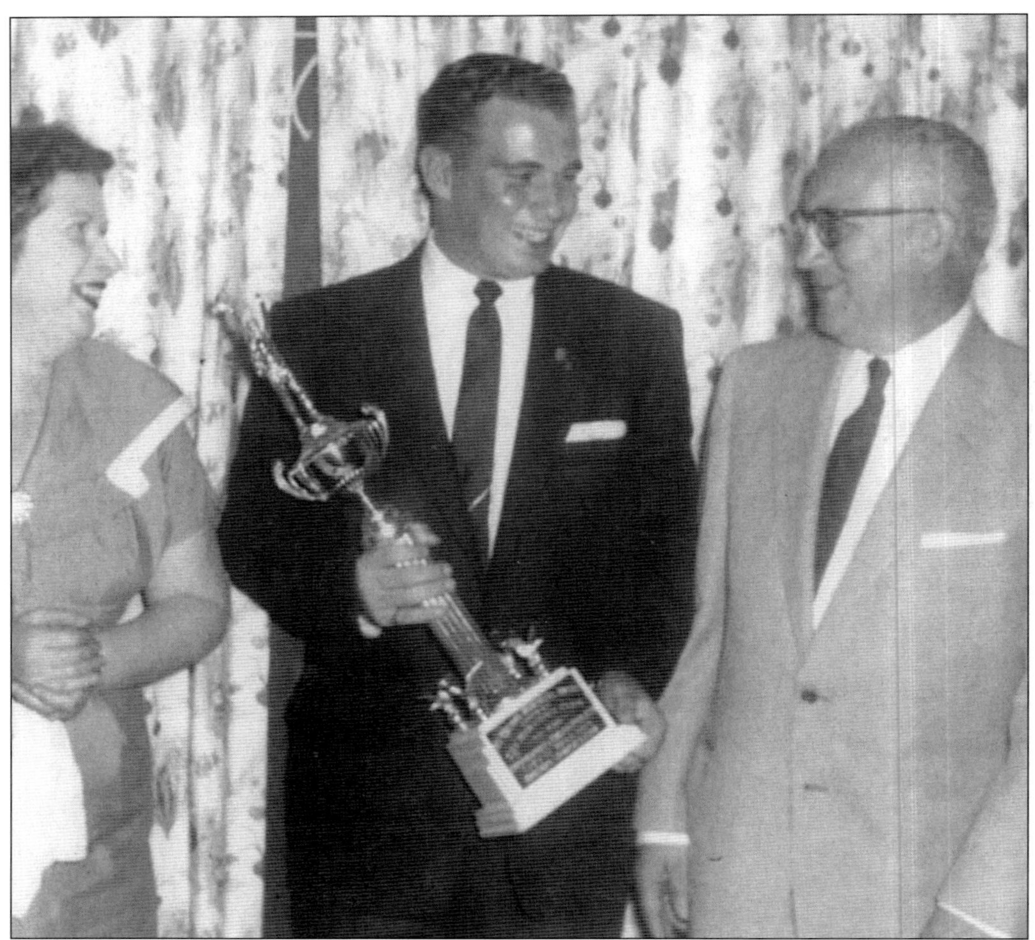

Marshall Levin, winner of the 1954 Mercury Club award, with his proud parents—Mildred and Sid, who had coached the Mercury football team in the 1930s. Young Jewish athletes organized the club in 1920 at Wells Memorial House; founders and early members included Sam London, Hy Kleinbaum, Herb Sorin, Michael Cuda, Hy Rapp, Al Berman, Dave Rosen, Nate Waldman, Joe and Sol Leader, Sam Paletz, Larry Walstein, Bill Kraines, Joe Milstein, Jack Tilsner, Sim Haskowitz, and Hy Truman. Members had to be highly skilled football, baseball or basketball players, but they also had to be scholars and be involved in Judaism and in the Jewish community. In 1936, the club created an annual award for the Minneapolis high school senior "who best exemplified athletic, scholastic, and civic excellence." It was named in memory of Mercury Club President Hy Truman, but is now known as the Hy Truman/Don Goldberg Award. Don (1953) and his sons, Nathan (1979) and Ross (1984), were all winners. Milton Minkin was the first winner, and others are Leonard (Butch) Levy (1937), Minnesota Timberwolves founders Marv Wolfenson (1944) and Bob Stein (1964), Marc Trestman (1973) and Arnold Lehrman (1940) and his son Jerry (1967). In 1987, when Marshall's daughter Deborah won a scholarship to the University of Missouri because she was a prize-winning gymnast at Southwest High School as well as a Phi Beta Kappa scholar, Mercury Club decided to choose two honorees each year, one male and one female. The winners that first year were Adam Lurie, an outstanding baseball and hockey player from Minnetonka, and Deborah Levin, which made Marshall and Deborah Mercury's first father-daughter winners. Mercury Club members still have an annual awards banquet, and meet regularly for lunch. (Courtesy of Bob Kleinbaum.)

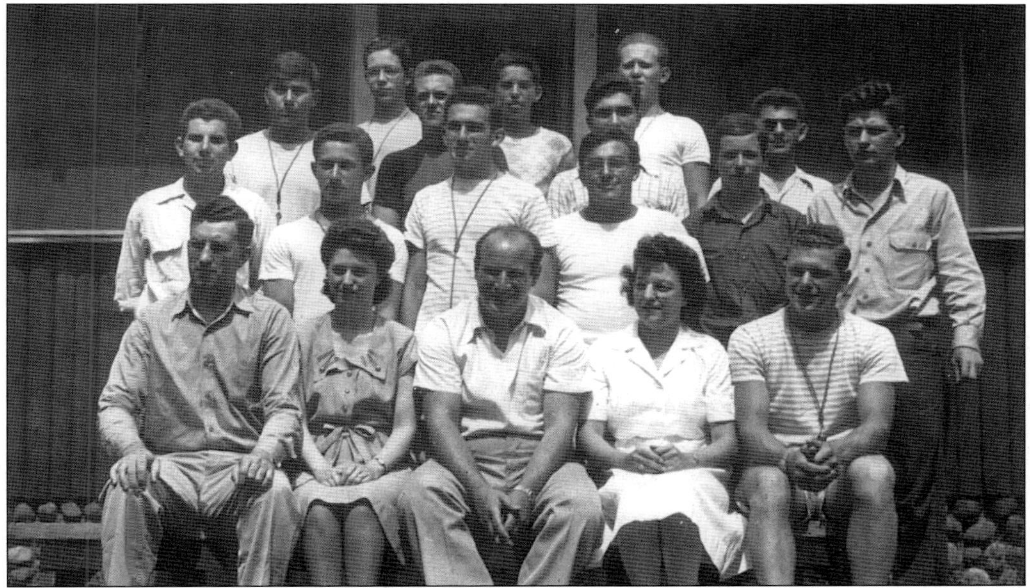

Council Camp, sponsored by the local chapter of the National Council of Jewish Women, opened on the St. Croix in the summer of 1938 to give children "two-week vacations in a wholesome Jewish atmosphere." More than 400 children attended camp the first year. By 1946, it was an independent operation, and moved to Aitkin, Minnesota. Shown here with founder and director Leonard Neiman, from left to right, are the following: (front row) maintenance workers Jim Clinger and his wife, Leonard Neiman, Miss Rudeman, the staff nurse, and counselors Mickey Nathanson; (second row) Leland Green, Fred Nathanson, Harold Kaiser, Marvin Kahner, Tom Lewin, and "Sparky" McCarthy; (third row) Milt Sidley, Dick Rubinstein, Don Goldstein, and Stan Stein; (fourth row) Bob Stone, Howard Karon, and Sheldon Epstein. Missing is counselor Joel Glotter. (Photo courtesy of Tom Lewin.)

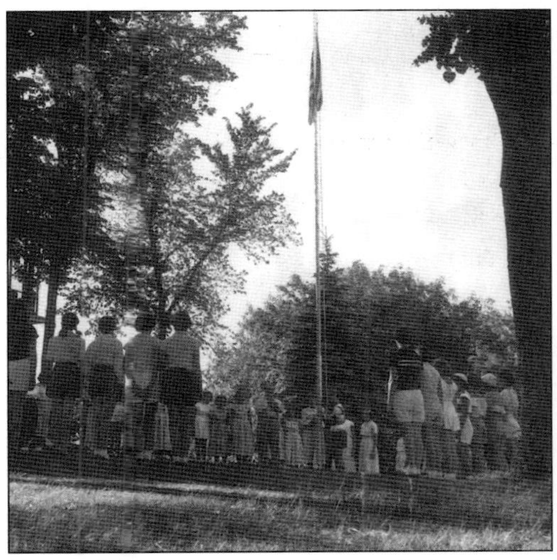

Council Camp students lowered the flag. It was a traditional Friday evening ceremony, with Camp Director Leonard Neiman playing the bugle (Photo by Tom Lewin.)

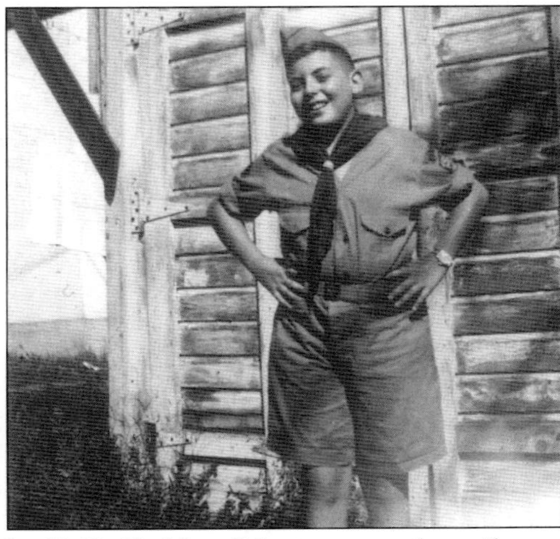

In 1942, Sheldon Schnitzer was also a "happy camper." His Boy Scout troop met at each others' homes and at the Emanuel Cohen Center, and went camping during the summer. (Courtesy of Marcia Schnitzer Hinitz.)

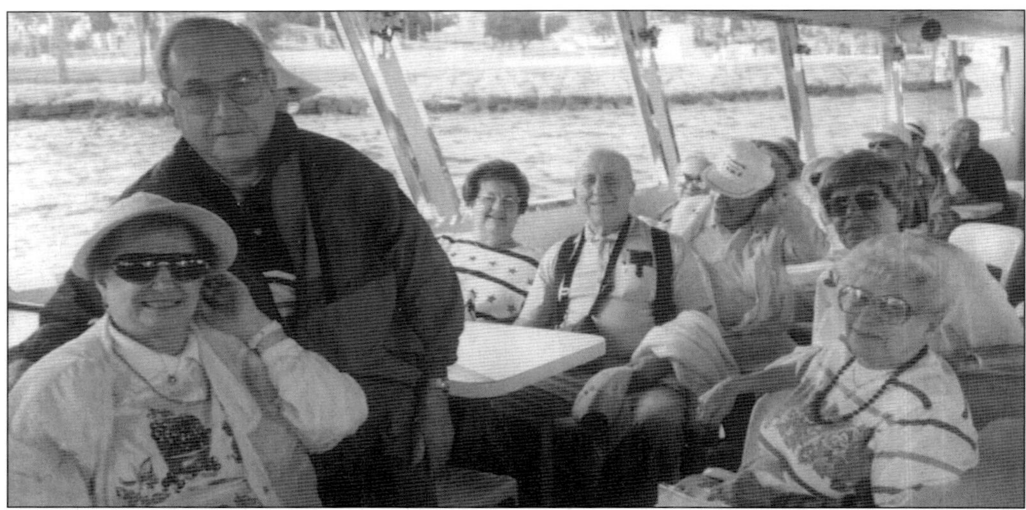

Mrs. Nathan Berman organized the Emanuel Cohen Center's Golden Age Club, for men and women over sixty. Thirty-two people attended the first meeting in November 1947, and membership grew to one hundred in just a few weeks! One year about 30 of them piled into a bus loaded with camping gear, much of it borrowed from their children or grandchildren, and headed for a week-long adventure at Council Camp. Most of them had never been camping before, but one member says, "They weren't just 'old people.' They were like kids. They'd sit on each other's bunks and talk, and throw frisbees or go swimming. They had more pep, more experiences—and more romances!" They also enjoy cruising on the Mississippi and the St. Croix, and at Big Lake and other scenic areas. (Courtesy of Minneapolis Jewish Community Center.)

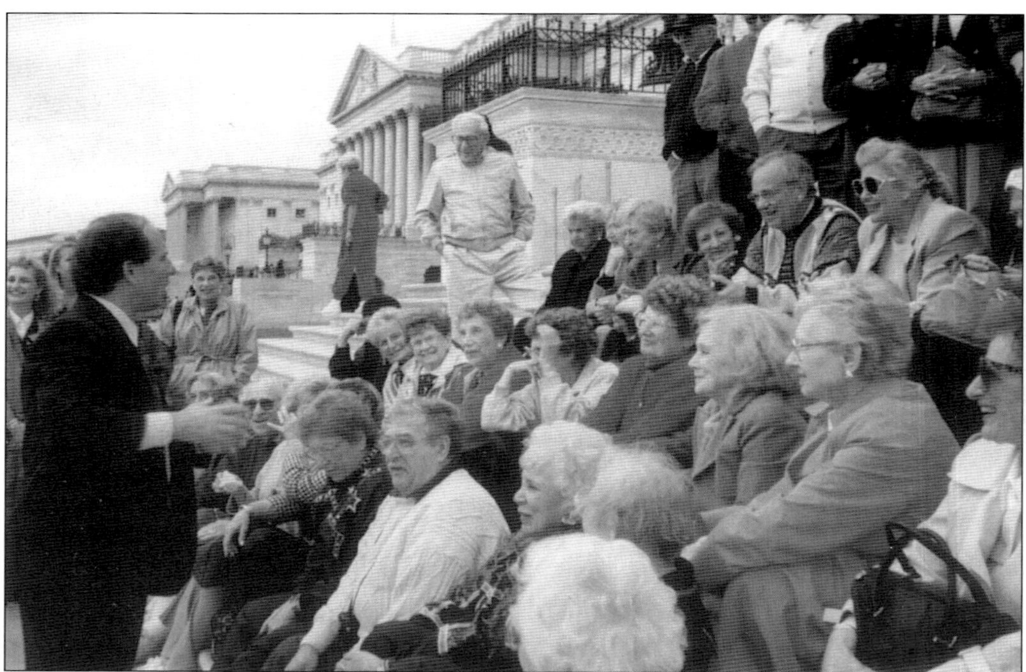

JCC Golden Agers went to St. Paul to tour the historic State Capitol and to meet Minnesota's Jewish senator, Paul Wellstone. (Courtesy of Minneapolis Jewish Community Center.)

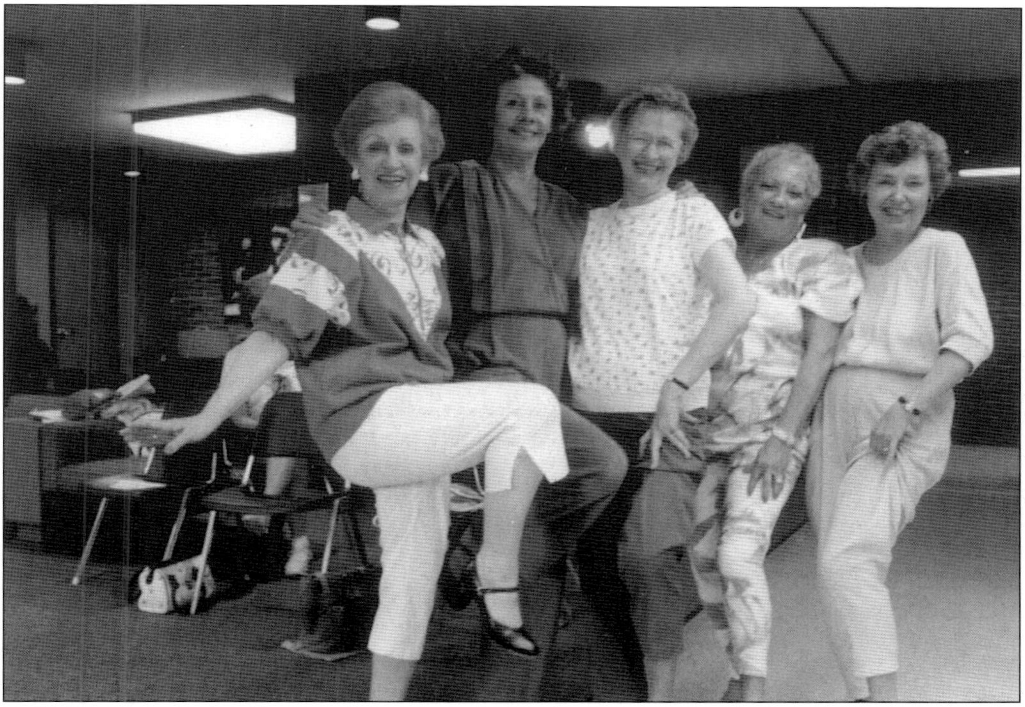

Golden Agers' vaudeville shows began at the JCC, but moved to the Prudential Building in St. Louis Park as audiences grew. The show goes on, with Golden Agers ranging in age from their late 50s to their 80s dancing and singing, playing solos on harmonica and other instruments, and doing stand-up comedy and skits. (Courtesy of Minneapolis Jewish Community Center.)

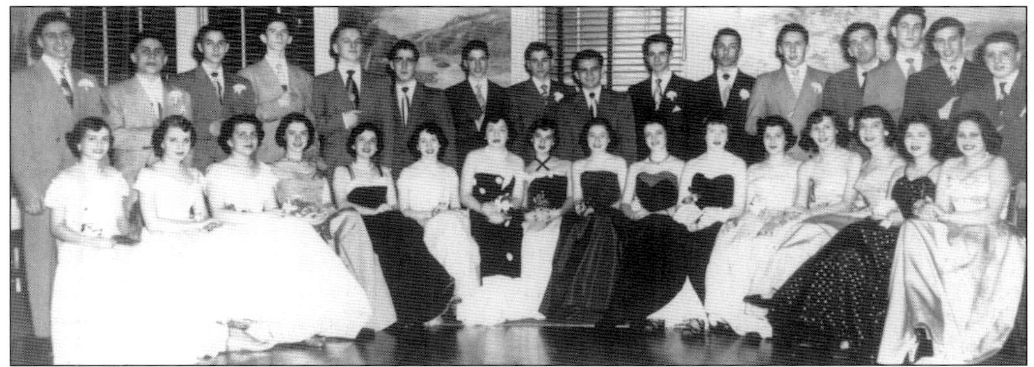

A Sweet Sixteen party was a tradition in the 1940s and 1950s. Phyllis Hirsch celebrated her 16th birthday at the Hasty Tasty, one of the community's favorite restaurants. Guests and their dates included, left to right, Marilyn Langfus and Dick Kunian, Ruth Lurie and Rod Cooperman, Maureen Lifson and Marvin Stillman, Sandy Silberman and Lloyd Sussman, Corrine Feinberg and Filmore Rodich, Bunny Efron and Howie Adler, Reva Margolis and Howard Simon, Reva Lear and Dick Hunegs, Phyllis Hirsch and Al Stein, Delores Wiesman and Jerry Rudolph, Sandra Schwartz and Stuart Bessler, Dobie Applebaum and Mickey Spector, Gloria Kushner and Allan Shinder, Renee Wasserman and Manny Cohen, Nat Warschauer and Alan Goldberg, Joanie Berkus and Art Rudick. (Courtesy of Jewish Historical Society of the Upper Midwest.)

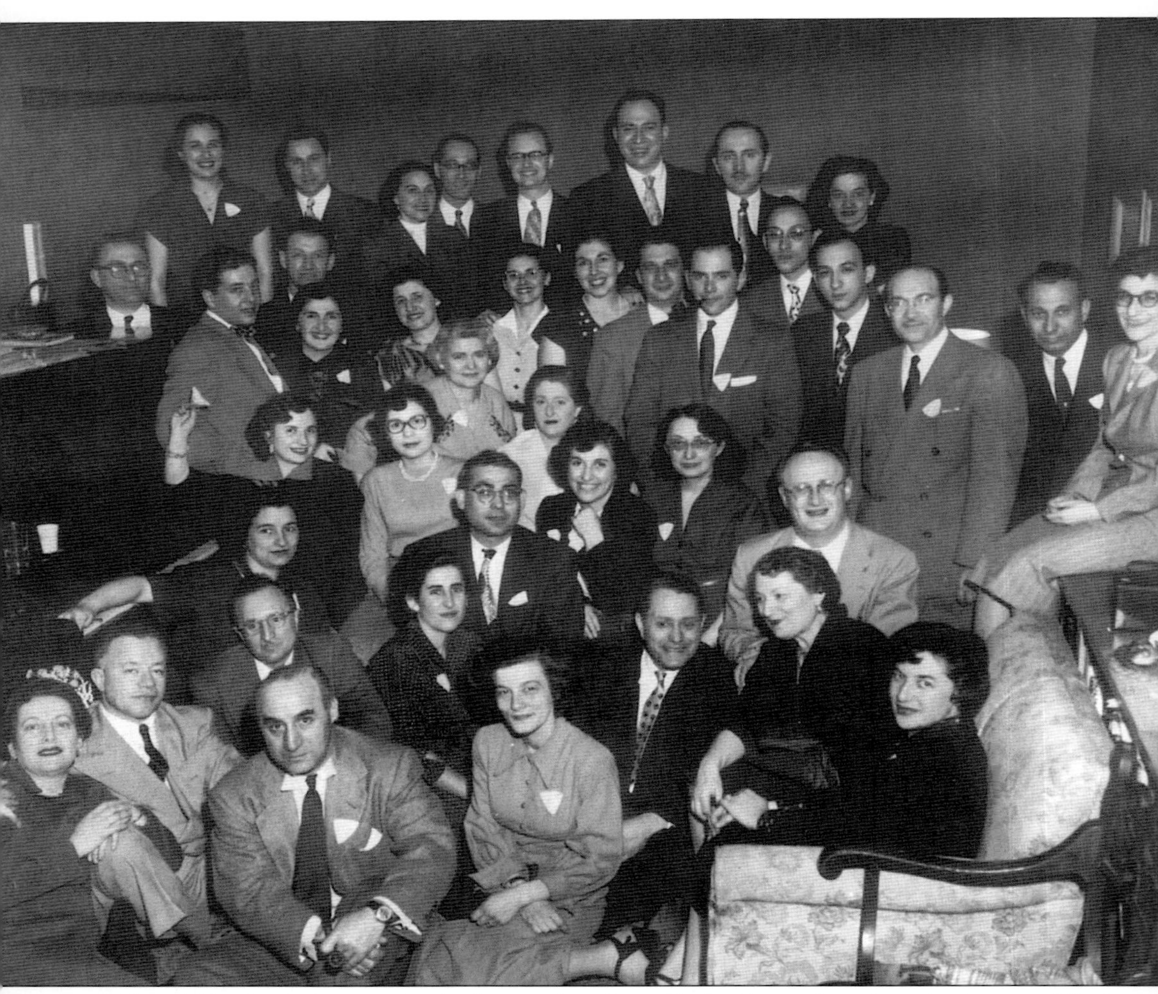

Talmud Torah graduates who had moved to New York City gathered at the home of Ruth Harris on March 9, 1952, for their annual Purim Party. Guests included Harry Korngold, Esther Sosewitz, Mr. and Mrs. Ted Chazin, J. Liss, Ted and Libby Cohen, Mr. and Mrs. Max Feder, Norman, Shirley and Rose Guttman, Peretz and Evelyn Friedman Rosenfield, Ruth Harris, Dr. Louis Gilman, H. and Arlene Davis, Carolyn Savitt, Libby Liss, Phyllis Blicker, N. Altrowitz, Norbert and Shirley Raucher, Dorothy Berman, Mervin and Helen Tomsky, David and Pearl Silver Ruskin, Sheldon Blicker, Bob Share, Rae and Hillel Aronson, Hirsch Gordon, Ben and Sarah Samsky, Naomi Hinitz, Reva and Herbert Stein, and Libby Schmitzer. (Courtesy of Helen Broude Tomsky.)

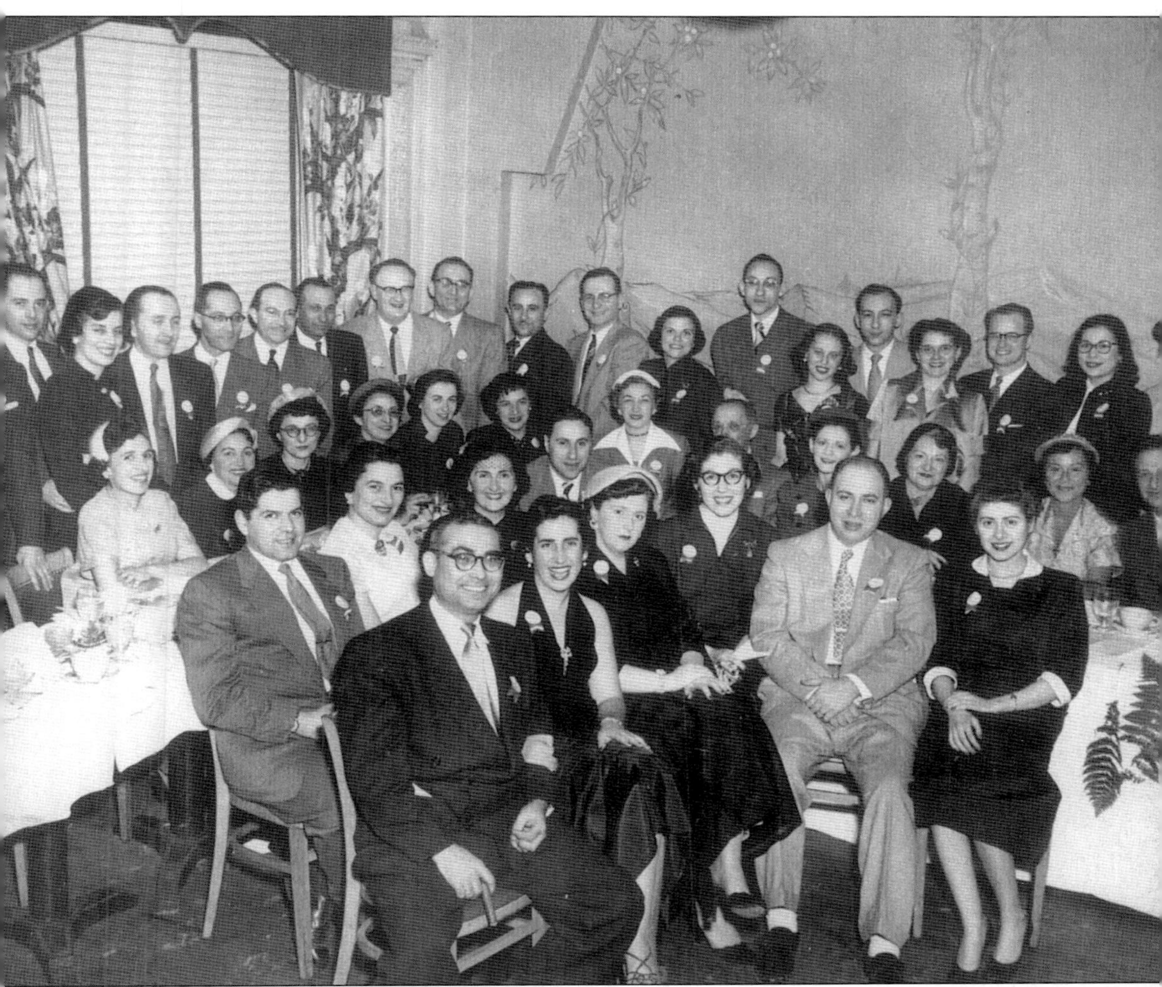

New York City's chapter of the Talmud Torah Alumni met for another Purim Banquet in 1953. Speakers included Carl Cowl, a member of Talmud Torah's first graduating class, and Rabbis Mervin Tomsky, David Aronson, Norman Frimer, Hirsch Gordon, and Moshe Goldblum. Mrs. Hillel Aronson led the singing, and party organizers included Libby Cohen, Evelyn Rosenfeld, Phyllis Furman Blicker, and Pearl Silver Ruskin. Attendees also included Sheldon Blicker, Mr. and Mrs. Bob Share, Peretz Rosenfield, Mr. Stern, Mr. Samsky, Dr. and Mrs. Gilman, Norman Guttman, Mrs. Goldblum, Rae Aronson, Hillel Aronson, Helen Tomsky, Carolyn Savitt, Naomi Hinitz, Reva Ziff Stern, Sarah Harris Samsky, Ruth Harris, Mrs. Norm Guttman, Bertha Aronson, Mrs. Frimer, Sarah Feder, Helen Cowl, Mr. and Mrs. Katzman (Rose Guttman), Mr. and Mrs Norman Raucher (Shirley Zimmerman), Ted Cohen, Dave Ruskin, and Zella Schneidman. (Courtesy of Helen Broude Tomsky.)

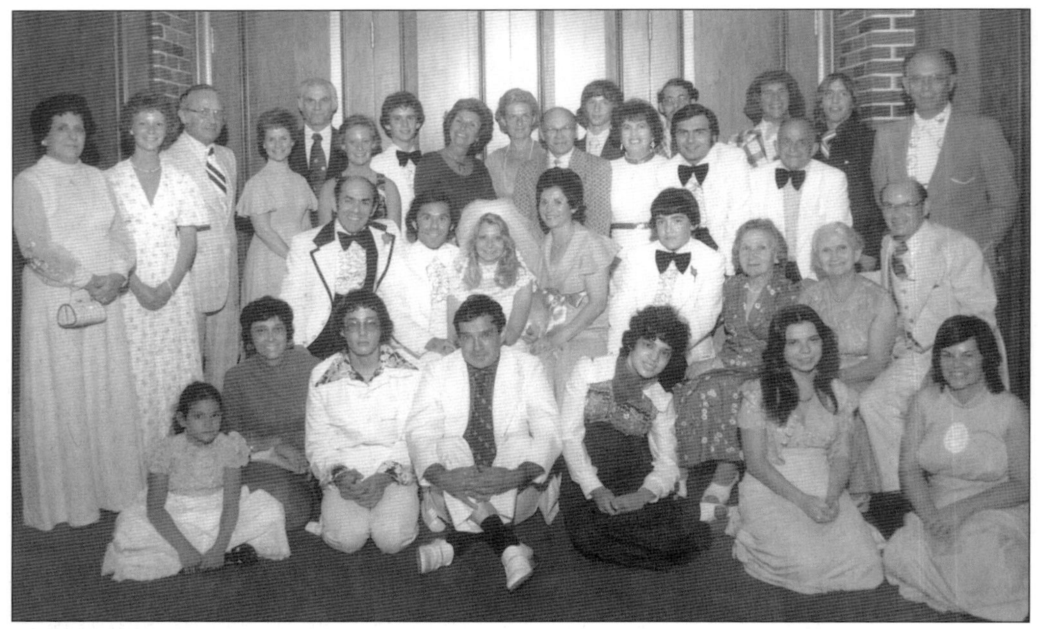

When Michael and Helen Getzkin were married, the groom's brother and his wife, Beatrice Beers Getzkin, served as best man and maid of honor. (Courtesy of Pacey Beers.)

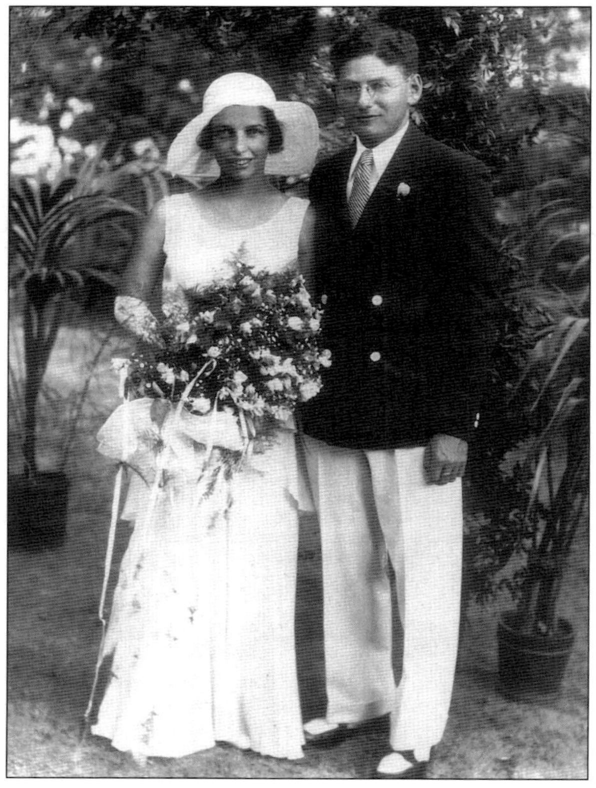

Reuben Berman was in medical school and Isabel Rosenstein was a graduate student in psychology at the University of Minnesota when they married on July 26, 1931—a marriage that lasted for 58 years, until Isabel died in 1989. Beth El Rabbi David Aronson performed their outdoor ceremony at Lake Minnetonka, and they honeymooned by going canoeing and camping in the Boundary Waters Canoe Area in northern Minnesota. The Berman family had left their home on Seventh and Elwood Avenues North a year earlier to move to California, but Reuben and Isabel stayed in Minneapolis, where he studied medicine at the University of Minnesota, was a founding member of Mt. Sinai Hospital, and practiced medicine from 1937 to 1985. Reuben is still active in the community, and plays the saxophone in the Jewish Community Center's orchestra. (Courtesy of Dr. Reuben Berman.)

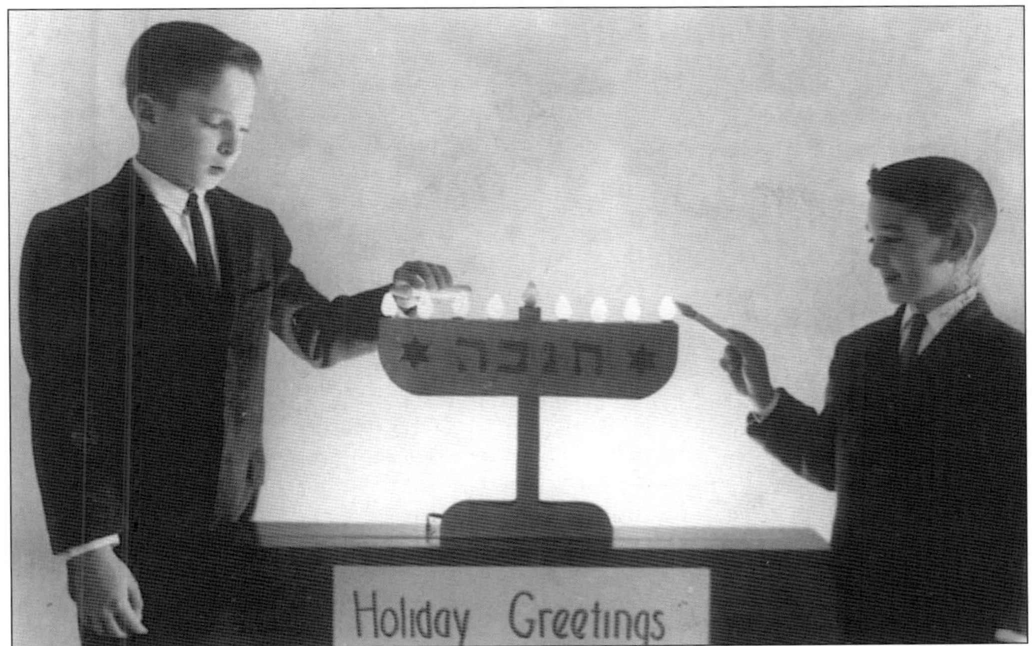

Many people made their own greeting cards—including these two very different Chanukah cards. The Nudell family's card features their sons Ricky and Irv lighting the Menorah. (Courtesy of Jewish Historical Society of the Upper Midwest.)

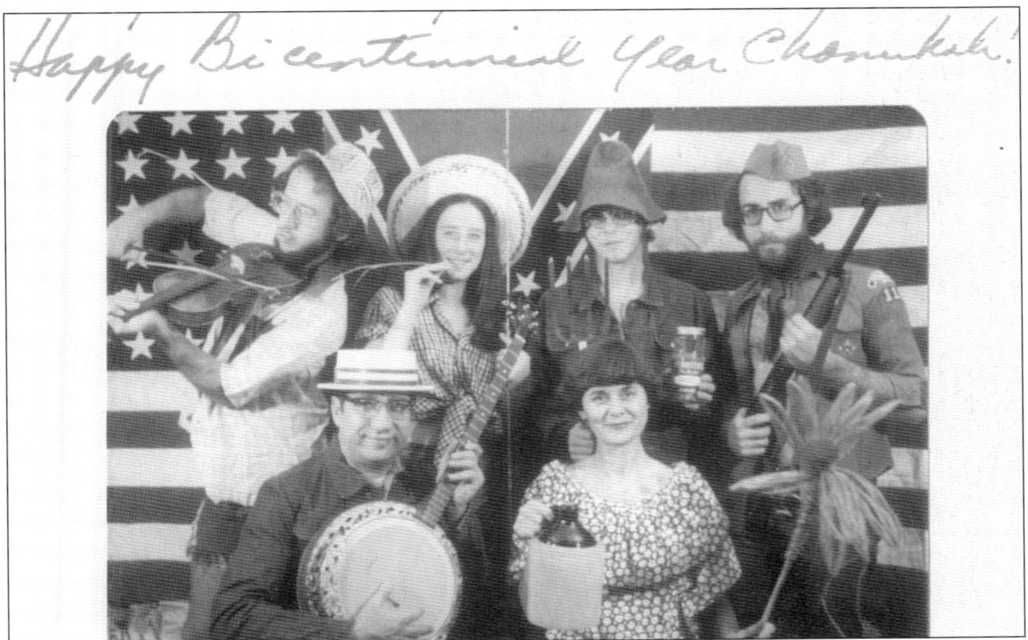

Farrell and Kathy Stiegler organized a Bicentennial Party in 1976 to celebrate America's 200th anniversary—and used this family photo from the party for their Chanukah card that year. In costume, shown here from left to right, are their children, Michael, Rebecca, and Jonathan, and their niece, Judy. (Courtesy of Jewish Historical Society of the Upper Midwest.)

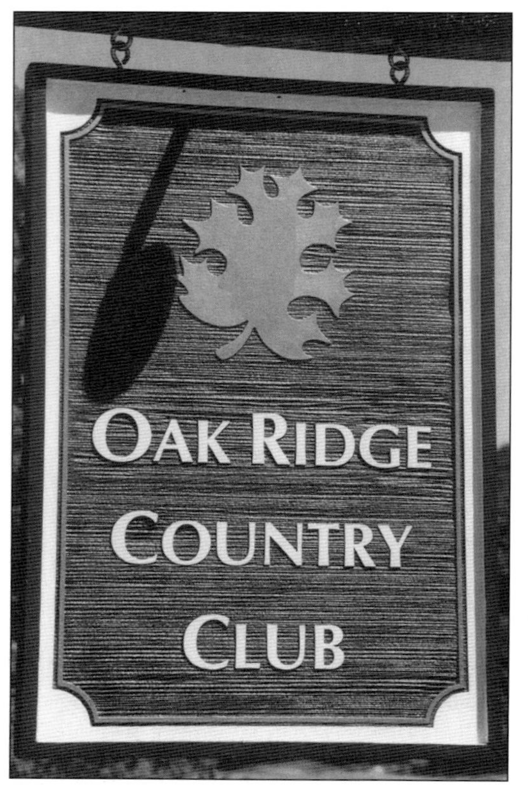

Members of the Jewish community founded their own Oak Ridge Country Club in 1921—an era when antisemitism was so rampant that when a Jewish sports reporter from the *Minneapolis Tribune* was assigned to cover a national golf tournament that was being held at an exclusive local country club, he was not permitted to enter the clubhouse, because he was a Jew! (Photo by Tom Lewin.)

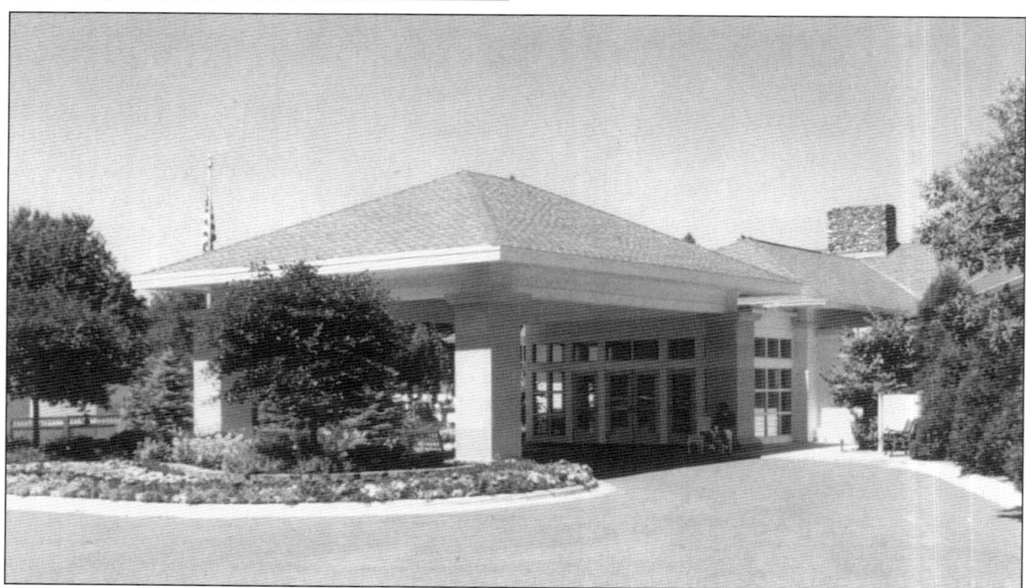

The original building has been remodeled and enlarged several times, most recently in 1995. Today Oak Ridge has an 18-hole golf course, a putting green, tennis courts, and a swimming pool, as well as dining rooms, meeting rooms, and a food and beverage dining service, which make it a popular location for Minneapolis Jewish Federation training sessions and other community and special events (Photo by Tom Lewin.)

Six

After World War II We Moved to the Suburbs—and Israel Became a State

As was happening in so many American cities, African Americans were moving into what had been Jewish neighborhoods as the Jews moved out. Young people coming home from World War II were getting married and starting families, and they couldn't find houses to buy in the North Side neighborhood they'd grown up in, so they began to buy newly built homes in inner-city suburbs like Golden Valley and St. Louis Park. Then older members of the Jewish community who were prospering in the postwar era began leaving their aging homes and small lots on the North Side for newer, larger homes in suburbia. It was the end of an era: when cousins James Gordon and Joan Barnett graduated from North High School in June 1958, they were third generation alumni, because their mothers and grandmothers, Guita Gordon and Etta Bearman, and Genevieve Barnett and Anna Goldblum, were also North High graduates, but they were the last members of their families to live on the North side.

The move to the suburbs quickly escalated—so much so that some of them began to jokingly call their new home "St. Jewish Park." By 1947 the Park Delicatessen, later known as Bernie's, had opened on Minnetonka Boulevard, and meeting notices for Hadassah and B'nai B'rith were being published in the St. Louis Park newspaper. And when B'nai B'rith conducted a community survey in 1952 to ask whether St. Louis Park needed synagogues, a community center, and a Talmud Torah, the answer was an overwhelming "yes."

Some of the gentile and Jewish teenagers on the North Side had always had problems getting along together, but now real trouble was brewing. Bob Latz says he signed up for boxing lessons at the Emanuel Cohen Center when he was a student at Lincoln Junior High School because "a black kid in my Shop Class taught me how to play a game they called Flinch. If they swung at you and you flinched, they'd get a free shot at your arm . . . so my arm was always black and blue! But after I took boxing lessons at the Center, I challenged the kid and 'cleaned his clock,' and that ended that problem." Later Latz joined the Golden Gloves high school boxing team at Ascension Catholic Church and decided to it was worth the risk to "make a statement" by wearing trunks with a Star of David on them.

Although children like Bob Latz were dealing successfully with racial and religious problems, and Stillman's Supermarket was sponsoring a black semi-professional baseball team and bought them two Lincoln sedans so they could tour the state, some members of the Jewish community were beginning to question whether North Minneapolis was still a place they could call "home." Some of their children were afraid to play or go ice skating at North Commons park, and there were more and more humiliating and cruel attacks on Jewish children by both non-Jews and their new African-American neighbors.

And then, on March 22, 1945, at a community event where police were present a car-full of gentile teenagers deliberately rammed into a car driven by Jewish teens. Luckily, nobody was seriously hurt, but eight of the community's rabbis got together and convinced city officials to join them for a public meeting at Lincoln Junior High School to discuss a solution to the growing violence on the North Side. On March 26, more than 2,000 members of the North Side Jewish community crowded into the school auditorium and several hundred more stood outside the building for almost 3 and 1/2 hours waiting to hear the results.

People who spoke up at the meeting included Mrs. Joseph Gordon, a relative of a child who'd been injured; I.S. Joseph, a member of the city's Public Welfare Board; Louis Gross, chair of the Minnesota Jewish Council; Reuben Latz, an officer in the AFL's Central Labor Union, Acting Chief of Police J.R. Lally, North Side Police Station Capt. Roland Helin, Juvenile Division Police Lt. Magni Palm, Park Police Chief S.T. Bloomgren, Park Board Director Karl B. Raymond, Jewish attorney and Third Ward Alderman Henry Bank, and Mayor Marvin Kline, who promised "to do everything in my power to cure the situation."

The police had arrested the young drivers for speeding recklessly through a crowd, but they were released immediately to their parents, and when Lt. Palm was asked why he had done nothing about the case, he said, "I think it is regrettable that a mass meeting should have been called for such a silly thing," and added that the boys had been released because "no complaints had been filed." Three men in the audience shouted that they had signed complaints and the North Side police station had said they'd call them the next morning, but instead they'd had to call the police, and that was when they learned that the boys had been released the night before! At that point Capt. Helin told them to meet him at the city attorney's office at 9 a.m. the next day, and he'd see that they would be permitted to file a complaint, and he'd make the arrests himself.

Some of the boys at the meeting also described how big groups of non-Jewish boys would surround a smaller group of younger Jewish boys and challenge them to a fight. If they denied they were Jews the mob might demand their wallets so they could see their ID, or just ask their names to see if they "sounded Jewish"—and then they were beaten up, ending up with black eyes, torn clothes, and sometimes broken teeth and broken noses.

Rabbi David Aronson pointed out two ways to deal with racial tension: the long-term approach through education, which would require cooperation of ministers, priests, rabbis, teachers and Boy Scout and other leaders; or the other approach—immediate law enforcement. Hubert Humphrey, who was campaigning for election as mayor of Minneapolis, outlined a five-point program to offset growth of racial prejudice in the city, and said he would ask business, labor, church, youth organization, and social agency leaders to create an overall organization that would effectively coordinate a city-wide program to prevent such incidents from happening.

However, many members of the Jewish community did not wait to see whether such problems could be solved, and the move to the suburbs escalated. The Emanuel Cohen Center combined with the Park Jewish Youth Service and the Jewish Camping Association to form the Jewish Community Center of Greater Minneapolis, and in 1963 they sold their building to the Minnesota Association for Retarded Children and began planning for a new building in St. Louis Park. In 1964, six rabbis, five of them with congregations that were still on the North Side—Kassel Abelson (Beth El), Jerome Herzog (Kenesseth Israel), Marc Liebhaber (Mikro Kodesh/Tifereth B'nai Jacob), Moses Sachs (B'nai Abraham), S.G. Sektor (Gemelus Chesed) and Arnold Goodman (Adath Jeshurun)—signed a joint proclamation supporting a $750,000 building fund campaign for a new Talmud Torah in St. Louis Park to "accommodate the school's 1,100 students . . . in a single efficient facility in the heart of our Jewish community." Three years later Talmud Torah sold their Queen Avenue building to the Minneapolis School Board and all classes moved to St. Louis Park, meeting in several locations until their current building at 3200 West 33rd Street was completed in 1970.

The community's synagogues had also begun to move. At first they simply built bigger buildings on the North Side. In 1945, Ahavath Achim moved to 1110 Morgan Avenue North. In 1948, Kenesseth Israel began planning a new synagogue and a Youth Center on land it owned at Plymouth and Thomas Avenues North. In 1954, Gemilus Chesed moved to Twelfth and Morgan, and in 1958, Tifereth B'nai Jacob bought land for a new building on 19th and Xerxes.

But by 1968 there were already 5,400 Jews living in St. Louis Park, and the North Side lost two of its synagogues that year. Kenesseth Israel moved to Kipling Avenue and West 28th Street in St. Louis Park and Beth El moved to its new synagogue on Highway 100 in St. Louis Park, built at a cost of almost $2 million, and sold its building at 14th and Penn to the city, which converted it to the Pilot City community center for the North Side's growing black population. The following year Tifereth B'nai Jacob decided not to build on Xerxes Avenue North, and instead merged with Mikro Kodesh and B'nai Abraham to form B'nai Emet and build a synagogue on Ottawa Avenue and Minnetonka Boulevard, and in 1967 Gemelus Chesed joined with Sharei Zedeck to form Sharei Chesed, and to build at 2734 Rhode Island Avenue.

Jewish involvement in the general community was broadening, too, and Jewish organizations were changing. The Jewish Family Welfare Association became the Jewish Family Service Association in 1943, and is now the Jewish Family and Children's Service. When the postwar immigration from Europe's Displaced Persons camps began, almost 50 percent of their staff resources were allocated to Holocaust survivors, including a Jewish Vocational Workshop organized in 1948, and 273 families started new lives in Minneapolis. Later, between 1973 and 1990, JFCS also resettled 825 families from what is now the former Soviet Union. Today, with an annual budget of more than two million dollars, and some 800 volunteers who give more than 36,000 hours per year, JFCS provides services for more than 6,000 clients, including continuing aid to Russian émigrés and other newcomers, and programs, transportation and counseling for children, the frail elderly, and mentally ill and developmentally disabled adults.

With racial and religious prejudice and discrimination continuing, and a growing focus on Holocaust education and interfaith studies, the Jewish Community Relations Council and the local chapter of the Anti-Defamation League combined in 1975 to become the JCRC/ADL, with Morton Ryweck as executive director and Marcia Yugend as its first president. After Ryweck retired in 1991, however, ADL decided it no longer needed a presence in the Twin Cities, and Stephen Silberfarb is the current executive director of what is now known as the JCRC.

The business community was also on the move. In 1956, Manny Swatez closed the family clothing store his father had started in 1914, because all his customers were moving to the suburbs. On May 5, 1967, Louis Greene wrote in his "About People" column in the *American Jewish World*, "The heart of the North Minneapolis Jewish business section stopped ticking Sunday . . . at the moment Ben Brochin closed down Brochin's Delicatessen . . . and tears were not uncommon in the eyes of third generation members of families which had obtained kosher foods at Brochin's." The Homewood Theater had also closed its doors, Margolis's Auto Repair was now a community youth center called The Way, and many other Plymouth Avenue businesses had relocated to St. Louis Park. And then, on the evening of July 21, 1967—as had already happened in 183 other cities—black youngsters rioted on Plymouth Avenue. The move to the suburbs quickly escalated, and in 1981 a Jewish Federation Population Study found as many Jews in Minneapolis and its suburbs as there had been 20 years earlier—but only 273 of them were still living in North Minneapolis!

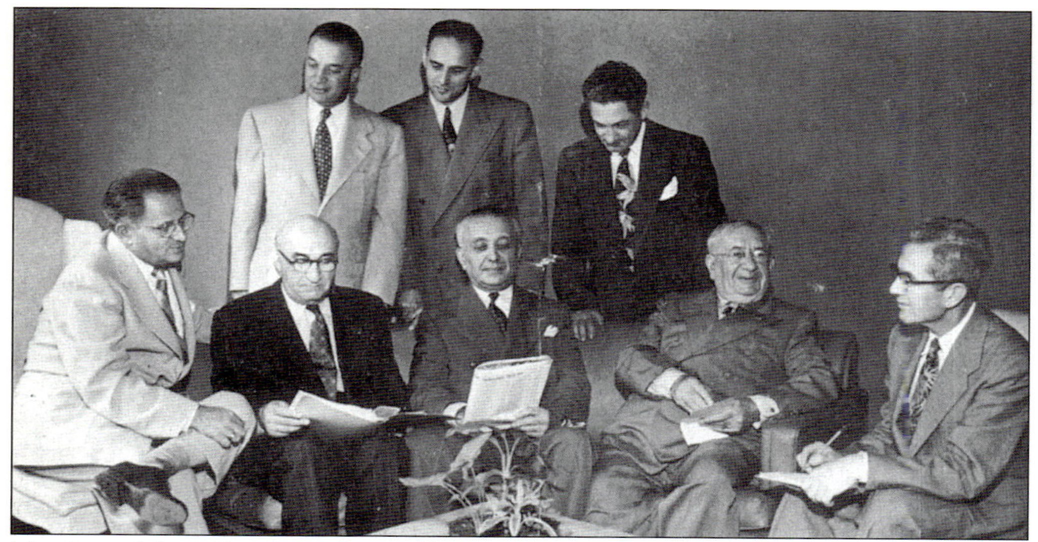

Members of the Talmud Torah's Building Project Administrative Committee met to discuss plans for a new building at 1616 Queen Avenue North. Left to right, are; (seated) Louis Shore, John Gelman, Max Zipperman, Benjamin Weisberg, and Talmud Torah Principal Leonard Kaiser; (standing) Max Sanders, Sam Ziff, and Carl Lifson. (Courtesy of Helen Broude Tomsky.)

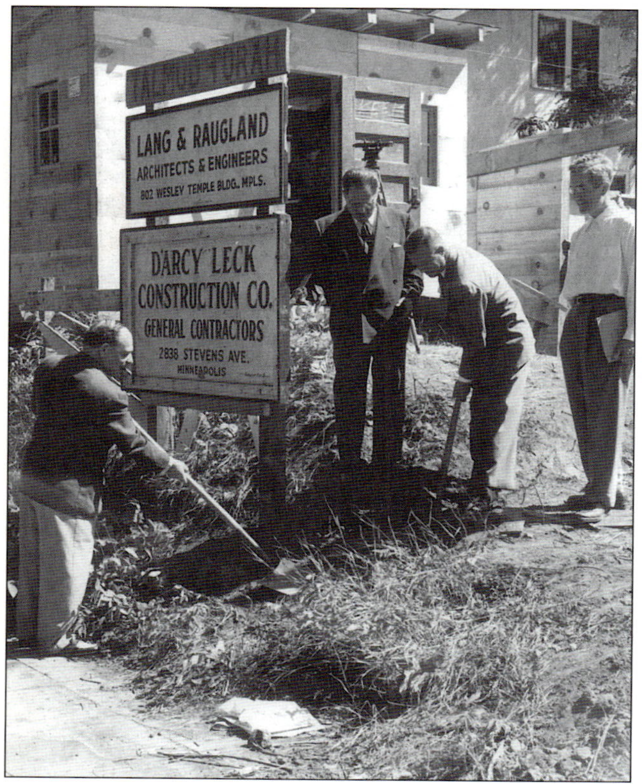

In July 1950 Talmud Torah held a symbolic groundbreaking ceremony for its new building, which was already under construction at 1616 Queen Avenue North, not realizing that within a few years almost all their students would be living in the suburbs. From left to right are J.L. Linoff, vice president; Max Sanders, chairman of the building committee; Louis Shore, and L.J. Kaiser, Talmud Torah's principal. (Courtesy of American Jewish World.)

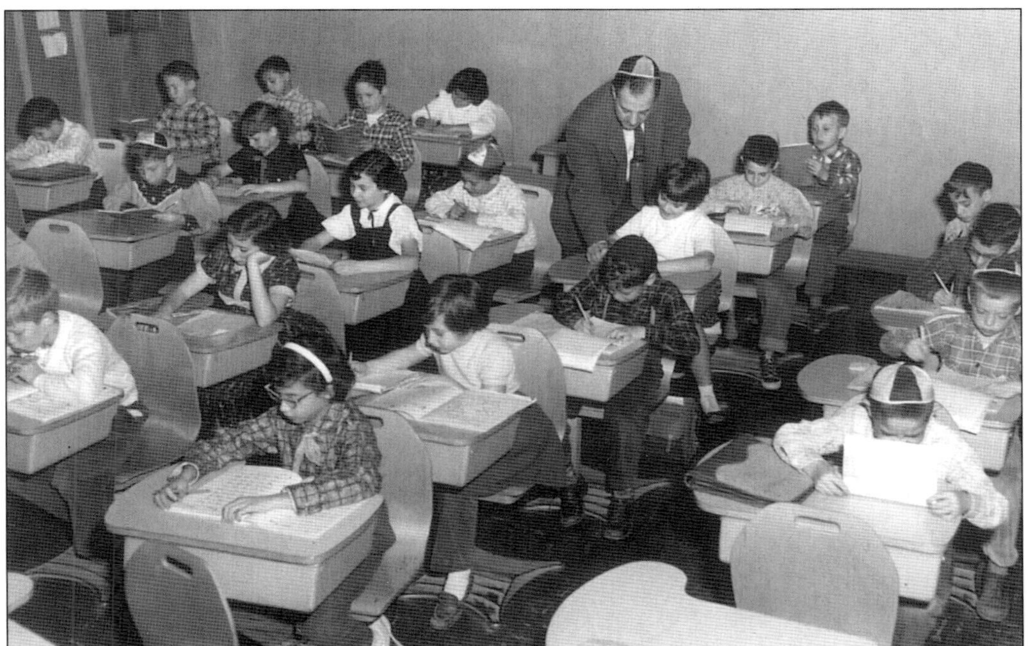

Sitting in their new, modern classroom in November 1956, Talmud Torah first-year students were just beginning to learn how to read and write in Hebrew. (Courtesy of American Jewish World.)

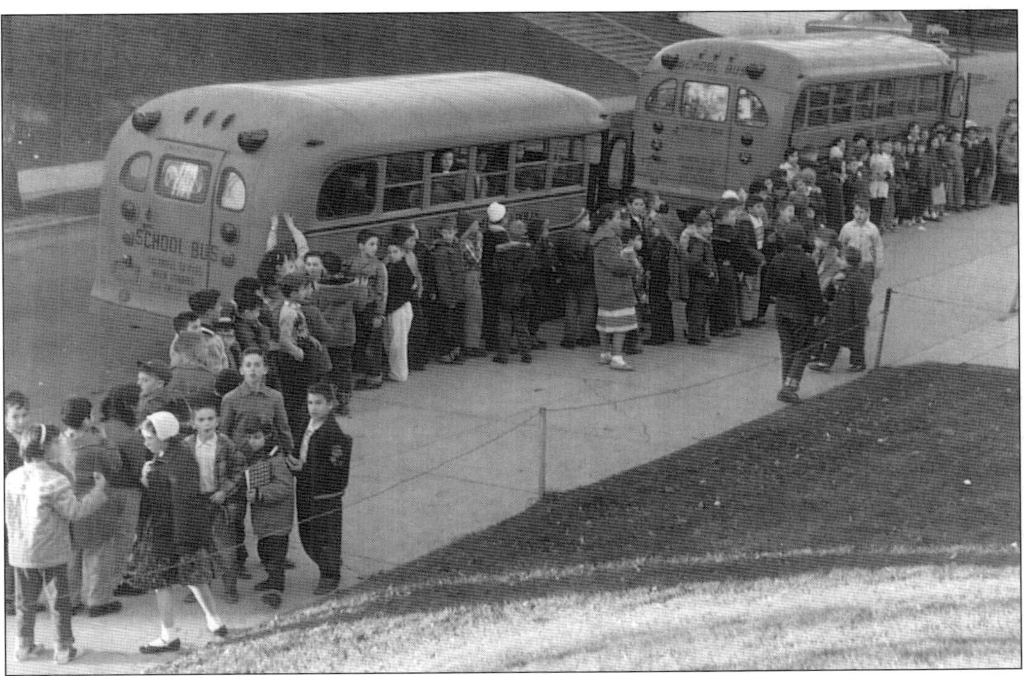

Most of Talmud Torah's students no longer lived within walking distance, however, and by 1959 they had a fleet of ten school buses and decided they needed a "Branch Building" in St. Louis Park. (Courtesy of American Jewish World.)

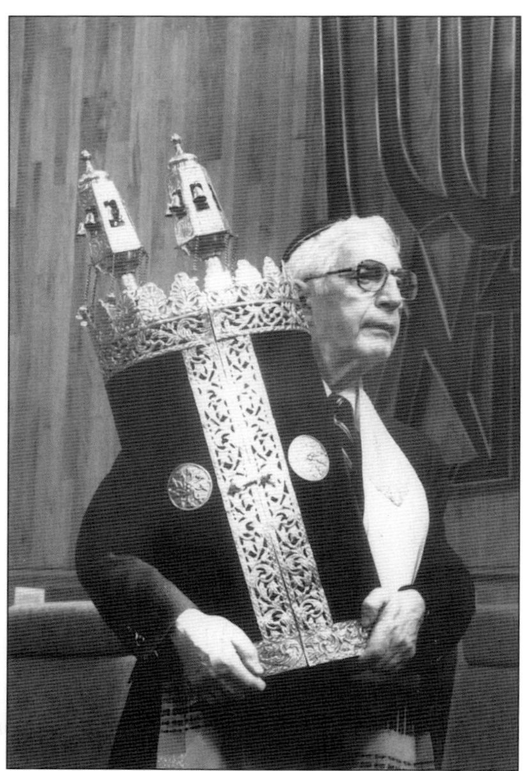

But some things remained the same, especially religious tradition. Beth El's congregation engaged in the *mitzvah* of writing a Torah for its new synagogue. The Torah was carried to the *Bima* by Nate Gottesman, in a parade led by Rabbi's wives Bertha Aronson and Shirley Abelson. (Courtesy of Bonnie Heller.)

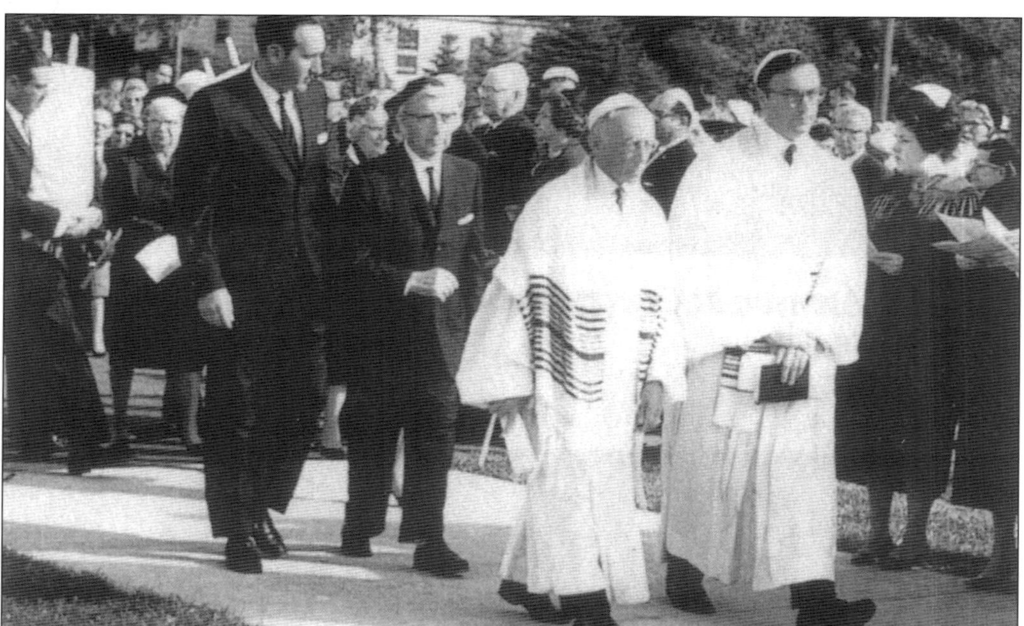

In 1963, this traditional "Processional with Torahs" heralded dedication of Beth El's new Activities Building in St. Louis Park. Senior Rabbi David Aronson and Assistant Rabbi Kassel Abelson lead the way, followed by Morris Trach and his son, David. (Courtesy of Bonnie Heller.)

NEWSLETTER

DECEMBER — 1947
VOL. 11, No. 4

MINNEAPOLIS
MINNESOTA

EDWARD P. SCHWARTZ, President
LOUIS GREENE, Editor

Our December Feature . . . .

Rev. John S. Simmons

PASTOR OF
ST. MARK'S LUTHERAN CHURCH
MINNEAPOLIS

SPEAKING ON

"Common Problems"

The Rev. Simmons is active in all community and city-wide projects of a constructive nature.

Tuesday, December 23, 1947

AUDITORIUM

Society for the Blind

CANTOR ILLYA KOHEN of Beth El Synagogue
in Traditional Chanukah Songs
FLORENCE ROSENBERG, Accompanist

Social Hour ★ Refreshments

WHAT HAVE YOU DONE TO GET A NEW MEMBER?

Meanwhile, though, North Minneapolis had continued to change—and not for the better. The Reverend John Simmons of St. Mark's Lutheran Church spoke on "Common Problems" at the December 1947 meeting of Minneapolis B'nai B'rith Lodge No. 271. (Courtesy of Florence Greene.)

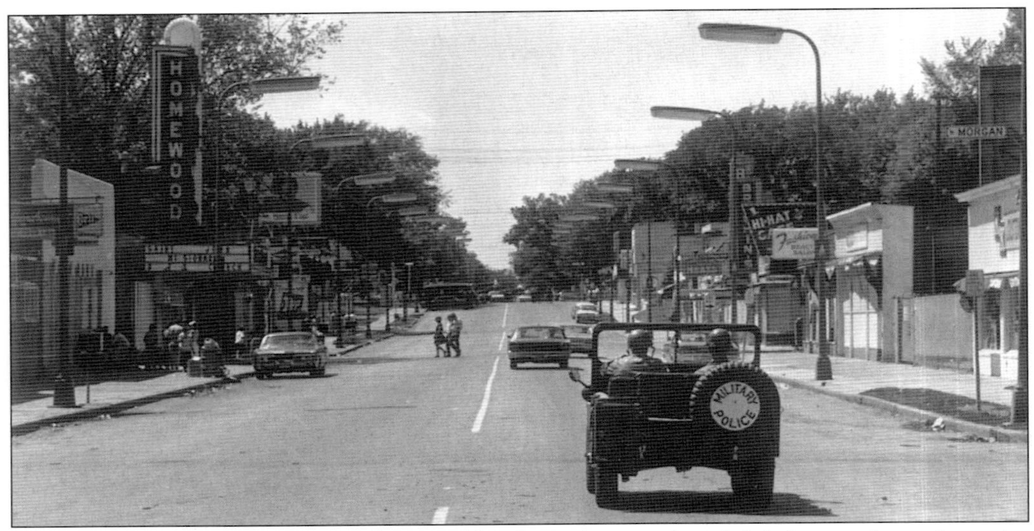

Allen Greenstein says he heard the "rumble" from the riot, but didn't know where the noise was coming from until Hymie Pessis, who also had a store on Plymouth Avenue, called him at 1 a.m. to tell him what was happening. Although a molotov cocktail sparked a fire that destroyed Stillman's, the supermarket next to Greenstein and Post, and Harold Sklar's bowling alley beneath it,"The cops let me through to my place," Greenstein recalls, "but there were no fires. I guess I didn't make anybody mad!" National Guardsmen continued to patrol the street the day after the fire. (Courtesy of Minnesota Historical Society.)

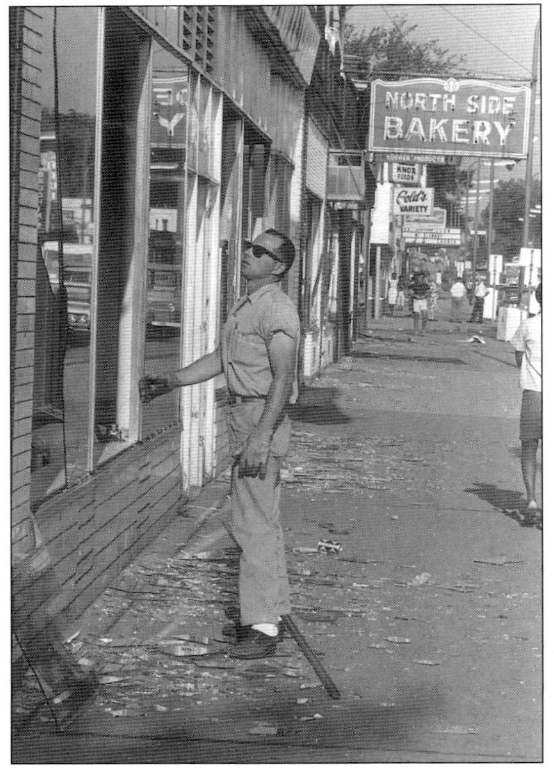

A National Guardsman assessed the damage the morning after the rioting began on July 21, 1967. The North Side Bakery, between Morgan and Logan on Plymouth Avenue North, had been co-owned by the Malinsky and Kaufman families, who by the late 1930s were baking more than 45 racks of *challah* on Fridays for customers who came early and waited in line to make sure they got their bread for the Sabbath. (Courtesy of Minnesota Historical Society.)

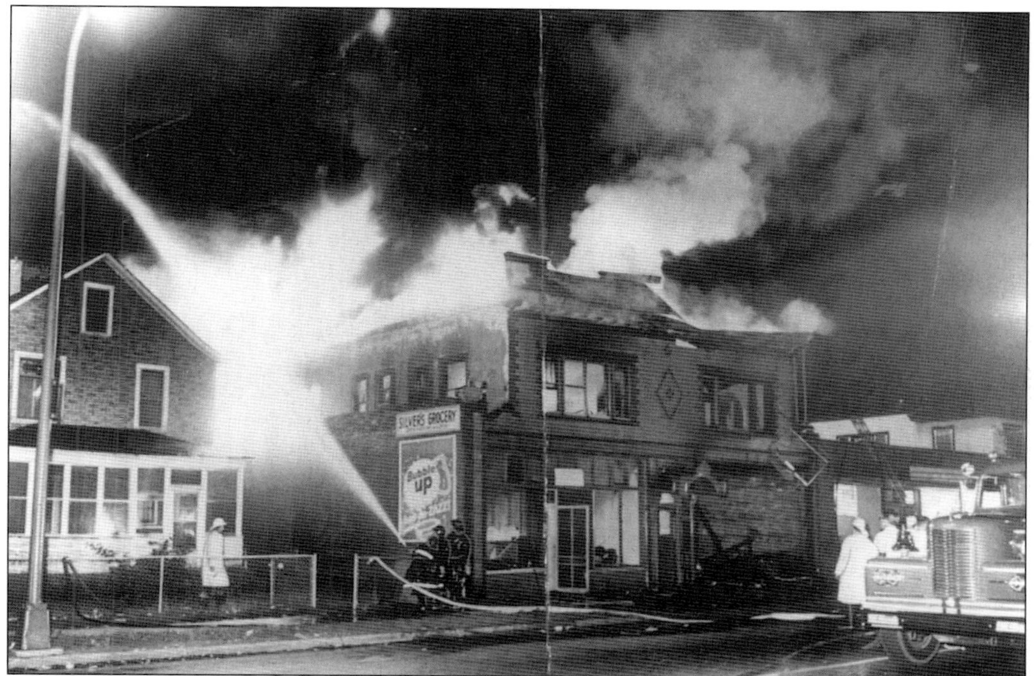

Neighbors who lived three blocks away still remember the screaming and the sound of glass breaking when rioting erupted on Plymouth Avenue in July, 1967. Firefighters at Silver's Food Market tried to keep the flames from spreading to the house next door. (Courtesy of Minnesota Historical Society.)

Harriet Kaplan worked at Koval Furniture and Appliances, 1601 Plymouth Avenue, which was one of the hardest-hit merchants, and had to help clean out the store after the riot. Koval lost more than 30 portable television sets and other merchandise, and moved his business to St. Louis Park the following month. The two police squads that answered a call at 1 a.m. were pelted with rocks by the rioters, but local police and the National Guard responded so quickly and in such large numbers—more than 130 policemen were sent to the area—that the violence quickly came to an end. (Courtesy of Minneapolis Tribune.)

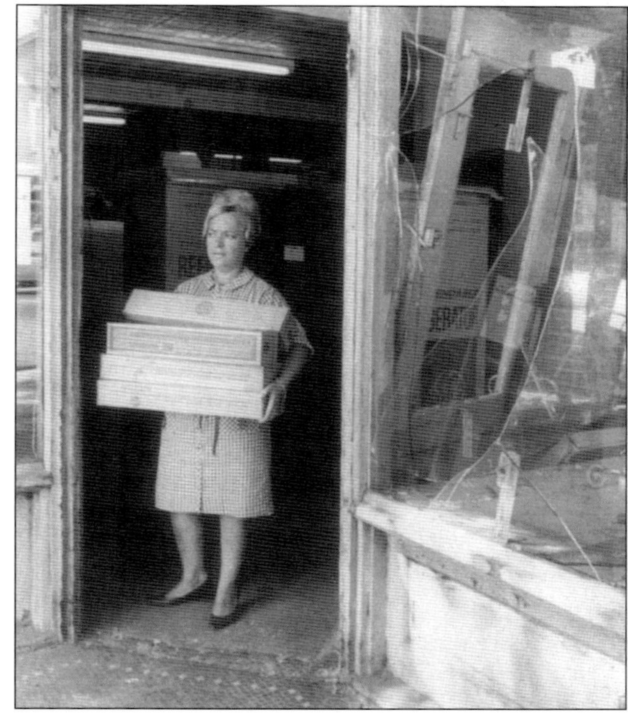

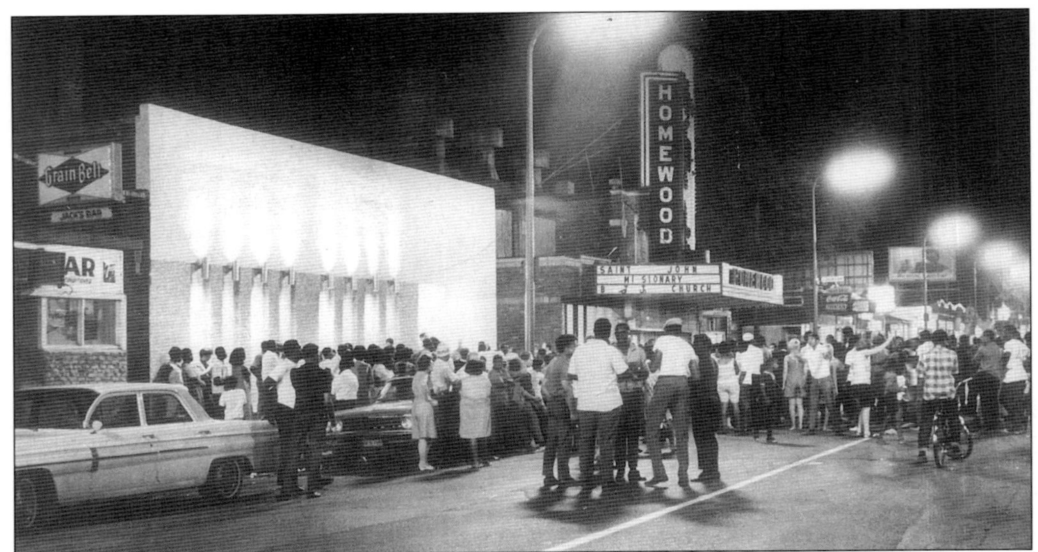

On what could have been a second night of rioting, Minneapolis's Jewish mayor, Arthur Naftalin, and his staff hired a band, set up a bandstand and food booths in front of The Way, a black community center on Plymouth Avenue next to what had been the Homewood Theater but was now a meeting place for St. John Missionary Baptist Church, and staged a street dance. Some 150 young people, most of them black, spent the evening jiving to the music, and the violence of the night before was now history. (Courtesy of Minneapolis Tribune.)

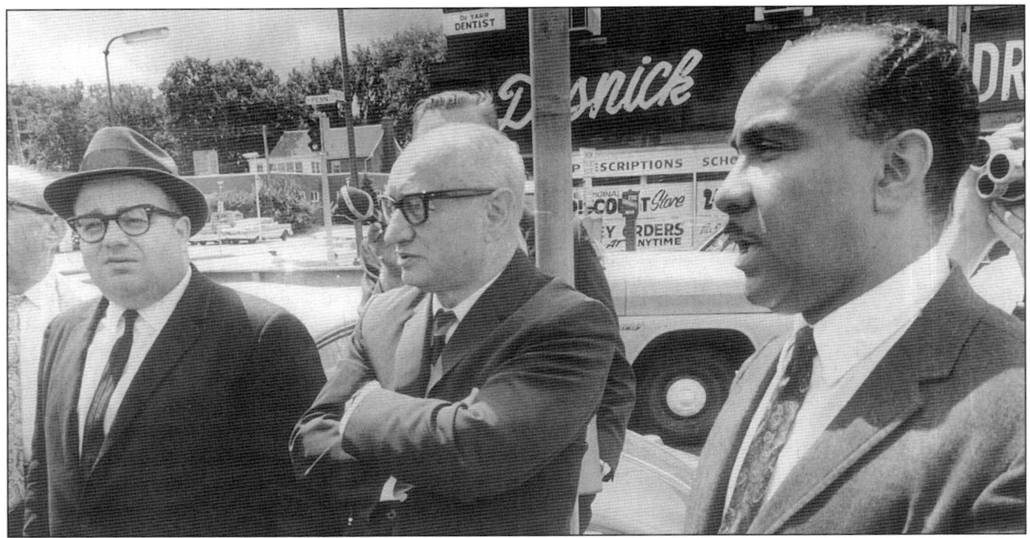

Some long-time residents had already decided it was time to create a working relationship between blacks and their Jewish neighbors, and began working together in organizations like MOER (Mobilization of Economic Resources) and TACTICS (Technical Advisory Committee to Implement Community Services). The week after the riot, Rabbi Louis Ginsberg (left), North Side resident Louis Greene, who was a board member of both MOER and TACTICS, and black community leader Harry Davis walked down Plymouth Avenue together to survey the damage and attend a meeting at Beth El Synagogue with 50 leading members of the Jewish community. (Courtesy of Minneapolis Tribune.)

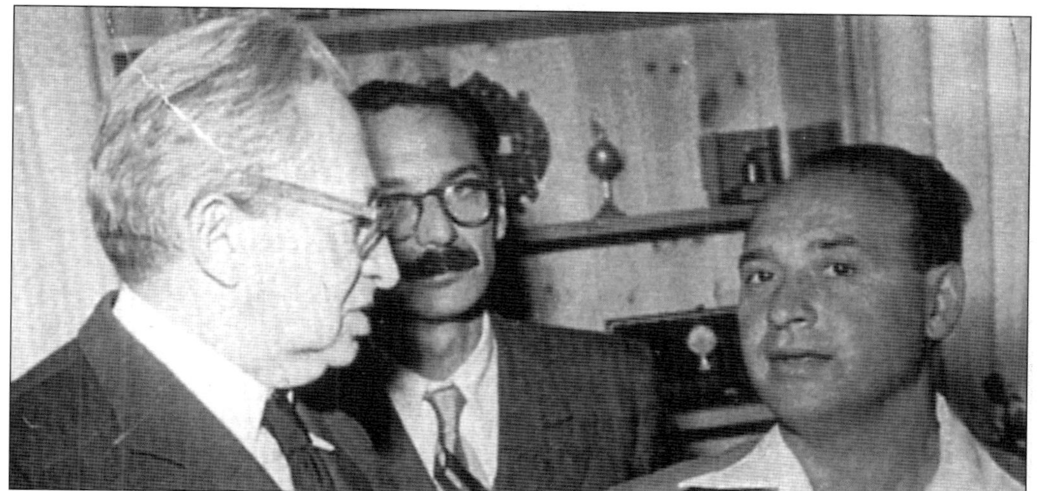

Saadia Gelb organized chapters of Habonim and Kadimah and a Young Poale Zion club for Hebrew-speaking young people while he was a student at the University of Minnesota in the 1930s. They established an *achsherah*—a training farm—in suburban Anoka, and young city dwellers came from all over the United States to learn how to farm. Saadia and his wife Helen made *aliyah* in November of 1947—just a few months before Israel was declared a State. Yitzhak Ben-Zvi, Israel's second president (left) was one of many Israeli leaders that Saadia (right) worked with as financial director of *kibbutz* Kfar Blum and an active member of Israel's Labor Party, Mapai. (From Saadia Gelb's autobiography, *The Chase Is the Game: The Journeys of an American-Israeli Pioneer*.)

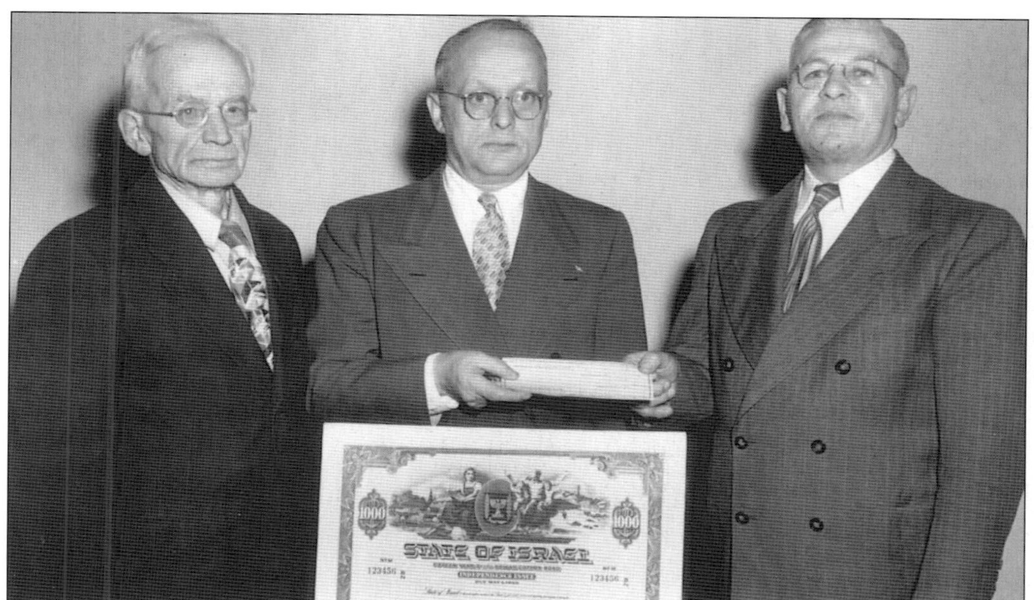

Buying Israel bonds was a commitment to Israel, and millions of American Jews looked on them as an investment, a contribution, or a gift to Israel, or to a new grandchild or a Bar Mitzvah boy. Gemelus Chesed Loan Society members, shown here from left to right, Vice President Philip Gold, President Jacob Liss, and Secretary Alan Levinson purchased two $1,000 bonds in 1949, which would mature in 1966. (Courtesy of American Jewish World.)

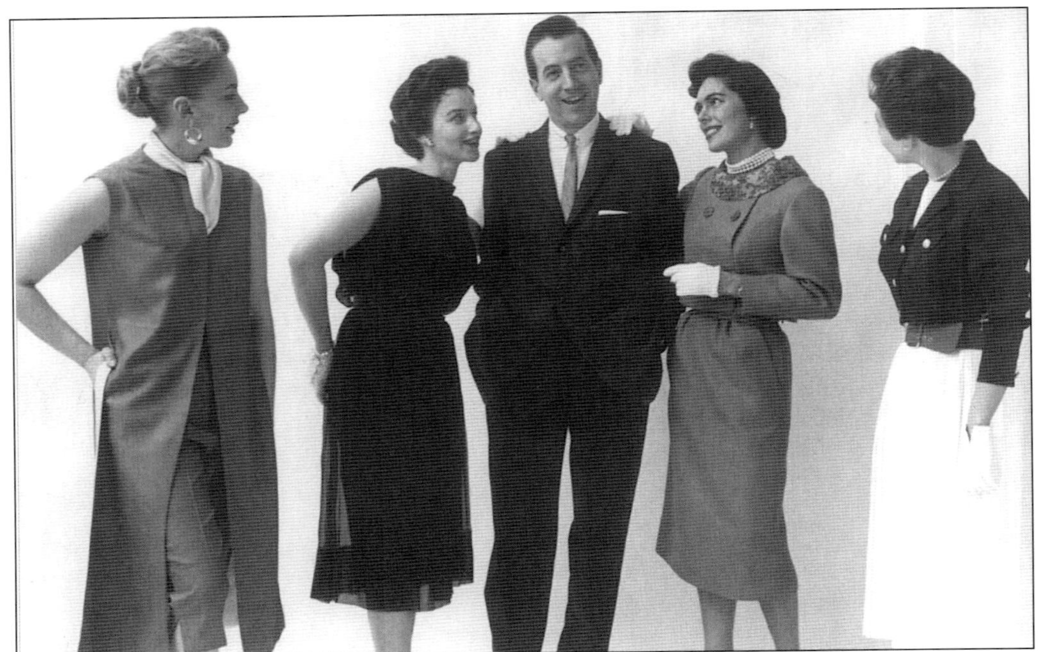

Special events also raised dollars for Israel, including Minneapolis Hadassah's annual "Funtennial" to help fund the Hadassah Medical Center in Israel. Their 1958 program included games, kiddie rides and pony rides, a chuckwagon and bake shop, and a "Color in Springtime" style show featuring clothes from Harold's and Liemandt's. Thirty members of the community volunteered as models, including, from left to right, Mmes. Stanley Beyer and Marvin Graybow, Bill Aberman, and Mmes. Harold Greenberg and Alvin Jaffe. (Courtesy of American Jewish World.)

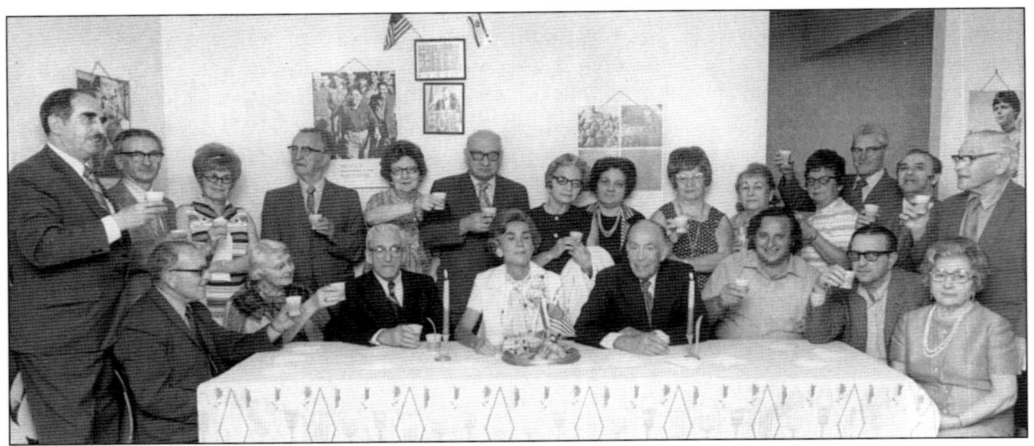

Former Minnesota Governor Karl Rolvaag and his wife were honored with a visit to Israel in September 1971, as guests of the Upper Midwest-Israel Histadrut Committee. Shown here from left to right are the following: (seated) David Turchick, Esther and Eli Rosenbloom, the Rolvaags, Regional Chair and National Vice-President Alen M. Herman, Prof. Emil Starr, and Mrs. Dorothy Weiner; (standing) Histadrut Regional Director Jay Wiseman, Mr. and Mrs. Joseph Blustein, William Mayberg, Florence and Louis Greene, Mrs. Sylvia Shure, Mrs. George Black, Women's Division Co-Chair Elizabeth Shrell, Mrs. Arthur Berman, Mr. and Mrs. Julius Manosevitz, (?) Black, and (?) Berman. (Courtesy of Florence Greene.)

Seven

North Minneapolis and the Jewish Community Today

In 1970, the North Side was still in the midst of transition caused by long-time residents reaching retirement age, aging housing, suburban growth, and the race riots and unrest in 1967. The neighborhood continued to lose residents to the suburbs, and housing prices were dropping as more and more members of the black community, many of whom were still underemployed and underpaid, were moving into the neighborhood because they could afford to buy homes there.

When Stillwater resident George Roberts was offered a job teaching history at North High School, he and his wife drove around North Minneapolis in search of a neighborhood that felt right, because he wanted to live close to where he worked. "The minute we saw this house on Sheridan Avenue North, we fell in love with it," Beverly says, and so the Roberts became early partners in a mix of young families, first-time home buyers, and young professionals, both black and white, who were moving into what had been the Jewish North Side because they were overwhelmed at being able to buy a 4-bedroom, 2-bath house for as little as $20,000.

By the 1990s, however, things were changing for the better. International Habitat for Humanity had played a role in the North Side's comeback, and continues to do so, buying as many as thirty or more homes each year for as little as one dollar each from the Minneapolis Housing and Redevelopment Authority, and doing extensive repairs and redecorating. The rehabilitated homes are then sold to low-income families on a no-interest, no-profit basis, on the condition that the new owners must have put 250 hours of "sweat equity" into their new home's rehabilitation, plus 100 hours of volunteer work on other homes. In 1999 Willard-Hay ranked as one of the top three Minneapolis neighborhoods—and the only one on the North Side—in terms of building permits, in part because many homes were getting the major repairs they needed, and brand-new homes were being built on vacant lots where homes owned by absentee landlords had been torn down after standing vacant and then boarded-up for years.

Sales of existing homes were also moving quickly because it had become a multicultural but friendly neighborhood, and it was the only place in the city where people, especially those who worked downtown, could buy conveniently-located houses with three or four bedrooms, two baths, and "a lot of character . . . high ceilings, solariums, balconies, and stone decks" for less than $100,000—a real gain from 1970s prices, but still a bargain compared to the $350,000 or more that homes like that were selling for in South Minneapolis. As one realtor put it, young buyers are choosing the North Side because "they're finding that they get way more house for their dollar than they can anywhere else."

Today, four architects, two teachers, and a college professor live on the same block as George and Beverly Roberts. Their house is worth almost five times what they paid for it, and continues to increase in value. New townhouses and apartment buildings are also springing up, and the *Star Tribune's* weekly Real Estate Transactions listings reflect the continuing up-swing. In July 1999, for example, a home at 1015 Queen Avenue North sold for $99,500. In the summer of 2001, a 1909 Tudor-style house with ornate woodwork and stained-glass windows sold for $109,000, a refurbished house across the street from Willard School sold for $126,500, two houses on 14th and Newton and 10th and Sheridan sold for $132,000 and $196,000 respectively, and houses adjacent to Wirth Park were selling for considerably more

And the community is also growing and changing in other ways. Pillsbury Neighborhood Services, now located in the old Emanuel Cohen Center building on Elwood Avenue, offers an ever-increasing range of services including child care, the Richard Green Early Learning Center, special programs for people with disabilities, training for people transitioning from welfare to work, small loans to low income parents looking for meaningful employment or in need of an automobile, car insurance, or uniforms and tools for work, and a summertime youth program that focuses on cultural enrichment through tutoring, arts and crafts, sports, music, history classes, and field trips. Black and white neighbors socialize and form Block Clubs to watch over each others' homes, and plan neighborhood picnics and holiday parties. They've come a long way since the days when Honeywell retiree Stan Stone, a black engineer who grew up on the North Side, remembers "hanging out" at Oak Ridge Country Club, where he and his pals earned spending money as golf caddies, and by cleaning and shining the members' golf shoes, fixing drinks, and making sandwiches for members who came to play gin rummy.

The Minneapolis Community Development Agency (MCDA) and the Minneapolis Neighborhood Revitalization Program (NRP) have also played a critical role in the comeback of Willard-Hay. In the past six years, more than 100 owners have purchased or fixed up their homes with MCDA below-market-rate loans, and NRP housing programs have helped owners and landlords purchase and rehab their properties. An NRP-funded Homewood Public Market will soon offer fresh produce and arts and crafts, and more is yet to come, according to city officials and neighborhood residents.

And last but not least, many men and women who grew up on the North Side are still friends, and many of them see each other at annual reunions or special events. The Monarchs, for example, now call themselves The Old Man's Club, because after 75 years of fellowship that began with a cooking class at the Emanuel Cohen Center in 1926, they still meet twice a month at restaurants or members' homes, except during January, February, and March, the "snow-bird" season when most of them migrate to winter homes in warmer climes like Arizona, California, and Florida. They play *schmeer* or other card games and reminisce about past years, laughing as they recall the banquet at the Calhoun Beach Club where a girl jumped out of the cake—a cardboard cake built and decorated by her mother!—and remembering golf outings at Breezy Point and Rolling Green, and formal dances at Oak Ridge Country Club.

Many former North Siders have also attended North High School's frequent alumni "graduation" ceremonies, a long-running tradition. In 1996, Gary Shapiro, class of '33, was the oldest alumnus present, and Art Felsen and Morrie Fruen were two of some 40 members of the class of '36 who came to celebrate the 60th anniversary of their graduation. And when North High School celebrated its 100th anniversary in June 1988, more than 3,000 of its estimated 37,000 alumni turned out for a two-day, triple-header celebration. They flew in from all over the United States to find a "Welcome North Alumni" information table at the airport main terminal, and charter buses for the official reunion hotels. At the Thursday evening "roll call" of members of the class of 1938, who were celebrating their 50th anniversary, those who responded included recently retired Federation executive Mitchell Lazarus, Earl Toberman, Bess Wilensky Berenbaum, Clara Lerner Robitz, Shirley Locketz Wilensky, Herman Ladin, Harold Gershgow, Morris Lehrman, Mischa Dworsky, and many others. The emcee for the evening was Jerry Teener, class of 1935 and had worked on reunion events for the past 2 1911–1913 but never graduated, was also th Nathan Light, class of 1933, and State Represe Orenstein Hecker, class of 1932, reminisced beginnings of Theatre in the Round Players, a c than 50 years, which Roz and her husband, unfortunately, wasn't taking place in the buildi imposing three-story building they all remembere in October 1973, and replaced with a new North l that some say speaks the architectural language of bunker with few windows, double doors that are o to keep out unwanted visitors, and painted-over gr

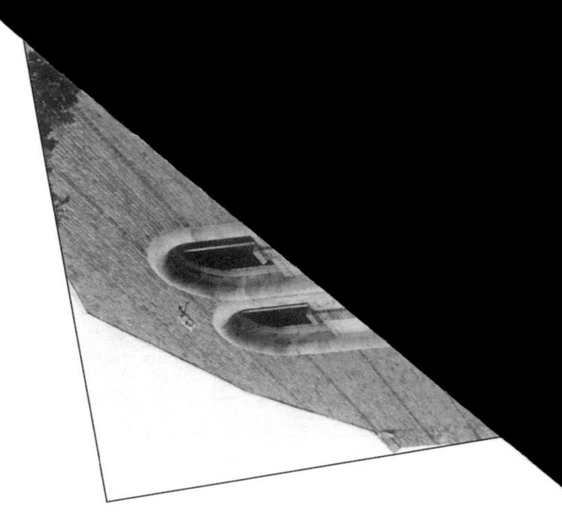

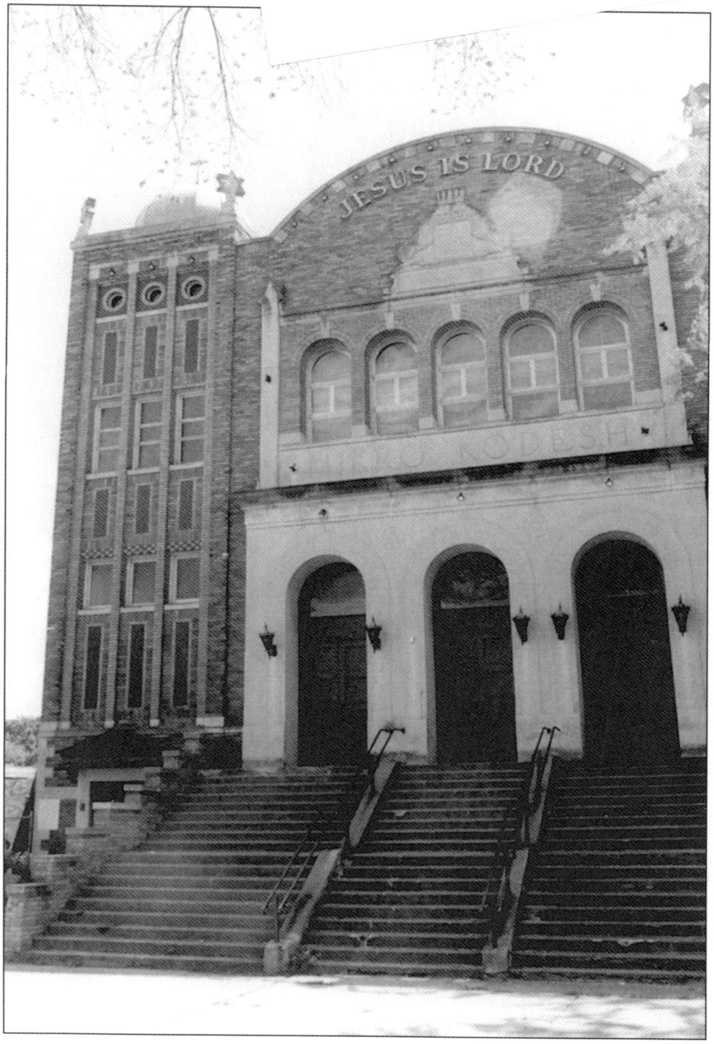

The building that was formerly Mikro Kodesh synagogue is now owned by Pastor Paul and his Greek Orthodox Disciples Ministry, offering meals, groceries, clothing, and other services to an estimated 35,000 needy individuals in the inner city. When they bought the building, which had been standing empty for almost 10 years after Mikro Kodesh became part of the new B'nai Emet congregation in St. Louis Park in the 1960s, they had to restore the once-vandalized synagogue. Its Jewish heritage remains, however, inside the building as well as outside, where the pews are still decorated with *Magen Dovids* and banners in the sanctuary have reminded worshipers to "Love the Lord with all your heart, with all your soul, with all your mind," and to "Love your neighbor as yourself." (Courtesy of Tom Lewin.)

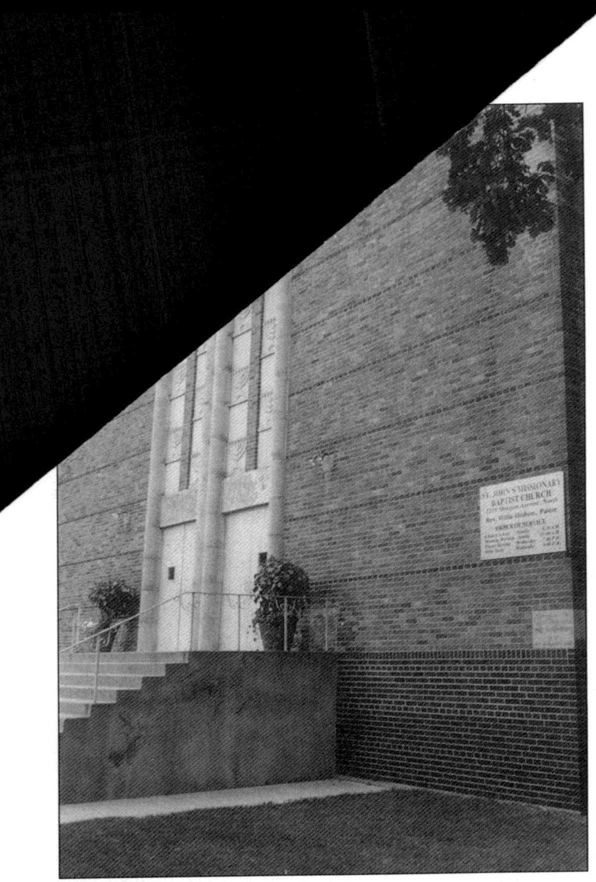

In 1969, St. John's Missionary Baptist Church bought Sharei Zedeck's building at 1119 Morgan Avenue North. The synagogue's name, engraved in Hebrew above the doors, has been obliterated, but the menorahs that decorated the front of the building are still there. (Photo by Tom Lewin.)

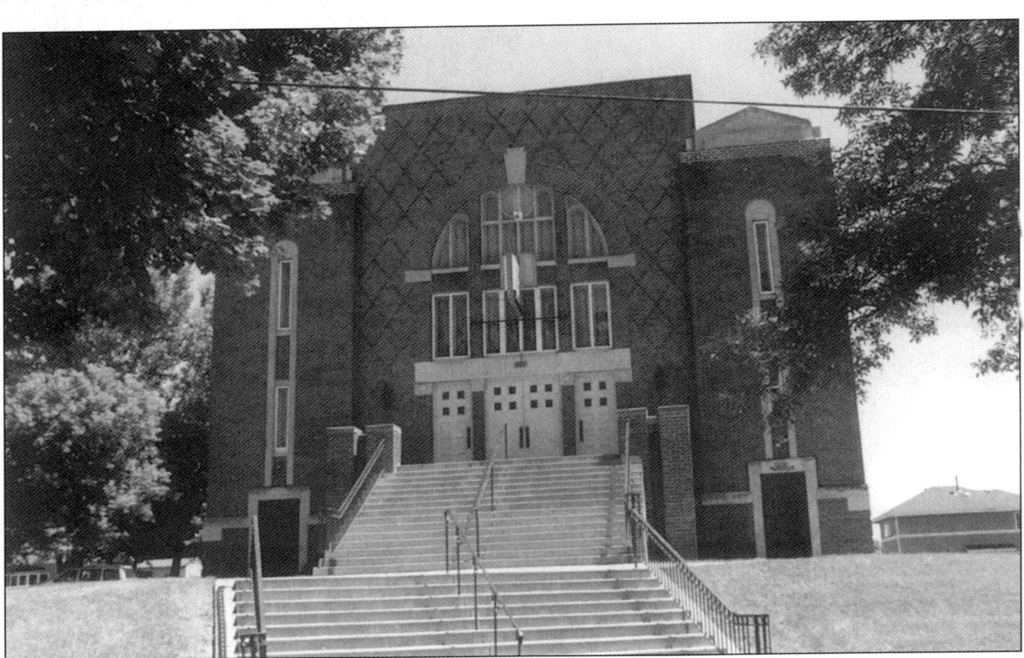

Tifereth B'nai Jacob, also known as the Elwood *shul*, is now Zion Baptist Church, and the Jewish stars on top of the building have been removed. (Photo by Tom Lewin.)

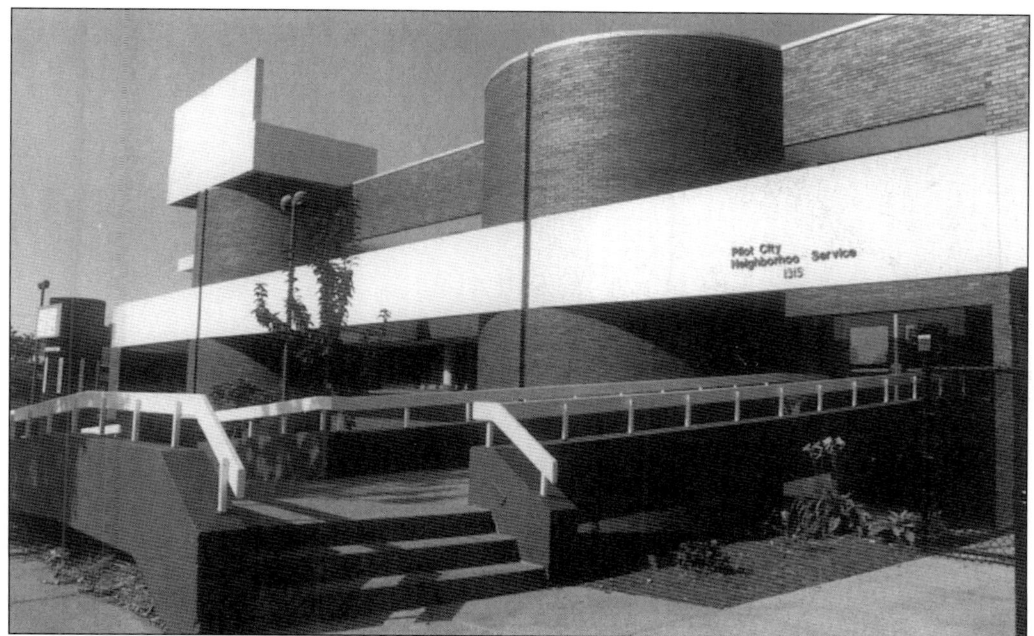

Beth El Synagogue is long gone from 14th and Penn Avenue North, and has been replaced by the Pilot City Community Center, a social service agency offering social programs, counseling, care, and economic and other assistance for neighborhood residents, including students, the unemployed, crime victims, and victims of domestic abuse. (Photo by Tom Lewin.)

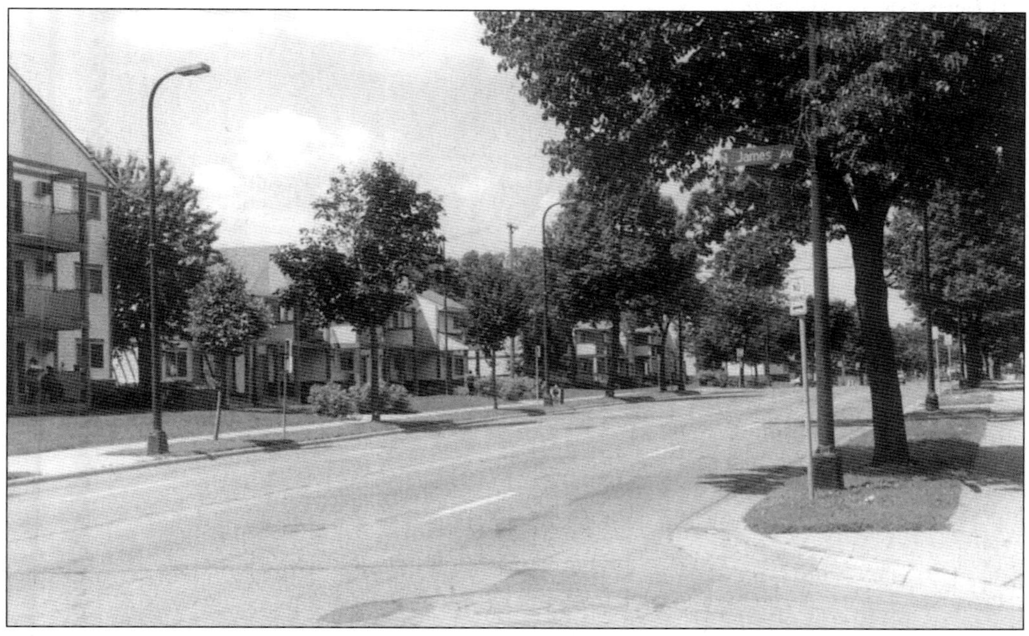

Like Olson Highway, Plymouth Avenue was once a thriving commercial area lined with family businesses. Today the businesses and streetcar tracks are long gone, and the streets are lined with apartment houses, condominiums, park areas, and single-family homes and duplexes. (Photo by Tom Lewin.)

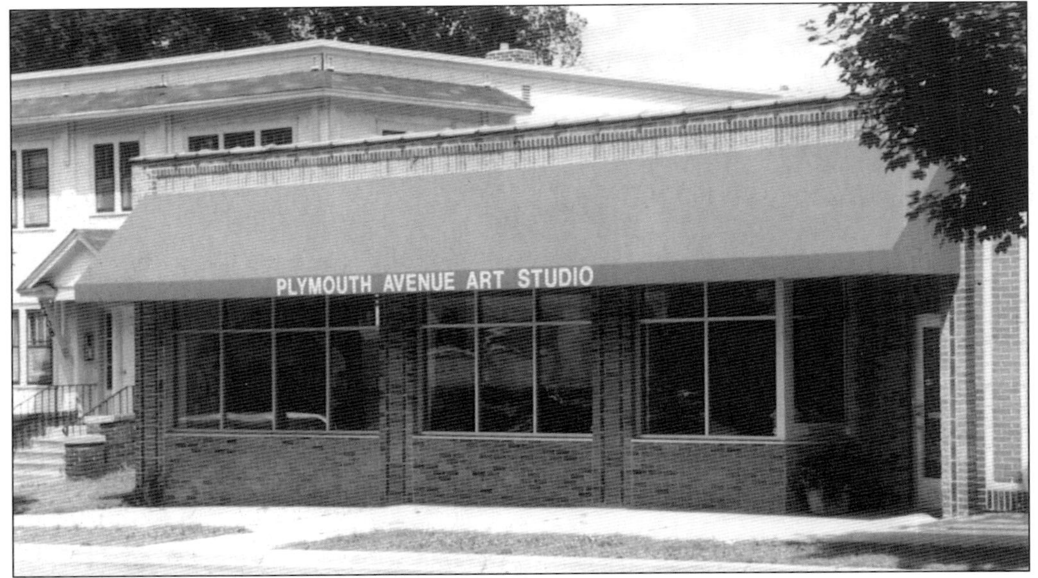

George and Beverly Roberts' newly-renovated Plymouth Avenue Arts Studio at Plymouth and Russell Avenues North is designed to encourage young artists of all races and colors, and includes five studios, an exhibit area, and a community meeting space. The building had been vacant for 10 years when the Roberts bought it and enlisted the help of North High School students and neighbors to gut it down to the sub-floor, studs and ceiling joists, and create a new space that will be "a visible presence for artists who will contribute to the community's vitality, self-image, and connectedness." (Photo by Tom Lewin.)

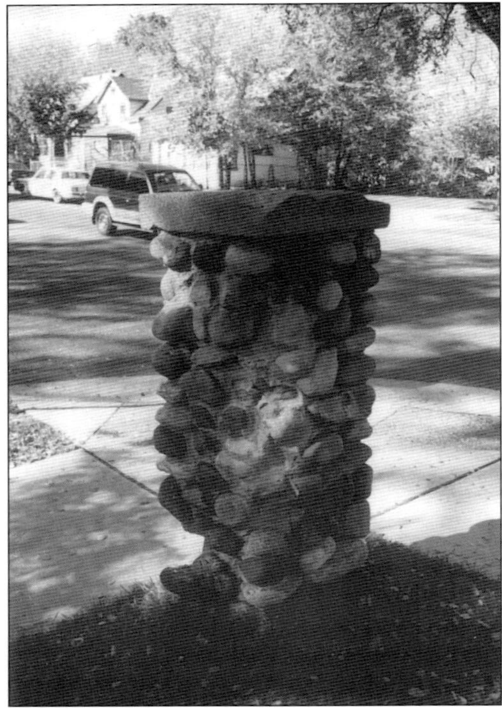

The Roberts' Homewood Markers Project has renovated or replaced the decaying stone pillars that had been built on each corner along the borders of the Homewood residential development in the 1920s. (Courtesy of Beverly Roberts.)

Houses like this 1920s home on the corner of Plymouth and Vincent Avenues North are now selling for $200,000 or more—a remarkable increase in value over the past few years, but still a bargain compared to prices for similar homes in South Minneapolis. (Photo by Tom Lewin.)

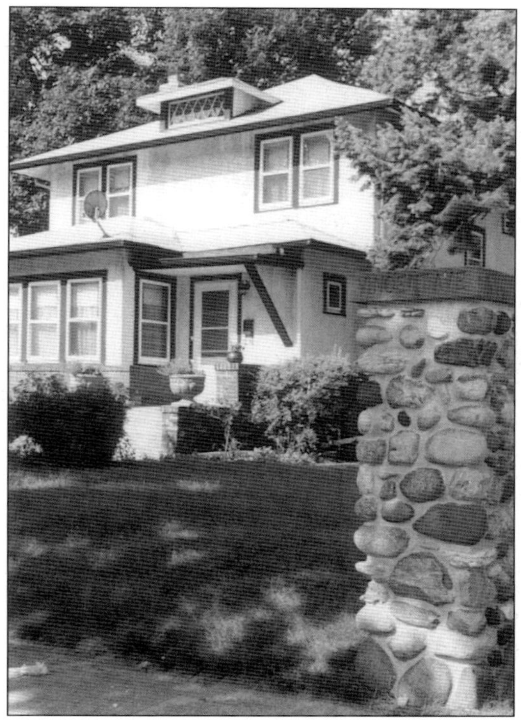

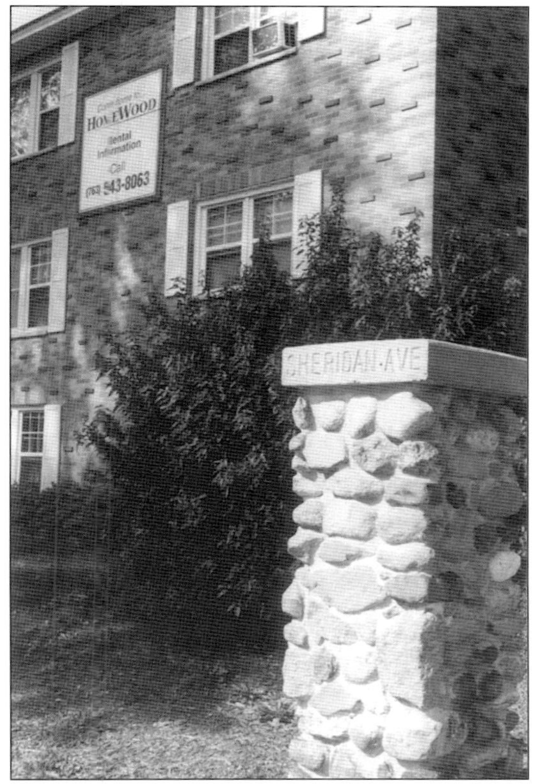

More and more apartment buildings and condominiums are also being built in North Side areas where houses which had stood empty for many years, or had been allowed to deteriorate, are now being torn down. (Photo by Tom Lewin.)

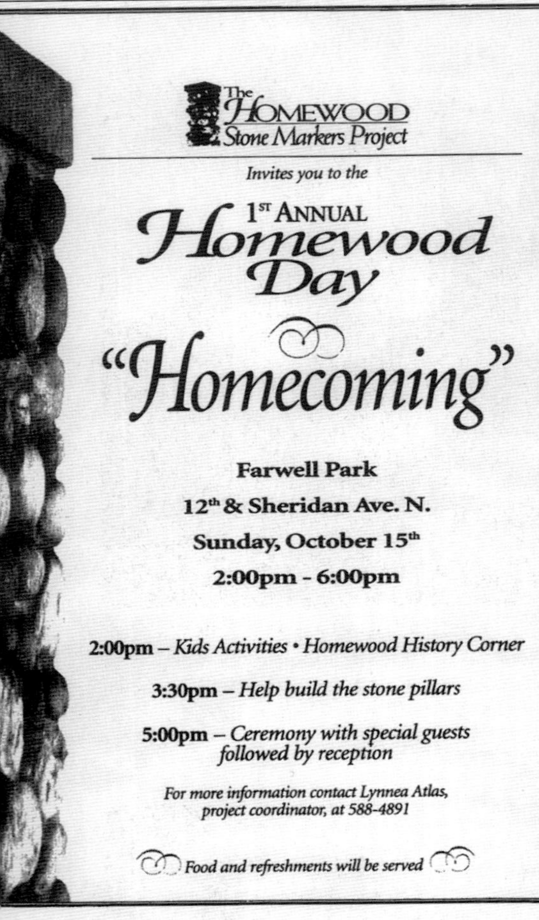

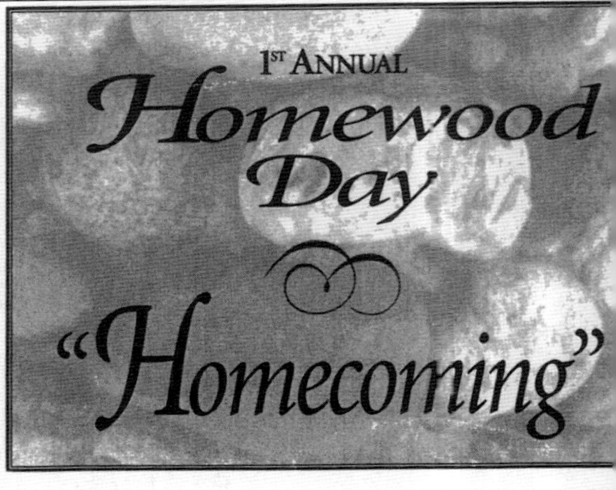

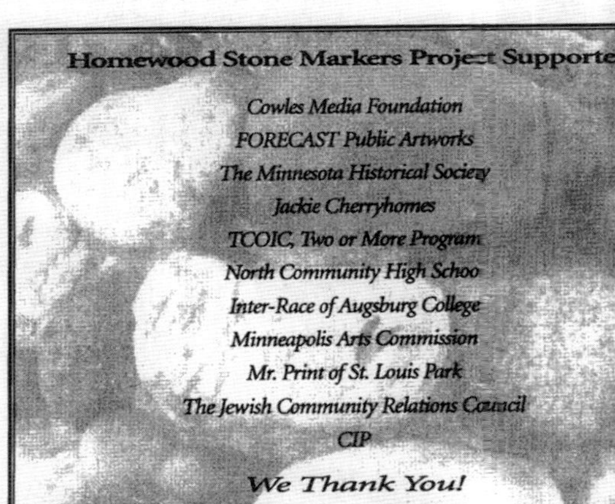

Today North Side homeowners of all races and religions live and work together as one community. They have annual Block Parties, and at their "Homewood Day Homecoming" hundreds of former North Side residents reunited and reminisced with friends and neighbors they hadn't seen for decades, and met the current owners of the houses they'd grown up in. (Courtesy of Beverly Roberts.)

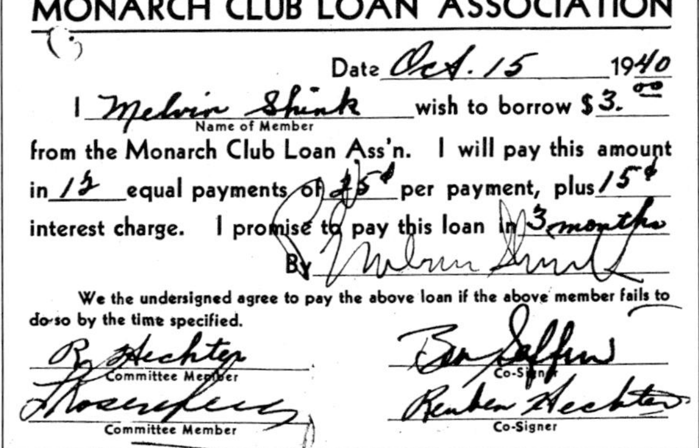

MONARCH CLUB LOAN ASSOCIATION

Date Oct. 15 1940

I Melvin Shink (Name of Member) wish to borrow $3.00 from the Monarch Club Loan Ass'n. I will pay this amount in 12 equal payments of 25¢ per payment, plus 15¢ interest charge. I promise to pay this loan in 3 months

By Melvin Shink

We the undersigned agree to pay the above loan if the above member fails to do so by the time specified.

R. Hechter — Committee Member | Ben Saffer — Co-Signer

Rosenfeld — Committee Member | Reuben Hechter — Co-Signer

If you joined the Monarchs Club at the Emanuel Cohen Center, you could borrow money—and $3.00 was a lot of money in 1940. It could buy you 20 corned beef sandwiches at Malcoff's, or 60 kids' tickets for Saturday matinees at the Homewood Theater! (Courtesy of the Jewish Historical Society of the Upper Midwest.)

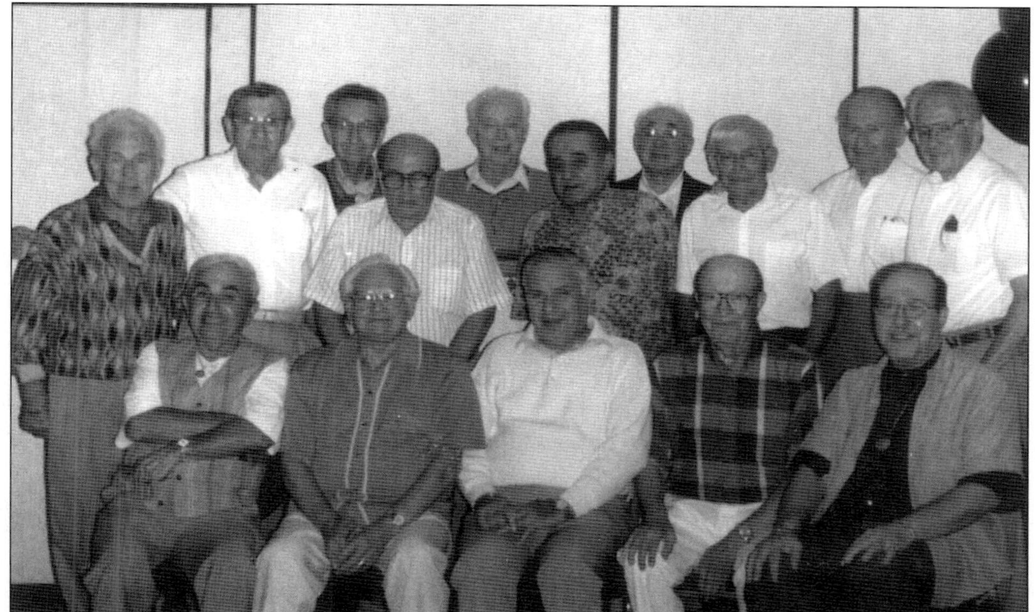

Monarch Club members recently celebrated more than 70 years of togetherness. Shown here from left to right are the following: (front row) Harold Herman (a founder), Ruby Leiderman, Al Kagin, Norton Rogin, and Norman Goldberg; (back row) Zollie Baratz, Conrad Solomon, Sheldon Pinck (a founder), Irv Efron, Johnny Kay, Sheldon Flom, Bernie Epstein, Len Goldman, Sam Benenson, and Izzy Milstein. Missing is Irv Herman—who was taking the picture. (Courtesy of Norman Goldberg.)

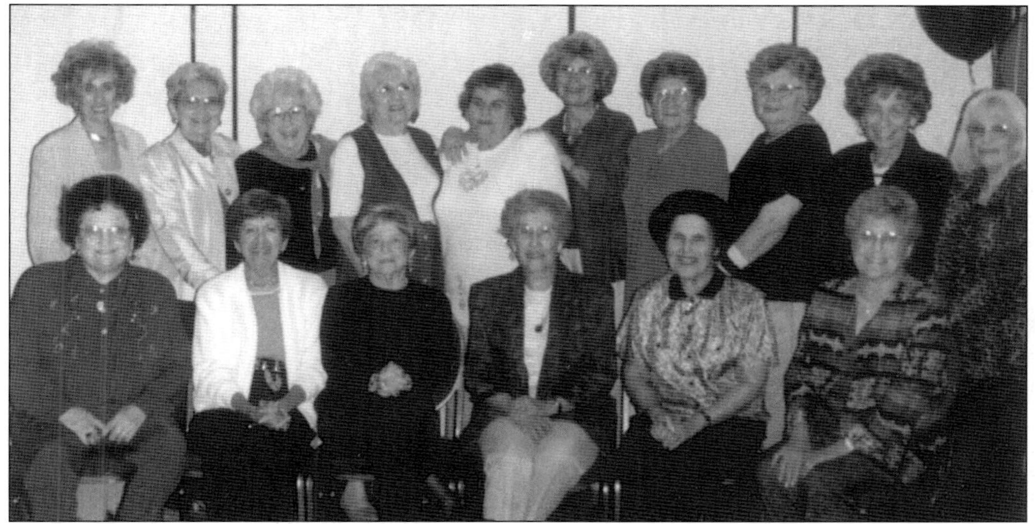

Monarch Club members invite their wives and widows of past members to their annual banquet, which was at Mystic Lakes Casino in 2001. From left to right are the following: (front row) Dorothy Epstein, Pearl Goldman, Helen Kagin, Ruth Leiderman, Elaine Rogin, and Jackie Herman; (back row) Shirley Baratz, Frances Herman, Reva Lear, Lillyan Solomon, Alice Flom, Gloria Pinck, Lillian Benenson, Rose Kay, Ilene Rosenberg, and Lee Goldberg. (Courtesy of Norman Goldberg.)

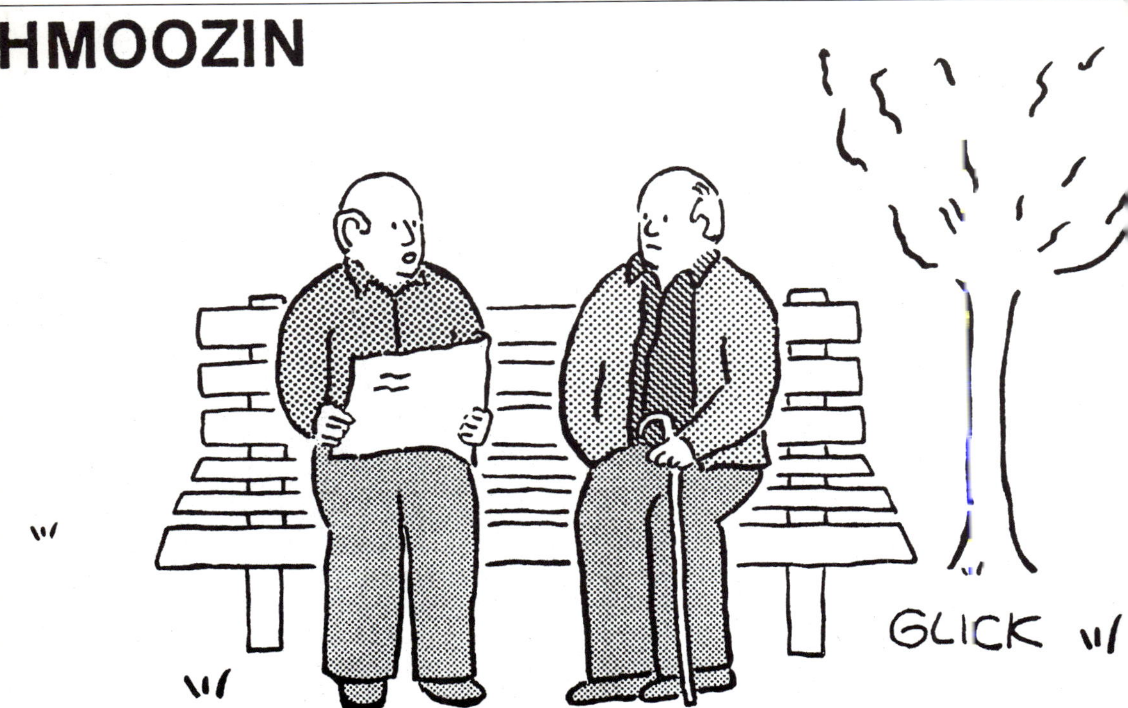

"When we were young, we didn't need any beepers, pagers, or cellular phones -- because anyone that we really needed to communicate with lived right on our block."

Many young people's parents still like to reminisce about those bygone days in their close-knit Jewish community, as shown in this cartoon by Arnold Glick, an attorney and an artist who now lives in Brookline, Massachusetts. The cartoon was published in the February 1999 issue of *American Jewish World.* (Courtesy of Arnold Glick and the *American Jewish World*.)